SOLICITATIONS, BIDS, PROPOSALS AND SOURCE SELECTION
Building a Winning Contract

GREGORY A. GARRETT
GAIL A. PARROTT

. Wolters Kluwer
Law & Business

AUSTIN   BOSTON   CHICAGO   NEW YORK   THE NETHERLANDS

Editorial Director: Aaron M. Broaddus
Cover and Interior Design: Craig L. Arritola

Copyright Notice

Notice of Trademarks

Product No.: 0-5190-400

ISBN: 978-0-8080-1612-0

CONTENTS

FOREWORD

The book *Solicitations, Bids/Proposals, & Source Selection: Building a Winning Contract* uses a simple, but, powerful process approach to explain in detail the Buying & Selling Life-Cycle used in both the public and private business sectors, with numerous case studies and dozens of best practices.

This fast-paced book walks you through the entire Buying & Selling Life-Cycle in just the first chapter. Chapters 2 - 7 then provide the detailed process inputs, proven tools & techniques, and desired outputs for all three phases and each of the seven key steps which both buyers and sellers must accomplish to achieve business success. Chapters 8, 9, and 10 each provide a thought-provoking discussion of proven effective best practices to improve buying and selling. Each chapter provides best practices in solicitations, bids/proposals, and contracts in a different marketplace. Chapter 8 addresses best practices in the U.S. Federal Government Marketplace. Chapter 9 provides best practices in the U.S. Commercial Marketplace. Finally, Chapter 10 discusses buying and selling best practices in the Multi-National/Global Marketplace.

This one-of-a-kind book provides both breath and depth of practical guidance, which few books have ever delivered. Plus, the authors have included numerous excellent interviews of buying and selling business professionals, from both the U.S. Government and industry. The interviews alone are worth the price of this book.

If you are a business professional involved in any aspect of buying or selling products, services, and/or solutions, then this book is a must buy, read, and do!

Sincerely,

William C. Pursch, Ph.D., CPCM
President, Pursch Associates
Past National President
National Contract Management Association

DEDICATION

Gregory A. Garrett

I would like to dedicate this book to my wfe Carolyn for her love, patience, and support! I would like to thank my many friends and associates who I have learned so much from, both what to do and what not to do!

Gail A. Parrott

I dedicate this book to my husband Terry for his love and support; to my daughter Caitlin for her creative inspirations and quick-witted humor; and to my parents, friends and mentors for always believing in me and daring me to be great.

ACKNOWLEDGMENTS

We would like to thank the following individuals for their guidance, support, and contributions to this book.

William C. Pursch, Ph.D., CPCM

Rene G. Rendon, D.B.A., CPCM, C.P.M., PMP

Linda F. Riviera

John A. (Jack) Bishop, Jr.

Philip E. Salmeri

Gregory Landon

John E. Stuart, CPCM, Col., USAF (Ret.)

Rex Elliott

Charles E. Rumbaugh, Esq.

Wayne E. Ferguson

Ron Smith, CPCM

Lenn Vincent, RADM, USN (Ret.)

Lee Ann Hunt, CPCM

Rick Diehl, CPCM, Col., USAF (Ret.)

A special thank you to Mrs. Barbara Hanson for her six years of outstanding administrative support and friendship.

ABOUT THE AUTHORS

Gregory A. Garrett

Gregory A. Garrett, is a best-selling and award-winning author, a dynamic speaker, international educator, and practicing industry leader. He currently serves as the Senior Principal and Account Executive for all U.S. Federal Government Civilian Agencies at the firm Acquisition Solutions, Inc. in Arlington, VA. He has successfully led more than $30 Billion of high-technology contracts and projects during the past 25 years. He has taught, consulted, and led contract and project teams in more than 40 countries. He has served as a lecturer for The George Washington University Law School and the School of Business and Public Management.

At Lucent Technologies, Mr. Garrett served as the Chief Compliance Officer, U.S. Federal Government Programs. He served as Vice President, Program Management, North America, Wireless, Chairman, Lucent Technologies Project Management Leadership Council, representing more than 2,000 Lucent project managers globally, and as Lucent Technologies first Director, Global Program Management at the company headquarters.

At ESI International, Mr. Garrett served as Executive Director of Global Business, where he led the sales, marketing, negotiation, and implementation of bid/proposal management, project management, commercial contracting, and government contract management training and consulting programs for numerous Fortune 100 multinational corporations, government agencies and small businesses worldwide, including: ABB, AT&T, BellSouth, Boeing, Dell, IBM, Inter-America Development Bank, Israel Aircraft Industries, Lucent Technologies, Motorola, NCR, NTT, Panama Canal Commission, United States Trade Development Agency, United Nations, United States Department of Energy, and the Department of Defense.

Formerly, Mr. Garrett served as a highly decorated military officer for the United States Air Force, awarded more than 17 medals, badges, and citations. He completed his active duty career as the youngest Acquisition Action Officer, in the Colonel's Group Headquarters USAF, the Pentagon. He was the youngest Division Chief and Professor of Contracting Management at the Air Force Institute of Technology where he taught advanced courses in contract administration and program management to more than 5,000 people from the Department of Defense and NASA.

Previously, he was the youngest Procurement Contracting Officer for the USAF Aeronautical Systems Center, where he led more than 50 multi-million dollar negotiations and managed the contract administration of over $15 billion in contracts for major weapon systems. He served as a Program Manager at the Space Systems Center, where he managed a $300 million space communications project.

Mr. Garrett is a Certified Purchasing Manager (C.P.M.) of the Institute for Supply Management (ISM). He is a Certified Project Management Professional (PMP) of the Project Management Institute (PMI) and has received the prestigious PMI Eric Jenett Project Management Excellence Award and the David I. Cleland Project Management Literature Award. He is a Certified Professional Contracts Manager (CPCM), a Fellow, and member of the Board of Advisors of the National Contract Management Association (NCMA). He has received the NCMA National Achievement Award, NCMA National Educational Award, the Charles J. Delaney Memorial Award for Contract Management literature, and the Blanche Witte Memorial Award for outstanding service to the contract management profession.

A prolific writer, Mr. Garrett authored 10 books including: *Managing Contracts for Peak Performance* (NCMA, 1990), *World-Class Contracting* (4th Ed., CCH, 2006), *Managing Complex Outsourced Projects* (CCH, 2004), *Contract Negotiations* (CCH, 2005), *The Capture Management Life-Cycle* (CCH, 2003), *Contract Management Organizational Tools* (NCMA, 2005), *Performance-Based Acquisition: Pathways to Excellence* (NCMA, 2005), *Leadership: Building High Performance Buying & Selling Teams* (NCMA, 2006), *U.S. Military Program Management: Lessons Learned & Best Practices* (Management Concepts, 2007), and he has served as principal author and series editor for the new *Federal Acquisition ActionPack Series* (Management Concepts, 2007). Plus he has authored more than 70 published articles on bid/proposal management, supply chain management, contracting, project management, and leadership.

He resides in Oakton, VA with his wife Carolyn and three children - Christopher, Scott, and Jennifer.

Gail A. Parrott

Gail A. Parrott currently serves as the contract management team focal point for the Boeing Company's Integrated Defense System (IDS) Tanker Japan Spares Program. Previously, she served as the eBusiness Site Leader of The Boeing Company's Integrated Defense System (IDS) for St. Louis. She led the site's Electronic Data Interchange (EDI) and Wide Area Workflow (WAWF) teams, and served as the contract management team focal point for Unique Item Identification (UID) and Radio Frequency Identification (RFID) programs. She also led a Web Services team, which developed a new system providing authorized Boeing users the autonomy to access at any time their related data from the government system called Mechanization of Contract Administration Services (MOCAS).

In 1997, Ms. Parrott joined McDonnell Douglas, which has since become a subsidiary of The Boeing Company. She has served in numerous accounting and financial management positions supporting various major aircraft programs, including: F/A-18, AV-8, and the Aircraft Spares programs. As the eBusiness Leader for the St. Louis site, Ms. Parrott has traveled amongst the many sites within the United States, as well as abroad to Europe presenting to the Ministry of Defense and BAE Systems.

Ms. Parrott has been very active in the National Contracts Management Association (NCMA) for several years. She has served as an officer in the NCMA St. Louis Gateway Chapter for the past four years. She currently is the Vice President of Operations, serving the previous two years as the Chapter President. Ms. Parrott served as the Program Chair for NCMA World Congress 2006. She has also partnered with the National Association of Purchasing Management (NAPM) St. Louis Chapter and is a member of the Consortium for Supply Chain Management Studies (CSCMS). She has received NCMA's Albert Berger Outstanding Leadership Award and Fellow Award.

Ms. Parrott has co-authored the article, *e-Business: Understanding Key Trends and Applying Best Practices,* which was published July, 2005 in Contract Management magazine. She has also received acknowledgement for contributions to the published book Performance-Based Acquisition authored by Gregory A Garrett.

Ms. Parrott holds a Bachelor's degree in Accounting from Southern Illinois University-Carbondale, Illinois and a MBA from Fontbonne University in St. Louis, Missouri. She is currently pursuing her Certified Commercial Contract Management (CCCM) certification. She resides in St. Louis, Missouri with her husband Terry and teenage daughter Caitlin.

INTRODUCTION

Building a contract, in both the public and private business sectors, which meets or exceeds the requirements of the buyer and seller is indeed a challenge, especially in a world of high expectations and demanding customers. This book provides a comprehensive roadmap or series of steps, which can be taken by both buyers and sellers to achieve mutual business success. The focus of this book is on the art and science of building a winning contract by: (1) creating appropriate and professional solicitations (Request for Quotes, Invitations for Bids, Request for Proposals, etc.), (2) developing successful bids/proposals (including oral presentations), and (3) conducting efficient, cost effective, and value-added source selection.

To help business professionals put all of these critical business activities into a proper context and workflow, we have developed a simple yet highly effective Buying & Selling Life-Cycle. The Buying & Selling Life-Cycle is focused on the activities surrounding solicitations, bids/proposals, and source selection. The Buying & Selling Life-Cycle is composed of three phases:

- Pre-Bid/Proposal Phase
- Bid/Proposal Phase
- Post-Bid/Proposal Phase

Chapter 1 begins by discussing the art and science of "the deal," which is comparable to partners learning how to Ballroom Dance. Later in Chapter 1, the Buying & Selling Life-Cycle is introduced as a set of moves composed of 3 phases and 7 steps to achieve business success. Chapters 2 through 7 discuss the three phases and one or more of the specific steps which buyers and/or sellers must take to achieve mutual business success. One of the very unique aspects of this book is the numerous interviews conducted of successful buying and selling business professionals from both the public and private business sectors, and the personal success stories learned and best practices expressed via those interviews, which are woven into the text of numerous chapters. This unique feature makes the book highly relevant and very practical. Chapters 8 through 10 provide even more detailed and specific market-based best practices for creating solicitations, developing successful bids/proposals, and conducting streamlined and effective source selections. In addition, the book provides several valuable appendices including:

- The Bid/No Bid Assessment Tool
- Glossary of Key Terms
- References

Further, the book provides a user-friendly index to aide the reader in easy referencing.

We hope you will find this book a valuable reference tool to help you build a winning contract!

Sincerely,

Gregory A. Garrett, CPCM, C.P.M., PMP
Gail A. Parrott

CHAPTER  1

THE BUYING & SELLING LIFE-CYCLE: LEARNING TO DANCE TOGETHER

INTRODUCTION

In both the public and private business sectors, buyers are far more knowledgeable about their rights, have higher expectations regarding the quality of products and services, have little tolerance for poor performance, are quick to change their minds, and frequently complain if they do not get what they want when they want it. Thus, winning a buyer's business and achieving customer loyalty is like learning to Ballroom dance with a partner who keeps setting a faster pace, changing the music, and varying the dance steps, all at the same time.

It is vital for sellers to learn how to dance with buyers in today's new business environment. Sellers must listen to the buyer's needs so they can proactively offer products, services, or business solutions to meet or exceed expectations. Buyer and seller partnership is important; however, like dancing you need to establish with your partner the dance space to determine how close is appropriate so you do not overstep your boundaries, or step on their foot, especially when dealing with government agency buyers.

Just like dancing, partner feedback is critical. You must know the difference between a partner's needs and desires. You must know how to treat your partner, so you do not start out or end up on the wrong foot. Business partners, must work together to achieve success, otherwise, one or both will stumble and fall.

Recognizing that the music keeps changing, just like technologies, requires sellers (both prime contractors and subcontractors) to be flexible and react quickly. Product innovation is essential to help sellers keep pace with the music of business and the beat of each industry in our global economy.

Despite these major challenges, some sellers are very successful at learning to dance with their buyers, thus improving execution and achieving customer loyalty. One of the key ingredients to becoming a successful business dance partner is understanding the buying and selling life-cycle.

The focus of this book is to provide an in-depth understanding of the buying and selling life-cycle. Specifically, the book focuses on how buyers and sellers must work together to build winning contracts throughout the solicitation, bid/proposal, and source selection process.

This book uses a three phase buying and selling life-cycle to illustrate the key dance steps required for a buyer and seller to work together to achieve mutual success. This chapter discusses the importance of buyers and sellers learning how to dance with each other, which is critical to developing winning contracts and ensuring end-customer satisfaction. Each subsequent chapter of the book examines one or more of the phases, steps, and best practices of the buying and selling life-cycle.

Bottom line – Buyer's and Seller's learning to dance with each other is not the action of just the purchasing manager, the sales manager, bid/proposal manager, and/or the contracts manager rather it is about a joint buyer-seller team effort. Integrating the discipline of customer-focused contract and project management in both a buyers and sellers organization, in a flexible and cost-effective manner, is critical to business success!

Contract and project management are vital to successfully dance with each other and deliver on promises. Contract and project management provide the teamwork, processes, tools and discipline, the dance steps, to allow buyers and sellers to build winning contracts, honor their commitments, and create long lasting customer loyalty.

Creating Value For Customers — "What it Takes to Build Winning Contracts"

Sellers of products, services and/or business solutions must create value for their buyers and their respective customers, otherwise, the buyers will select a new dance partner. Value creation drives today's business, which causes organizations to form partnerships. Creating value for buyers over a sustained period of time, at a fair and reasonable market-based price is why buyers want to dance with a seller. So, what exactly are the key elements of creating value?

There are several key elements, which are typically linked to sellers creating value for buyers resulting in high performance and greater customer loyalty.

Figure 1-1 illustrates some of the key elements, which affect a buyer's perception of value, thus either increasing or decreasing their loyalty to a seller/dance partner. As is illustrated in Figure 1-1, trust is critical to building a winning contract and achieving end-customer loyalty, and many factors can and do affect how trust is gained or lost. It is important to note that perceptions, more than facts, in some cases will dramatically impact buyer loyalty. Thus, building a winning contract and achieving end-customer loyalty is a blend of art and science – like demonstrating the concept of rigid-flexibility when dancing a tango or when developing a project plan while the buyer continually changes its requirements.

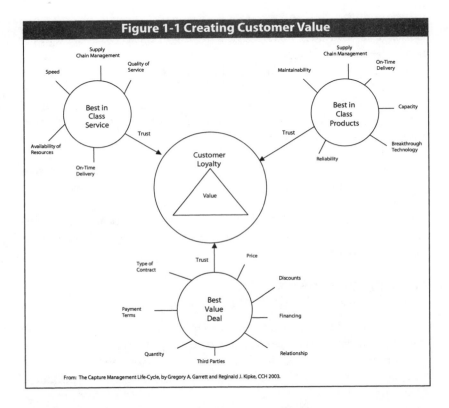

Figure 1-1 Creating Customer Value

From: The Capture Management Life-Cycle, by Gregory A. Garrett and Reginald J. Kipke, CCH 2003.

Value Challenges: Inadequate Customer Value

There are numerous reasons why buyers become dissatisfied with their dance partners/sellers. The following diagram, Figure 1-2, illustrates several of the major causes of inadequate buyer/customer value. While every industry has certain unique aspects, the major causes to inadequate customer value are pretty much the same everywhere.

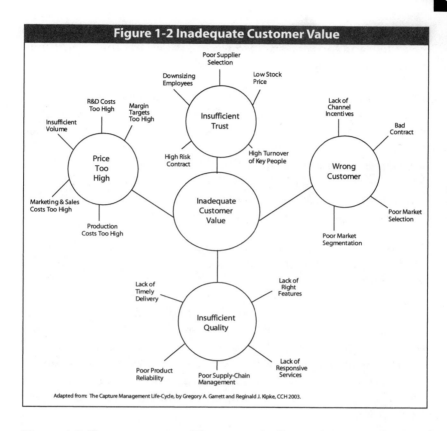

Figure 1-2 Inadequate Customer Value

Adapted from: The Capture Management Life-Cycle, by Gregory A. Garrett and Reginald J. Kipke, CCH 2003.

Figure 1-2 illustrates some of the many challenges buyers and sellers typically face in creating real value for their customers.

The Buying & Selling Life-Cycle

Increasingly, the dance between buyers and sellers required to build winning contracts has become complex, lengthy and dynamic. With the constant demands of customers for rapid response and best value, combined with widespread application of sophisticated technology in nearly every industry, buyers have increasingly become more sophisticated in their source selection practices. This same availability of technology has also reduced the barriers to market entry in many industries such that new competitors arise on an almost daily basis. Buyers are looking for ways to reduce their costs and improve performance. Traditional sellers are finding they must cut costs at every turn to compete with newer, smaller and more nimble competitors. All these trends converge to make it essential that buyers and sellers regardless of size or industry, work together via a structured approach to prioritize and focus scarce resources to maximize the opportunity to achieve mutual success.

The buying and selling life-cycle is just such a structured approach. It can be used in the commercial and government marketplace for domestic, international or global opportunities. It can be used to respond in a "reactive mode" to a buyer solicitation, such as a Request for Information (RFI), Requests for Quotation (RFQ), Request for Proposal (RFP), or Request for Tender (RFT). It can equally be used in a "pro-active mode" to generate an unsolicited offer to a buyer.

Whether you work in a large government agency, small start-up company, or a global corporation, we are all part of a virtual workplace that is no longer bordered by geography or time zone. Traditional face-to-face communication and interaction has been largely replaced by teleconference, email, instant messages, and webinars. The buying and selling life-cycle provides a framework that is geography and time zone independent. It can be used effectively in single-location organizations where everyone is "under one roof" as well as global corporations where employees will never meet each other in-person and may not even have a live conversation.

Sellers are driven by a profit motivation and procure products and services to either increase revenues or reduce expenses. Although not driven by a profit motivation, government buyers are focused on delivery of a specific program or service at a fair and reasonable price. As a seller, even if you have the best technology or service in the world, you will not win new business unless you can show the buyer how to apply your technology or services to increase their performance or reduce expenses. Sellers must demonstrate value to buyers by making or providing products or services which make business and life better, faster, and/or cheaper.

The foundation of the buying and selling life-cycle is the focus on the customer's business problems or objectives. Simply stated, this process is all about creating mutually beneficial offers which solve the buyer's business problems or objectives and meets the seller's requirements for profitability and risk. When you focus on the customer's business problems or objectives, you are looking at business from the customer's perspective, which will drive both the buyer and the seller to the best solution.

The buying and selling life-cycle, as depicted in Figure 1-3, is separated into three phases: the Pre-Bid/Proposal Phase, Bid/Proposal Phase, and the Post-Bid/Proposal Phase. The Pre-Bid/Proposal Phase is the up front period where the buyer develops their requirements and the solicitation (i.e. Request for Information (RFI), Request for Quote (RFQ), or Request for Proposal (RFP)) and the seller conducts pre-sales activities, including Bid/No Bid decision making. The Bid/Proposal Phase is the period during which the customer bid/proposal is developed by the seller and the buyer finalizes their source selection process. The Post-Bid/Proposal Phase is the period after the Bid/Proposal has been submitted to the buyer.

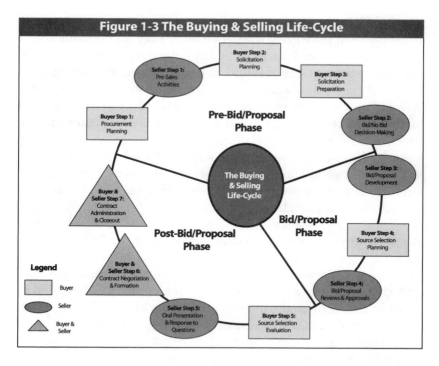

Figure 1-3 The Buying & Selling Life-Cycle

Pre-Bid/Proposal Phase

Buyer Step 1: Procurement Planning

Procurement planning is determining what to procure and when. The first contract management problem for the buyer is to decide which goods and services to provide or perform in-house and which to outsource. This *make-or-buy or outsourcing decision* requires consideration of many factors, some of which are strategically important. The decision to outsource creates a project that will be implemented in cooperation with an outside organization that is not entirely within the buyer's control. Market research is an essential element, which enables the buyer to more fully understand their purchasing options.

The relationship between buyer and seller is a legal, if not economic, relationship of equals. The contract binds them to one another but does not place one under the other's managerial control. Sometimes the seller's economic position may be so powerful, however, that the *terms and conditions* (Ts and Cs) of the contract are ineffective in protecting the interests of the buyer.

For the seller, the contract will present an opportunity to succeed, but it also will pose great risks. The seller may find that the buyer has specified its need inadequately or defectively; the seller's marketing department has oversold its products, services, or capabilities; faulty communication has transpired between the two parties during contract formation; or more likely, some combination of all three has occurred. In any of these cases, performance may be much more demanding than originally contemplated and may even be beyond the seller's capabilities. In addition, the buyer may wield great economic power, which effectively outweighs the contract Ts and Cs designed to protect the seller from the buyer's potentially unreasonable demands.

All the communication break downs, misunderstandings, conflicts, and disputes that can occur within virtually every organization also can occur between organizations, often with greater virulence and more disastrous effect. Although the contract is intended to provide a remedy to the injured party if the other fails to fulfill its contractual obligations, it is not a guarantee. Legal remedies may be uncertain and, even if attained, may not fully compensate the injured party for the other party's failure.

The outsourcing decision can be a critical one for any organization. After the decision to contract for goods or services is made, the buyer must plan carefully and implement the decision properly.

Buyer Step 2: Solicitation Planning

In the course of planning, the buyer must:

- Conduct market research
- Determine how to specify its requirements or deliverables
- Identify potential sources
- Analyze the sources of uncertainty and risk that the purchase will entail
- Develop performance-based standards, metrics, and incentives
- Choose the methods for selecting a seller and for proposal evaluation, negotiation, and contract formation
- Arrange for effective administration of the contract

Developing a Statement of Work (SOW) or Performance Work Statement (PWS), or Statement of Objectives (SOO) is one of the most difficult challenges in procurement planning. First, the buyer must understand its own requirements - quite a difficult task. Second, the buyer must be able to communicate those requirements, typically in the form of either specific deliverables or some form of a level of effort, to others outside the buyer's organization - an even more difficult task. Because developing and communicating performance-based requirements is one of the most critical functions in contract management.

Buyer Step 3: Solicitation Preparation

Buyers may request bids, quotes, tenders, or proposals orally, in writing, or electronically through procurement documents generally called *solicitations.* Solicitations can take the following forms: request for proposals, request for quotations, request for tenders, invitation to bid, invitation for bids, and invitation for negotiation.

Solicitations should communicate the buyer's needs clearly to all potential sellers. Submitting a high-quality solicitation is vital to the buyer's success. Better solicitations from the buyer generally result in having better bids, quotes, proposals, or tenders submitted by the seller in a more timely manner. Poorly communicated solicitations often result in delays, confusion, fewer bids or proposals, and lower-quality responses. Increasingly, buyers are using electronic data interchange and electronic commerce to solicit offers from sellers of products and services worldwide.

Seller Step 1: Presales Activities

Presales activities are the proactive involvement of the seller with prospective and current buyers. Presales activities include identifying prospective and current customers, determining their needs and plans, appropriately influencing customer requirements, and evaluating competitors. The most successful of these activities include proactive sales management and the extensive use of market research, benchmarking, and competitive analysis as proven tools and techniques to improve customer focus, gain insight, and provide advantage over competitors.

Seller Step 2: Bid/No Bid Decision

Making the bid/no-bid decision should be a multi-part process: evaluating the buyer's solicitation, understanding the competitive environment, and assessing the risks against the opportunities for a prospective contract. This step is critical to the contract management process; however, far too many sellers devote too little time and attention to properly evaluating the risks before they leap into preparing bids and proposals.

Effectively managing risk is one of the keys to the success of sellers in today's highly competitive global business environment. Several world-class companies have developed tools and techniques to help their business managers in evaluating the risks versus the opportunities of potential contracts. The tools they use involve risk identification, risk analysis, and risk mitigation.

Bid/Proposal Phase

Buyer Step 4: Source Selection Planning

Clearly, seller selection is one of the most important decisions a buyer will make. Contract success or failure will depend on the competence and reliability of one or more key sellers and their subcontractors. Procurement planners must identify potential sources of goods and services, analyze the nature of the industry and market in which they operate, develop criteria and procedures to evaluate each source, and select one for contract award. No single set of criteria or procedures is appropriate for all procurements; thus, to some extent, original analyses must be made for each contract.

Source selection may be as simple as determining which competing set of bid prices is the lowest. On the other hand, it may involve weeks or even months of proposal analysis, plant visits, prototype development, and testing. The selection may be accomplished by one person, or it may require an extended effort by a panel of company managers.

Today, companies are spending more time planning and conducting source selection than ever before. The industry trend is toward more comprehensive screening and selection of fewer suppliers for longer duration contracts.

Seller Step 3: Bid/Proposal Development

Bid or proposal development is the process of creating offers in response to oral or written solicitations or based on perceived buyer needs. Bid and proposal development can range from one person writing a one- or two-page proposal to a team of people developing a multivolume proposal of thousands of pages that takes months to prepare.

As you develop the solution in more detail, you should take steps to ensure it is holistically compliant with the customer's technical, delivery, financial and contractual requirements. You also need to ensure the design is consistent with the description in the proposal and the pricing developed. Finally, you need to develop a delivery plan which addresses the fundamentals of who, what, when, where and how the solution will be delivered.

As you develop the solution, you will likely find gaps or potential adverse situations which could occur. These are risks that need to be addressed. For each of these risks, you need to develop a Risk Mitigation Plan using one or more strategies designed to avoid, transfer, share or reserve the risk. These plans will become an important part of the review with Stakeholders later to obtain their authority to bid.

As the solution takes shape, you will develop one or more business cases. Ideally, you will develop a customer business case showing the costs and benefits of the solution in the customer's financial terms. At a minimum, you need to develop an internal business case on the profitability of the opportunity for review with the Stakeholders in order to obtain their authority to bid.

Finally, you need to develop the proposal or customer deliverable(s). Although the actual format will vary, major components of a customer proposal typically include:

a) Executive Summary,
b) Technical Response,
c) Delivery Response,
d) Pricing Response, and
e) Contractual Response.

The Executive Summary provides an overview of the offer and is targeted to executive decision makers in the customer's organization. The win strategy and solution architecture serve as the skeleton for the Executive Summary, which is augmented with key details from the Technical Response, Delivery Response, Pricing Response, and Contractual Response.

The Technical Response describes the products and services being offered and explains how they solve the customer's business problems. The Delivery Response describes the specifics of "how," "when" and "who" will deliver and support the offer and may include such items as an Implementation Plan, Delivery Schedule, Transition Plan, Maintenance Plan or Support Plan. Even if the Delivery Response is not delivered to the customer, a well thought out and realistic Implementation Plan should be developed for internal purposes to understand how the project will be delivered. Depending upon the scope and complexity of what is being offered, it may be appropriate to operationally view the Technical and Delivery Response as a single deliverable for proposal development and review purposes.

The Pricing Response describes how the offer is priced and price terms. The Contractual Response describes the terms and conditions under which the offer is being made and typically includes such topics as internal commitments, warranty, payment terms and liabilities. If financing is being offered to the customer, this would typically be described in the Pricing Response, but may alternatively appear in the Contractual Response. Depending upon the scope and complexity of what is being offered, it may be appropriate to operationally view the Pricing and Contractual Responses as a single deliverable for proposal development and review purposes.

Seller Step 4: Bid/Proposal Reviews & Approval

The type and number of Bid/Proposal Reviews is based on the scope and complexity of the opportunity and the time available. Bid/Proposal Reviews can be classified into two types: a) internally focused review and b) externally focused review.

An internally focused review, typically referred to as a Pink Team Review, is usually conducted by members of the Bid/Proposal or Capture Team reading what others on the team have written. The chief focus of an internal Pink Team review is to ensure the proposal is complete and accurate. Depending upon the complexity and scope of the offer and the time available, there may be multiple Pink Team Reviews. Due to specialization of resources, there will frequently be different review team members for the major sections of the proposal (e.g., Executive Summary, Technical Delivery, Pricing and Contractual).

Externally focused reviews, typically referred to as a Red Team Review, are conducted by individuals who are not members of the Capture Team. These "unbiased" and "impartial" individuals will read what has been written from the customer's perspective. The chief focus of an external Red Team review is to ensure the proposal makes sense and addresses specified customer requirements. Depending upon the scope and complexity of the offer and time available, there may be multiple Red Team reviews. Due to specialization of resources and complexity of the proposal, there will frequently be different review team members for the major sections of the proposal (e.g., Executive Summary, Technical, Delivery, Pricing, Contractual).

It is recommended that you document all reviews and the completeness of the bid. This not only provides a record of the review, it also creates a sense of formality that will motivate the reviewers to take the sessions more seriously. This documentation can take many forms, but typically consists of an Offer Certification by team leaders or reviewers that the bid is compliant with all technical, delivery, financial and contractual requirements. Areas of non-compliance need to be identified as either exceptions that will be highlighted to the customer or risks your company is assuming in the bid.

During the executive review and approval, typically referred to as a "Gold Team Review/Approval," you should review all of the key information from the earlier reviews. You need to gauge the level of executive review required based on numerous factors such as: the scope of the opportunity, complexity, urgency of the requirements, knowledge of the customer's needs, goals, budget, competition in the market, etc. Additional key information that should be reviewed and includes:

- Changes in Opportunity Profile
- Solution Developed
- Risk Mitigation Plans
- Business Case (Including Profitability of the Offer)

You should also hold a "roll call" confirming the executives support and approval. Depending upon the scope of the opportunity, and the seller's corporate Schedule of Authorizations or Approvals, you may also need to obtain approval of senior executives in your company (i.e., CEO or President) or potentially even the Board of Directors.

Post-Bid/Proposal Phase

Having submitted your bid or proposal to the buyer, now the real dancing begins. The Post-Bid/Proposal Phase starts once the proposal is submitted to the buyer and includes all the key actions required to close the sale, negotiate the deal, deliver the solution, look for process improvements, and identify follow-on opportunities.

Buyer Step 5: Source Selection Evaluation

Source selection is all about the buyer evaluating the seller's offers (bids, proposals, tenders, and/or oral presentation) and all of the seller's appropriate qualifications – past performance, use of small business, financial strength, reputation, use of break through technologies, etc. Selecting the right source, like selecting the right dance partner, is critical to ultimate business success. The key to source selection is to make the right partner selection as efficiently, quickly, and cost-effectively as possible. Source selection is typically driven by the people chosen to serve on the source selection team, the source selection process, the source selection evaluation criteria & weightings, and the source selection authority or key decision maker.

Seller Step 5: Oral Presentation & Responses to Questions

For most strategic bids or proposals sellers will have an opportunity to provide an oral presentation of their bid or proposal to a select group of the buyer. If the buyer does not offer this opportunity, the seller should request permission to provide such a presentation. This will give the seller a chance to review the bid or proposal and reinforce their win strategy with the Buyer's key influencers and decision makers. Depending upon the scope of the bid or proposal, this may involve multiple presentations to multiple audiences. If the seller is not given the chance to provide an oral presentation, then the Buyer will typically transmit numerous questions via email to the seller(s) requesting their timely responses. Thus, the seller(s) will often reconvene their respective capture team to prepare appropriate responses to all of the Buyer's questions.

Buyer & Seller Step 6: Contract Negotiation and Formation

After a source is selected, the parties must reach a common understanding of the nature of their undertaking and negotiate the Ts and Cs of contract performance. The ideal is to develop a set of shared expectations and understandings. However, this goal is difficult to attain for several reasons. First, either party may not fully understand its own requirements and expectations. Second, in most communication, many obstacles prevent achieving a true "meeting of the minds." Errors, miscues, hidden agendas, cultural differences, differences in linguistic use and competence, haste, lack of clarity in thought or expression, conflicting objectives, lack of good faith (or even ill will), business exigencies – all these factors can and do contribute to poor communication.

In any undertaking, uncertainty and risk arise from many sources. In a business undertaking, many of those sources are characteristic of the industry or industries involved. Because one purpose of a contract is to manage uncertainty and risk, the types and sources of uncertainty and risk must be identified and understood. Then buyer and seller must develop and agree to contract Ts and Cs that are designed to express their mutual expectations about performance and that reflect the uncertainties and risks of performance. Although tradition and the experiences of others provide a starting point for analysis, each contract must be considered unique.

The development of appropriate Ts and Cs is an important aspect of contract negotiation and formation. (Common Ts and Cs include period of performance, warranties, intellectual property rights, payments, acceptance/completion criteria, and change management.) Some organizations spend a lot of time, perhaps months, selecting a source, but they hurry through the process of arriving at a mutual understanding of the contract Ts and Cs. A "let's get on with it" mentality sets in. It is true that contracts formed in this way sometimes prove successful for all concerned. However, when both sides involve large organizations, difficulties can arise from the different agendas of the functional groups existing within each organization's contracting party.

Some world-class organizations have developed internal electronic systems to help their contract managers in negotiating, forming, and approving their contracts.

Buyer and Seller Step 7: Contract Performance, Administration & Closeout

Contract performance is essentially doing what you said you were going to do. Contract administration is the process of ensuring compliance with contractual Ts and Cs during contract performance and up to and including contract closeout or termination.

After award, both parties must act according to the Ts and Cs of their agreement; they must read and understand their contract, do what it requires of them, and avoid doing what they have agreed not to do.

☆ BEST PRACTICES: IN CONTRACT ADMINISTRATION

- Reading the contract
- Ensuring that all organizational elements are aware of their responsibilities in relation to the contract
- Providing copies of the contract to all affected organizations (either paper or electronic copies)
- Establishing systems to verify conformance with contract technical and administrative requirements
- Conducting preperformance (or kickoff) meetings with the buyer and seller
- Assigning responsibility to check actual performance against requirements
- Identifying significant variances
- Analyzing each such variance to determine its cause
- Ensuring that someone takes appropriate corrective action and then follows up
- Managing the contract change process

- Establishing and maintaining contract documentation: diaries and telephone logs, meeting minutes, inspection reports, progress reports, test reports, invoices and payment records, accounting source documents, accounting journals and ledgers, contracting records, change orders and other contract modifications, claims, and routine correspondence.

Periodically, buyer and seller must meet to discuss performance and verify that it is on track and that each party's expectations are being met. This activity is critical. Conflict is almost inescapable within and between organizations. The friction that can arise from minor misunderstandings, failures, and disagreements can heat to the boiling point before anyone on either side is fully aware of it. When this happens, the relationship between the parties may be irreparably damaged, and amicable problem resolution may become impossible. Periodic joint assessments by contract managers can identify and resolve problems early and help to ensure mutually satisfactory performance.

Some world-class companies use electronic systems to assist them with contract monitoring, performance measurement, progress reporting, and contract compliance documentation.

Contract Closeout or Termination

After the parties have completed the main elements of performance, they must settle final administrative and legal details before closing out the contract. They may have to make price adjustments and settle claims. The buyer will want to evaluate the seller's performance. Both parties must collect records and prepare them for storage in accordance with administrative and legal retention requirements.

Unfortunately, contracts are sometimes terminated due to the mutual agreement of the parties or due to the failure of one or both of the parties to perform all or part of the contract. After a termination notice is received, the parties must still go through the same closeout actions as for a completed contract.

SELECTED INTERVIEW

Name: Linda Riviera

Job Title: Contracting Officer

Organization: National Aeronautics and Space Administration (NASA), Office of Procurement, Johnson Space Center (JSC)

Location: Houston, TX

Major Responsibilities: Currently supporting source selection evaluation board activities within the Center Operations Directorate as the Contracting Officer on a major acquisition. Other major activities include supporting the Institutional Procurement Office as a Contracting Officer in the contract extension activities for a major contract within the Center Operations Directorate.

Background: Linda Riviera is a Level III Contracting Officer working for the Office of Procurement at the NASA Johnson Space Center in Houston, Texas. During her 15 year career with NASA, she has supported various center organizations including the Mission Operations Directorate, the International Space Station Program and most recently the Center Operations Directorate. During her career at JSC, she has also supported several source evaluation boards and was named to the Source Evaluation Board Review committee that was charted to review and recommend improvements to the SEB process at JSC. For this effort, she was awarded the Space Flight Awareness Team Award and the Acquisition Improvement Award. For her "outstanding efforts in supporting professional development and training within the Office of Procurement," Linda was awarded the Center Director Commendation which is JSC's highest honor. Linda began her contracting career working for the International Business Machines Corporation in Arlington, Virginia. Linda is a graduate of New Mexico State University where she received a bachelor's degree in Business Administration. Linda is a 15 year member of NCMA and is the former President of the Space City Chapter in Houston, Texas. Linda now serves on the Chapter's Board of Advisors.

QUESTIONS & ANSWERS:

Question: What do you consider to be proven best practices for Buyers when conducting procurement planning and developing solicitations?

Answer: I consider the best proven best practice for buyers when conducting procurement planning and developing solicitations is for the buying team to allow time in the initial stages of the acquisition cycle for planning the strategy. I have participated in several acquisition teams that developed a vision statement and statement of objective for the acquisition as the initial step in planning the strategy. This process clearly set the objectives of the acquisition team and clearly defined the needs of the customer and the agency. Once the strategy has been defined, the next most important step is to share the strategy with industry. The Johnson Space Center recently initiated "Industry Day" in its acquisition planning. The purpose of Industry Day is to promote competition on the proposed acquisition, increase industry understanding of the existing requirements and to allow NASA/JSC to utilize and incorporate selected industry comments to improve the acquisition strategy. Industry Day is held early in the acquisition planning cycle, prior to release of any draft documents such as the Draft Request For Proposal and well in advance of the pre-proposal conference. The comments that JSC has received from the selling community as a result of implementing Industry Day has been overwhelming positive. The potential offerors have an opportunity to understand the acquisition strategy and provide comments, begin developing partnering arrangements, and meet the members of the acquisition team. This added step in the procurement planning and solicitation phase of the acquisition has proven to be a best practice for JSC.

Question: What actions do you suggest sellers take to ethically and appropriately influence buyer's requirements?

Answer: The best opportunity for sellers to influence buyer requirements is in the initial stages of the acquisition planning. The Government buyer may solicit from industry comments to the acquisition strategy in general and to specific areas of the strategy such as contract type, period of performance, and performance incentives. Sellers should articulate their understanding of the strategy, provide positive or negative comments with supporting rationale and provide examples of their company best practices with similar types of contracts. In addition to soliciting written comments from sellers, the buying team may allow sellers to have one-on-one visits with the buying team. JSC has initiated "Discussions with Industry" which was initiated to foster open communications with industry. Prospective offerors are invited to meet with the buying organization management team as well as the buying team. The meetings are limited in time and frequency and include guidelines as to what may and may not be discussed. Using these examples and following the requests of the RFI and ground rules for industry discussions, the sellers have the opportunity to ethically and appropriately influence buyer requirements.

Question: What do you consider to be the top five Seller best practices for developing a winning bid or proposal?

Answer: 1. The seller must develop their internal acquisition strategy which includes market research, know the competition and understand the buyer requirements.

ONE

2. The seller must read the requirements of the Request For Proposal (RFP) and generate a technical and cost proposal that clearly articulate the sellers methodology for fulfilling the buyer requirements.

3. The seller must prepare for oral discussions by clearly identifying the roles of the selling team, articulating the selling team's commitment and understanding of the acquisition, and being prepared with solutions to any weaknesses identified to the seller prior to oral discussions.

4. The seller should ensure that all issues or questions regarding the solicitation are asked early on by submitting questions to the RFP to the buying team.

5. The seller should ensure that the best and final proposal has been reviewed, over and over again, to ensure that it's the best product that it can be and that weaknesses identified in oral discussions have been addressed.

Question: How can U.S. Government agencies truly streamline and improve their source selection process?

Answer: Although government agencies follow source selections procedures identified in the Federal Acquisition Regulation, there is always room for improvement for internal agency processes. In recent years, JSC has been proactive in the improvement of their internal source selection process. The most significant change was the implementation of procurement websites for all major acquisitions at JSC. The procurement websites include items that were generally not available to the public such as identifying the members of the source evaluation board, the source selection authority, copies of the current contract, which was once available only via a FOIA request, and the posting of the

Building a Winning Contract

source selection statement. In my opinion, this website is a tool that has leveled the playing field for all sellers. JSC is making available as much information as possible to industry regarding the acquisition as a supplement to FEDBIZOPPS. JSC has also created an external website that provides general information and is the portal that links to the specific JSC acquisition websites.

Below is an example of the external JSC Office of Procurement website.

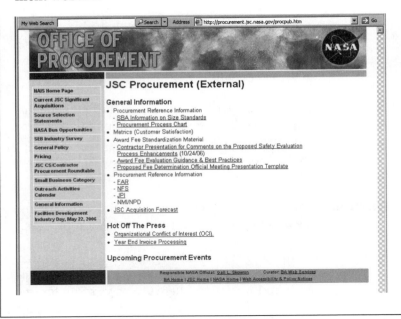

ONE

Below is an example of a specific aquisition website at JSC.

 Occupational Medicine and Occupational Health Contract Acquisition Website

Acquisition Information Links

Source Selection Statement

Any inconsistencies between the electronic copy of the Source Selection Statement and the original signed document contained in the contract file, the original signed document prevails.

- Synopsis
- Request For Information (RFI)
- Statement of Work Summary
  - DRAFT RFP Statement of Work (2/2/05)
  - Statement of Work (12/5/01)
- Schedule (3/10/05)
- Request For Proposal
- Membership
  - Procurement development Team (PDT)
  - SSA Contacts
  - SEB Membership
- Anonymous Questions to the Contracting Officer
- Procurement Strategy
- Pre-Proposal Conference

- Site Visit Schedule
- Official Updates & Info
- NASA Acquisition Internet Service (NAIS)
- Official Questions & Answers
- Official Questions & Answers #2
- Official Questions & Answers #3
- Vendors Expressing Interest
- Discussion with Industry
- Technical Library
- Contacts
- Feedback
- Industry Feedback Survey

Question: Please share a brief personal success story regarding: Solicitations, Bids/Proposals, or Source Selection – Building a Winning contract.

Answer: During the past several years I have been assigned to serve as the Contracting Officer for several very large acquisitions at the Johnson Space Center (JSC). One of my assignments included supporting the Mission Integration Contract (MIC) source evaluation board (SEB) which provides mission integration and language translations in support of the International Space Station Program (ISS). This SEB was one of several that were initiated to support the new requirements of the ISS program. It was at this time that JSC first implemented the use of websites for their acquisitions to ensure that as much information that the buying team could share, would be shared with industry. All of the ISS SEB's engaged in extensive market research and relied on industry comments to help formulate the ISS procurement strategy. The MIC team that I supported utilized the comments from industry to develop their strategy and to define their requirements. The team worked diligently to ensure that the RFP was the best it could be. Every detail of the Pre-proposal conference, site tours, and oral discussions, were carefully planned incorporating best practices whenever we could or redefining and improving the SEB process. The result was award of a contract to a company demonstrating technical excellence at a reasonable cost to the Government. Equally important, the unsuccessful offerors were satisfied that their proposals had been treated fairly in the evaluation process. After debriefings were held, questionnaires were sent out to all the interested parties asking for feedback and comments to our acquisition process. The procurement team received very positive feedback and industry applauded the open lines of communications that began with the initial phase of the acquisitions and continued to source selection. Many procurement processes initiated with the ISS SEBs resulted in improvements to JSC source selection process. In my opinion, this was a great example of a buying government team working together to build a winning contract.

Note: The subject interview solely expresses the informal opinions' of the interviewee, they do not necessarily represent the views or opinions of the organization, company, or agency which they are employed.

ONE

Summary

In this chapter, we have discussed the need for buyers and sellers to work together to create and deliver value to their end customers through quality contracts. Like projects, contracts must be managed effectively to be successful. Business professionals are responsible for managing contracts - how you will be affected by a particular contract and how you will manage it will depend on whether you are acting as the buyer or the seller of the product or service.

The buying and selling life-cycle is composed of three phases and seven steps required by the buyer and seven steps by the seller. However, even the most effective business process can work only if the senior management and all team members commit to making it happen. At the end of each subsequent chapter there will be a brief section entitled "Straight Talk: Suggestions for Significant Improvement." This Straight Talk section will include very candid and sometimes controversial suggestions for business changes which some individuals may view as radical and perhaps politically incorrect. However, we believe these suggestions need to be put on the table for discussion to help both the public and private business sectors find ways to reduce costs and improve performance results. This book is focused on providing a detailed discussion of the three phases, seven steps, and numerous best practices contained within the buying and selling life-cycle, with special emphasis on the planning, preparation, and execution of solicitations, bids/proposals, and source selection to build a winning contract.

Questions to Consider

1. Does your buying organization follow a well documented, mutually agreed to, and effectively executed procurement process – from requirement determination through product/service/solution delivery?

2. Does your selling organization follow a well documented, mutually agreed to, and effectively executed sales/business development capture process – from opportunity identification through product/service/solution delivery and payment?

3. What do you consider to be your organization's buying/selling strengths?

4. What do you consider to be your organization's buying/selling weaknesses?

CHAPTER  2

PRE-BID/ PROPOSAL PHASE: PROCUREMENT PLANNING, SOLICITATION PLANNING AND PREPARATION

INTRODUCTION

Said simply, procurement planning, solicitation planning and preparation is the buyer's process of identifying which business needs can best be met by procuring products or services outside the organization and then requesting the desired products or services from qualified sellers. The buyer's procurement planning, solicitation planning, and solicitation preparation process involves determining: whether to outsource, how to solicit bids/proposals, what to buy, how much to buy, when to buy, how much seller participation is appropriate, what type of pricing arrangement is appropriate, and what resources are needed. Market research is vital to selecting the right source and obtaining the best deal.

According to the May 2006 – Center for Advance Purchasing Studies (CAPS) Cross-Industry Benchmarking results, outsourcing continues to grow throughout the 300+ companies in more than 20 industries studied. In fact, the average company spends 43.69 percent of their sales dollars purchasing products and services from other companies, this percentage has continually grown over the past five years.

The CAPS Cross-Industry Benchmarking results indicate some business processes and actions are clearly changing, while others are remaining pretty much the same. For example, the CAPS Cross-Industry Benchmarking results show that most industries spend a lot of their money purchasing products and services, but are continually reducing their number of suppliers. To further illustrate, just a few years ago, the number of Active Suppliers who accounted for 80 percent of Purchase Spend was approx. 10 percent. Today, the average number of Active Suppliers who account for 80 percent of Purchase Spend is 6.46 percent. Also changing, is the percent of Purchase Spend with diversity suppliers, which a few years ago was approximately 5 percent. Today the average number is 9.63 percent – it has nearly doubled! Further, a key item to watch is the percent of companies outsourcing some of their purchasing activities, which a few years ago the average was approximately 10 percent. Today the average number is 29 percent – it has nearly tripled!

As stated earlier, based upon the subject survey results some procurement activities are staying the same. An example includes the percent of active suppliers who are e-procurement enabled, which was about 11 percent a few years ago and today remains about the same. In addition, the percent of purchases via e-auctions remains between 2 to 3 percent, and the percent Purchase Spend via procurement cards remains between 1 to 2 percent. Table 2-1 provides a quick summary of some of the key results of the CAPS Research – Report of Cross-Industry Benchmarks (May 2006).

Table 2-1 Center for Advanced Purchasing Studies CAPS Research Report of Cross-Industry Benchmarks (May 2006)			
Benchmark	Cross-Industry Average	Telecommunications Average	Aerospace & Defense Average
Purchase Spend as a Percent of Sales Dollars	43.69%	43.46%	44.77%
Purchase Operating Expense as a Percent of Sales Dollars	0.39%	0.24%	1.05%
Purchasing Operating Expense per Purchasing Employee	$110,320	$124,908	$120,238
Percent Spend Managed by Purchasing	80.62%	76.31%	93.28%
Percent of Companies Outsourcing Some of Their Purchasing Activities	29.00%	30.00%	30.00%
Active Suppliers Accounting for 80% of Purchase Spend	6.46%	1.73%	4.79%
Percent of Active Suppliers Who are e-Procurement Enabled	11.16%	8.53%	8.42%
Percent Purchase Spend via e-Procurement	16.45%	7.00%	5.65%
Percent of Purchase spend with Diversity Suppliers	9.63%	7.27%	12.69%

This chapter will provide an in depth discussion of the procurement planning, solicitation planning and preparation process (see Figure 2-1, "The Buying & Selling Life-Cycle"). This chapter will also offer numerous proven effective best practices, and provide selected interviews from U.S. Government and industry experts.

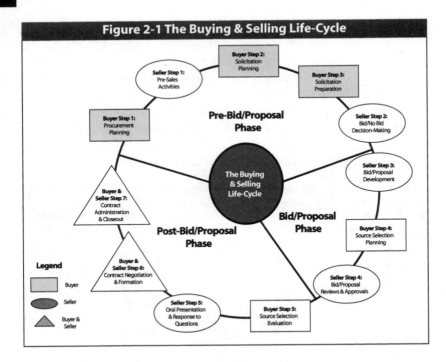

Figure 2-2 illustrates the Buyer's Step 1: Procurement Planning Process including key inputs, proven tools and techniques, and desired outputs.

Figure 2-2 Buyer Step 1: Procurement Planning Process

Input	Tools & Techniques	Output
• Similar past Performance Work Statements (PWS), Statement of Objectives (SOO), or Solicitations • Procurement Resources • Market Conditions • Business Constraints • Business Assumptions	• Outsource Analysis • Market Research • Expert judgment • e-Procurement and Contracting Methods • Contract type or Pricing Arrangements	• Procurement Management Plan • Seller Participation and Feedback

*Adapted from: "World Class Contracting," by Gregory A. Garrett, CCH, 2006.

TWO

Key Inputs

- Similar past Performance Work Statements (PWS), Statements of Objectives (SOO), or Solicitation documents.
- *Procurement resources:* If the organization does not have contract management resources, the business team managing the contract process must supply both the resources and the expertise to support procurement activities.
- *Market conditions:* The procurement planning process must include consideration of what products and services are available in the marketplace, from whom, and under what terms and conditions.
- *Business constraints:* Constraints are factors that limit the buyer's options. Constraints typically include: funds availability, past experience, resource availability, urgency of the requirements, etc.
- *Business assumptions:* Assumptions are factors that, for planning purposes, are considered to be true, real, or certain. Assumptions made should always be documented.

Tools and Techniques

The following tools and techniques are used for procurement planning:

- *Outsource Analysis:* The decision to outsource must be based upon effective market research, experience, and made in cooperation with a multifunctional team, the precise size and identity of which depends on the nature of the undertaking and the buyer's business and organization. The purchasing or contracting department should be consulted for obvious reasons, but other interested or affected functional organizations could include research and development, marketing and sales, finance, engineering, manufacturing, human resources, security, and legal, to name a few.

    The decision to outsource or buy is essentially a decision to meld the seller's organization with the buyer's. However, the decision casts the business professional's usual challenges of communication and control in an unusual light, because he or she must communicate and exercise control through the special medium of the contract.

    Outsource analysis must reflect the perspective of the performing organization as well as the immediate business needs. For example, purchasing a capital item (anything from a construction crane to a personal computer) rather than renting it is seldom cost-effective. However if the performing organization has an ongoing need for the item, the portion of the purchase cost allocated to the project may be less than the cost of the rental.

■ *Market research:* It is imperative to take the time to conduct effective market research to understand what best-in-class companies are doing in terms of products, services, and solutions. Further, it is very important to gather information either via web-based surveys, telephone surveys/interviews, or more detailed one-on-one meetings to determine what are the proven effective performance standards, measures, metrics, and incentives to achieve excellent results.

■ *Expert judgment:* Assessing the input to the procurement planning process often requires expert judgment. Such expertise may be provided by any group or individual with specialized knowledge or training and is available from many sources, including other units within the performing organization, consultants and educators, professional and technical associations, and industry groups.

e-Procurement and Contracting Methods

There are two main approaches to contracting: *competitive methods,* such as purchase cards, imprest funds, auctioning, net marketplaces, vertical exchanges, horizontal exchanges, web portals, sealed bidding, private exchanges, two-step sealed bidding, and competitive negotiations, and *noncompetitive methods,* such as purchase agreements and sole-source or single-source negotiations (see Table 2-1).

Table 2-1: Two Approaches to Contracting		
	Competitive	**Noncompetitive**
Simplified	• Purchase Cards • Imprest funds or petty cash • Auctioning • Net marketplaces • Vertical exchanges • Horizontal exchanges • Web portals	• Purchase agreements
Formal	• Sealed bidding • Private exchanges • Two-step sealed bidding • Competitive proposals • Competitive negotiations	• Sole-source negotiation • • Single-source negotiation

Using Competitive Contracting Methods

Many competitive contracting methods to obtain products and services exist, ranging from simple to highly complex; all involve aspects of e-procurement.

Simplified Competitive Contracting Methods

Simplified competitive contracting methods include:

- *Purchasing or procurement cards (P-cards):* An organization's credit card commonly used to purchase low-price, off-the-shelf products and services. The degree of competition depends on the guidelines that the procurement organization provides to the individuals empowered to use the P-card. Most companies set predetermined spending limits on employee usage and track purchases to ensure that purchases are for business purposes only.
- *Imprest funds or petty cash:* A small amount of money used to pay for small purchases of common products or services. Source selection depends on the company's or organization's purchasing guidelines.
- *Auctioning:* A widely practiced head-to-head bidding method, typically done face-to-face or via teleconferences, that is used to increase direct competition and that can be applied to the purchase of any product or service.
- *Net marketplaces:* Two-sided Internet-based exchange where buyers and sellers negotiate prices, usually with a bid-and-ask system, and where prices move both up and down.
- *Vertical exchanges:* A form of net marketplace that is specific to a single industry.
- *Horizontal exchanges:* A form of net marketplace that deals with goods and services that are not specific to one industry.
- *Web portal:* A public exchange, which may be a vertical exchange or horizontal exchange, in which a company or group of companies lists products and services for sale and/or shares other business information.

Formal Competitive Contracting Methods

Formal competitive contracting methods are controlled bidding processes that keep pressure on competitors throughout the source selection process. Most of that pressure bears on price. Thus, from the buyer's point of view, competitive bidding is a highly effective technique for keeping prices low.

However, several disadvantages are associated with competitive bidding. First, it can be a costly process to administer because of the need to evaluate multiple formal proposals, and it can occupy a buyer's personnel for an extended time. Second, it can stifle communication between the buyer and seller during contract formation because of the need to protect confidential information in the competitor's proposals. This increases the risk of misunderstandings and disputes during contract performance. Third, the pressure to keep prices low can drive them below the point of realism, increasing cost risk and the attendant risk of poor seller performance and disputes. Competitive bidding, more so than other approaches, may create an adversarial relationship between buyer and seller, especially when the process takes on the characteristics of sealed bidding.

Nevertheless, competitive bidding can be effective, especially for purchasing commodities and for simple projects in which price is the most important factor. Most contracts for construction projects are still awarded through competitive bidding, as are most government contracts worldwide.

Sealed Bid

Competitive bidding usually takes the form of *sealed bidding,* in which price is the only criterion for selecting a source from a set of competing, prequalified sources. This technique entails soliciting, typically electronically, firm bids. The solicitation describes what the seller must do or deliver, the performance terms and conditions (Ts and Cs), and the deadline and location for submitting the bids. The bids usually state nothing more than the offered price. Sometimes bidders state their own Ts and Cs.

After the deadline passes, the buyer reviews the bids and evaluates them by comparing the prices offered. Buyers usually select the lowest bidder, but not always. The buyer may reject the lowest bids because they are too risky or because the bidder is not qualified. In the commercial world, the parties may negotiate after bid opening to reach agreement on details. Some buyers negotiate prices even after soliciting low bids, but this technique is ill-advised because bidders will anticipate the practice in the future and adjust their bids accordingly.

To use sealed bidding, the buyer must have a specification that clearly and definitively describes the required product or service.

For bid price comparison to be meaningful, all bidders must be pricing the same requirement. Otherwise, the bids will not be truly comparable. In addition, the specification must be free of errors, ambiguities, and other defects. If a bidder thinks that the buyer will change the specification during contract performance, that bidder may submit a below-cost bid to win the competition, anticipating the opportunity to increase the cost while negotiating for the change. This practice is called *buying in*.

In addition, because sealed bidding makes sense only for the award of firm-fixed-price contracts, performance cost uncertainty must be low. Otherwise, selecting the lowest bid will be a decision to select the proposal with the highest cost risk, which as already discussed, can have serious consequences. In a firm-fixed-price contract awarded by sealed bidding, an adversarial relationship is likely to develop between buyer and seller.

When using sealed bidding, the buyer must prequalify bidders or provide another way to ensure that the low bidder is competent to perform the work satisfactorily. Most buyers have a standard procedure by which potential sources can get on the *bidder's mailing list* or *qualified suppliers' list*. Many buyers will not entertain a bid from a source that is not prequalified by the quality and purchasing departments. Some buyers wait until after bids are reviewed and the low bidder is identified to determine its competence to perform, but this procedure is a wasteful one that frequently delays contract award.

Private Exchanges

Today many companies have developed private exchanges to procure goods and services from prequalified or preauthorized sellers. A private exchange is hosted by a single company and is located behind or inside the company's firewall. A private exchange typically operates using either a sealed bidding process or an e-auction process. More and more companies are using private exchanges to get the benefit of competition, but are doing it in a controlled and secure electronic environment.

Two-Step Sealed Bidding

The *two-step sealed bidding* method requires sellers to first submit their technical proposal, typically electronically, and all other management and company qualification information, including past performance information. The buyer evaluates all the technical and other data – everything except pricing information – to determine whether the potential seller is a qualified supplier of the needed products or services.

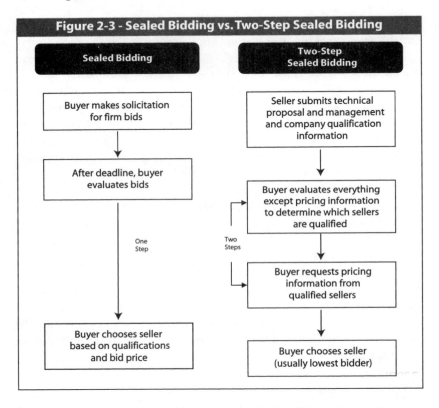

Figure 2-3 - Sealed Bidding vs. Two-Step Sealed Bidding

Sealed Bidding

Buyer makes solicitation for firm bids

After deadline, buyer evaluates bids

One Step

Buyer chooses seller based on qualifications and bid price

Two-Step Sealed Bidding

Seller submits technical proposal and management and company qualification information

Buyer evaluates everything except pricing information to determine which sellers are qualified

Two Steps

Buyer requests pricing information from qualified sellers

Buyer chooses seller (usually lowest bidder)

The buyer then requests that the qualified sellers submit their respective pricing information for evaluation. Typically, the buyer then awards the contract to the qualified seller with the lowest price. Figure 2-3 compares sealed bidding and two-step sealed bidding.

Competitive Negotiations

Sometimes buyers will use *competitive negotiations*, in which they solicit formal proposals from, and have discussions with, several competitors simultaneously. They may request formal *best and final offer (BAFO)* before making a source selection decision. This approach is used commonly in government work and, in recent years, with increasing frequency in the commercial world at large.

In these competitions, technical considerations, such as system design, are often more important than price, and the award is often made to someone other than the lowest bidder.

Competitive negotiations – even with electronic transmission of documents – can be time-consuming, labor-intensive, and costly for both buyers and competitors. Competing businesses must often prepare voluminous proposals full of technical detail, make oral presentations, and prepare numerous proposal revisions and written responses to buyer inquiries. Proposal preparation costs can be high.

Competitive bidding and competitive negotiations have the common trait of merging source selection and contract formation. Combining these steps is accomplished through the buyer's solicitation (invitation for bids, tender, or request for proposals), which not only asks for proposals but also specifies what the buyer wants included as contract terms and conditions (Ts and Cs). The proposal, which is accompanied by other information intended to persuade the buyer that the firm submitting the proposal is the best qualified, is usually a promise to comply with the Ts and Cs in the buyer's solicitation.

If the source has not taken exception to any Ts and Cs in the solicitation and if the buyer is willing to accept all aspects of the proposal, selecting the best-qualified source is tantamount to accepting that firm's proposal. If the source has taken exception or if the buyer does not like all aspects of the source's proposal, the parties must negotiate to reach an agreement.

Using Noncompetitive Contracting Methods

Simplified Noncompetitive Contracting Methods

When a buyer has selected a seller and wants to establish a successful, long-term contract relationship involving repetitive transactions, buyer and seller will commonly use simplified noncompetitive contracting methods to facilitate the process.

These methods include oral contracts, oral contract modifications, and written agreements known as basic ordering agreements, purchase agreements, sales agreements, general agreements, master agreements, distributor agreements, and universal agreements, among other things. These written agreements establish standard

Ts and Cs by which the parties can reduce administrative costs and cycle time and increase customer satisfaction.

Noncompetitive contracting methods can be applied to either single-source or sole-source negotiation.

Formal Noncompetitive Contracting Methods: Single-Source vs. Sole-Source Negotiation

Single-source negotiation occurs when the buyer selects a single company or seller to provide the product or services. In single-source situations, the buyer has the opportunity to select other sellers but has a preference for a specific seller. Sole-source negotiation occurs when there is only one seller that can provide the needed product or service. Thus, a sole-source seller has a monopoly in its market and tremendous leverage with most buyers. Increasingly, buyers are reducing their use of competitive-bidding and relying on negotiation with only one company as a means of awarding contracts. This process entails a more rigorous separation between source selection and contract formation than does competitive bidding.

Source selection is carried out through relatively informal processes of inquiry. Market research provides a short list of potential sources. The companies on this list are contacted usually electronically and asked to complete questionnaires or prepare information packages, or the buyer may simply use the Web and search for specific goods or services via supplier electronic catalogs without preparing a formal request for proposal. The buyer may visit the source to evaluate their facilities and capabilities in person or virtually via videoconferencing, net-meeting, or video tapes.

The buyer may shorten the list to two or three companies to contact for more extensive discussions. When enough information is gathered, the buyer evaluates it and selects a single source for negotiation, leading to contract award. The parties may communicate several times before the source finalizes its proposal. When the source submits its proposal to the buyer, much of it will not be new but will merely confirm agreements reached during preliminary discussions.

After receiving the proposal, typically electronically, and conducting a preliminary analysis, the buyer may engage in *fact finding,* seeking to understand all elements before deciding whether to bargain for better terms. With all the facts in hand, the buyer performs a thorough cost and technical evaluation of the proposal. During this evaluation, the buyer identifies every aspect of the proposal that must be modified through bargaining.

If the buyer decides to bargain, the negotiator develops a *negotiation objective* and presents it to company superiors for approval. If the objective is approved, the negotiator communicates with the source and bargains until the parties reach an agreement or a stalemate. The parties then prepare a document describing the Ts and Cs of their agreement and sign it to complete the source selection and contract formation processes.

Figure 2-4 compares competitive bidding, competitive proposals and negotiations, and single-source and sole-source negotiation.

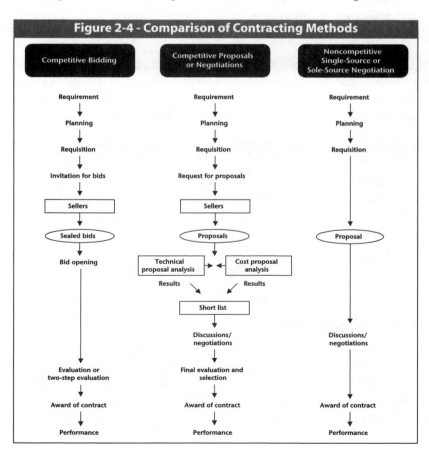

Figure 2-4 - Comparison of Contracting Methods

These proven successful contracting methods may be used in either a paper/written mode or electronically. Competitive contracting methods are used most frequently for the transaction of products and services globally. However, today most of the money is exchanged on large-dollar, multi-year, complex contracts that integrate products, services, and solutions through noncompetitive contracting methods.

Contracting Type or Pricing Arrangements

Over the years some standard pricing arrangements have evolved. These arrangements fall into three categories: *fixed-price, cost-reimbursement,* and *time-and-materials* contracts (PMI designates unit-price contracts as a separate category.) These contract categories have developed as practical responses to cost risk, and they have become fairly standard formal arrangements. Incentives can be added to any of the contract types in these three categories and are discussed in detail later in this chapter. Table 2-1 lists several types of common contracts in these categories.

These pricing arrangements, however, are manifested in the specific terms and conditions of contracts, hence, the contract clauses. No standard clauses for their implementation exist. Therefore, the contracting parties must write clauses that describe their specific agreement.

Table 2-1 Contract Categories and Types			
	Fixed-Price	**Cost-Reimbursement or Unit Price***	**Time-and-Materials**
Types of Contracts	Firm-fixed-price	Cost-reimbursement	Time-and-materials
	Fixed-price with economic price adjustment	Cost-plus-a-percentage-of cost	Unit-price
		Cost-plus-fixed-fee	
	Fixed-price incentive	Cost-plus-incentive fee	
		Cost-plus-award fee	

Fixed-Price Category

Fixed-price contracts are the standard business pricing arrangement. The two basic types of fixed-price contracts are *firm-fixed-price (FFP)* and *fixed-price with economic price adjustment (FP/EPA).* Firm-fixed-price contracts are further divided into *lump-sum* and *unit-price* arrangements.

TWO

Firm-Fixed-Price Contracts

The simplest and most common business pricing arrangement is the FFP contract. The seller agrees to supply specified goods or deliverables in a specified quantity or to render a specified service or level of effort (LOE) in return for a specified price, either a lump sum or a unit price. The price is fixed, that is, not subject to change based on the seller's actual cost experience. (However, it may be subject to change if the parties modify the contract.) This pricing arrangement is used for the sale of commercial goods and services.

Some companies include a complex clause in their FFP contracts. Such a clause may read in part as follows:

Prices and Taxes

> The price of Products shall be ABC Company's published list prices on the date ABC Company accepts your order less any applicable discount. If ABC Company announces a price increase for Equipment, or Software licensed for a one-time fee, after it accepts your order but before shipment, ABC Company shall invoice you at the increased price only if delivery occurs more than 120 days after the effective date of the price increase. If ABC Company announces a price increase for Services, Rentals, or Software licensed for a periodic fee, the price increase shall apply to billing periods beginning after its effective date.

Note that this clause was written by the seller, not the buyer, and reflects the seller's point of view and concerns. Nevertheless, the pricing arrangement it describes is firm-fixed-price, because the contract price will not be subject to adjustment based on ABC Company's actual performance costs.

Clauses such as "Prices and Taxes" frequently form part of a document known as a *universal agreement.* Such a document is not a contract, it is a precontract agreement that merely communicates any agreed-to Ts and Cs that will apply when an order is placed by the buyer. After an order is accepted by the seller, the company's published or announced list prices become the basis for the contract price according to the terms of the universal agreement (this agreement is discussed later in this chapter in "Purchase Agreements").

Firm-fixed-price contracts are appropriate for most commercial transactions when cost uncertainty is within commercially acceptable limits. What those limits may be depends on the industry and the market.

Fixed-Price with Economic Price Adjustment

Fixed-price contracts sometimes include various clauses that provide for adjusting prices based on specified contingencies. The clauses may provide for upward or downward adjustments, or both. Economic price adjustments are usually limited to factors beyond the seller's immediate control, such as market forces.

This pricing arrangement is not *firm*-fixed-price, because the contract provides for a price adjustment based on the seller's actual performance costs. Thus, the seller is protected from the risk of certain labor or material cost increases. The EPA clause can provide for price increases based on the seller's *costs* but not on the seller's decision to increase the *prices* of its products or services. Thus, there can be a significant difference between this clause and the "Prices and Taxes" clause discussed previously.

The shift of risk to the buyer creates greater buyer intrusion into the affairs of the seller. This intrusion typically takes the form of an audit provision at the end of the clause, particularly when the buyer is a government.

EPA clauses are appropriate in times of market instability, when great uncertainty exists regarding labor and material costs. The risk of cost fluctuations is more balanced between the parties than would be the case under an FFP contract.

Cost-Reimbursement Category

Cost-reimbursement (CR) contracts usually include an estimate of project cost, a provision for reimbursing the seller's expenses, and a provision for paying a fee as profit. Normally, CR contracts also include a limitation on the buyer's cost liability.

A common perception is that CR contracts are to be avoided. However, if uncertainty about costs is great enough, a buyer may be unable to find a seller willing to accept a fixed price, even with adjustment clauses, or a seller may insist on extraordinary contingencies within that price. In the latter case, the buyer may find the demands unreasonable. Such high levels of cost uncertainty are often found in research and development, large-scale construction, and systems integration projects. In such circumstances, the best solution may be a CR contract—but only if the buyer is confident that the seller has a highly accurate and reliable cost accounting system.

The parties to a CR contract will find themselves confronting some challenging issues, especially concerning the definition, measurement, allocation, and confirmation of costs. First, the parties must agree on a definition for acceptable cost. For instance, the buyer may decide that the cost of air travel should be limited to the price of a coach or business-class ticket and should not include a first-class ticket. The buyer will specify other cost limitations, and the parties will negotiate until they agree on what constitutes a reimbursable cost.

Next, the parties must decide who will measure costs and what accounting rules will be used to do so. For example, several depreciation techniques are in use, some of which would be less advantageous to the buyer than others. Which technique will the buyer consider acceptable? How will labor costs be calculated? Will standard costs be acceptable, or must the seller determine and invoice actual costs? What methods of allocating overhead will be acceptable to the buyer? How will the buyer know that the seller's reimbursement invoices are accurate? Will the buyer have the right to obtain an independent audit? If the buyer is also a competitor of the seller, should the seller be willing to open its books to the buyer?

If these issues remain unsettled, the buyer is accepting the risk of having to reimburse costs it may later find to be unreasonable. This issue is the central problem with cost-reimbursement contracting, and it has never been resolved entirely.

Clearly, the CR contract presents the parties with difficulties they would not face under a fixed-price contract. First, the parties must define costs and establish acceptable procedures for cost measurement and allocation. Second, the buyer takes on greater cost risk and must incur greater administrative costs to protect its interests. Third, the seller faces greater intrusion by the buyer into its affairs. Nevertheless, many contracting parties have found a CR contract to be a better arrangement than a fixed-price contract for undertakings with high cost uncertainty.

Types of CR contracts include *cost, cost-sharing, cost-plus-a-percentage-of-cost (CPPC)*, and *cost-plus-fixed fee (CPFF)*.

Cost Contracts

The cost contract is the simplest type of CR contract. Governments commonly use this type when contracting with universities and nonprofit organizations for research projects. The contract provides for reimbursing contractually allowable costs, with no allowance given for profit.

Cost-Sharing Contracts

The cost-sharing contract provides for only partial reimbursement of the seller's costs. The parties share the cost liability, with no allowance for profit. The cost-sharing contract is appropriate when the seller will enjoy some benefit from the results of the project and that benefit is sufficient enough to encourage the seller to undertake the work for only a portion of its costs and without fee.

Cost-Plus-a-Percentage-of-Cost Contracts

The CPPC contract provides for the seller to receive reimbursement for its costs and a profit component, called a *fee*, equal to some predetermined percentage of its actual costs. Thus, as costs go up, so does profit. This arrangement is a poor one from the buyer's standpoint, as it provides no incentive to control costs, because the fee becomes greater as the costs increase. This type of contract was used extensively by the U.S. government during World War I but has since been made illegal for U.S. government contracts, for good reason. It is still occasionally used for construction projects and some service contracts in the private sector.

The rationale for this pricing arrangement was probably "the bigger the job, the bigger the fee," that is, as the job grows, so should the fee. This arrangement is similar to a professional fee, such as an attorney's fee, which grows as the professional puts more time into the project. This arrangement may have developed as a response to the cost-growth phenomenon in projects that were initially ill-defined. As a seller proceeded with the work, the buyer's needs became better defined and grew, until the seller felt that the fees initially agreed to were not enough for the expanded scope of work. Again, while there was a place for CPPC in the past, today it is rarely used.

TWO

Cost-Plus-Fixed Fee Contracts

Cost-plus-fixed fee is the most common type of CR contract. As with the others, the seller is reimbursed for its costs, but the contract also provides for payment of a fixed fee that does not change in response to the seller's actual cost experience. The seller is paid the fixed fee on successful completion of the contract, whether its actual costs were higher or lower than the estimated costs.

If the seller completes the work for less than the estimated cost, it receives the entire fixed fee. If the seller incurs the estimated cost without completing the work and if the buyer decides not to pay for the overrun costs necessary for completion, the seller receives a portion of the fixed fee that is equal to the percentage of work completed. If the buyer decides to pay overrun costs, the seller must complete the work without any increase in the fixed fee. The only adjustment to the fee would be a result of cost growth, when the buyer requires the seller to do more work than initially specified.

This type of contract is on the opposite end of the spectrum from the FFP contract, because cost risk rests entirely on the shoulders of the buyer. Under a CR contract, a buyer might have to reimburse the seller for the entire estimated cost and part of the fee but have nothing to show for it but bits and pieces of the work.

Classification of Contract Incentives

The fundamental purpose of contract incentives is to motivate desired performance in one or more specific areas. Contract incentives are generally classified as either objectively based and evaluated or subjectively based and evaluated. Further, both classifications of contract incentives are typically categorized as either positive incentives (rewards—get more money) or negative incentives (penalties—get less money) or some combination thereof.

Those incentives that use predetermined formula-based methods to calculate the amount of incentive, either positive or negative, in one or more designated areas are objectively based and evaluated. Facts and actual events are used as a basis for determination. Therefore, individual judgment and opinions are not considered in an evaluation of performance.

Objectively based and evaluated contract incentives commonly include the following designated performance areas:

- Cost performance
- Schedule or delivery performance
- Quality performance

Subjectively based and evaluated contract incentives are those incentives that use individual judgment, opinions, and informed impressions as the basis for determining the amount of incentive, either positive or negative, in one or more designated areas. These incentives can and often do contain some objective aspects or factors. However, subjective contract incentives are ultimately determined by one or more individuals making a decision based on their experience, knowledge, and the available information—a total judgment.

Subjectively based and evaluated contract incentives typically include the following:

- Award fees
- Award Term
- Other special incentives

Figure 2-5 summarizes the link between rewards and penalties and contract incentives as described in the following paragraphs.

Objective Incentives

Incentives Based on Cost Performance

Cost is the most commonly chosen performance variable. For fixed-price (cost) incentive contracts, the parties negotiate a *target cost* and a *target profit* (which equals the *target price*), and a *sharing formula* for cost overruns and cost underruns. They also negotiate a *ceiling price*, which is the buyer's maximum dollar liability. When performance is complete, they determine the final actual costs and apply the sharing formula to any overrun or underrun. Applying the sharing formula determines the seller's final profit, if any.

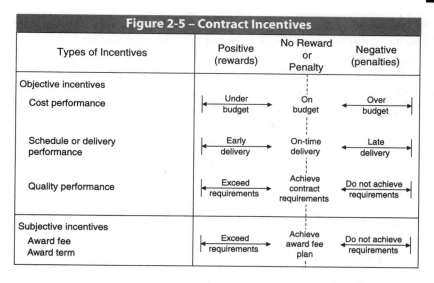

Figure 2-5 – Contract Incentives

Types of Incentives	Positive (rewards)	No Reward or Penalty	Negative (penalties)
Objective incentives			
Cost performance	Under budget	On budget	Over budget
Schedule or delivery performance	Early delivery	On-time delivery	Late delivery
Quality performance	Exceed requirements	Achieve contract requirements	Do not achieve requirements
Subjective incentives Award fee Award term	Exceed requirements	Achieve award fee plan	Do not achieve requirements

Consider an example in which the parties agree to the following arrangement:

Target cost: $10,000,000
Target profit: $850,000
Target price: $10,850,000
Sharing formula: 70/30 (buyer 70 percent, seller 30 percent)
Ceiling price: $11,500,000

Assume that the seller completes the work at an actual cost of $10,050,000, overrunning the target cost by $50,000. The seller's share of the overrun is 30 percent of $50,000, which is $15,000. The target profit will be reduced by that amount ($850,000 – 15,000 = $835,000). The seller will then receive the $10,050,000 cost of performance plus an earned profit of $835,000. Thus, the price to the buyer will be $10,885,000, which is $615,000 below the ceiling price. The $35,000 increase over the target price of $10,850,000 represents the buyer's 70 percent share of the cost overrun.

Had the seller overrun the target cost by $100,000, raising the actual cost to $10,100,000, the seller's share of the overrun would have been 30 percent or $30,000. That amount would have reduced the seller's profit to $820,000.

Basically, at some point before reaching the ceiling price, the sharing arrangement effectively changes to 0/100, with the seller assuming 100 percent of the cost risk. This effect is implicit in fixed-price incentive arrangements because of the ceiling price and is not an explicit element of the formula. The point at which sharing changes to 0/100 is called the *point of total assumption (PTA)*, which represents a cost figure. Indeed, the PTA is often appropriately referred to as the *high-cost estimate*. Figure 2-6 depicts these relationships and outcomes in graphical form. (Note that the graph describes a first-degree linear equation of the form $Y = A - BX$, with cost as the independent variable X, and profit as the dependent variable Y. B, the coefficient of X, is equal to the seller's share).

The PTA can be determined by applying the following formula:

$$PTA = \left(\frac{\text{Ceiling price - Target price}}{\text{Buyer share ratio}} \right) + \text{Target Cost}$$

In the event of an underrun, the seller would enjoy greater profit. If the final cost is $9,000,000 (a $1,000,000 underrun), the seller's share of the underrun is 30 percent, which is $300,000. Thus, the price to the buyer would include the $9,000,000 cost and the $850,000 target profit plus the seller's $300,000 underrun share (total profit of $1,150,000). Thus, $9,000,000 actual cost plus $1,150,000 actual profit equals $10,150,000 actual price, reflecting precisely the buyer's 70 percent share of the $1,000,000 underrun [$10,850,000 target price – 70 percent of the $1,000,000 underrun ($700,000) = $10,150,000].

Incentives Based on Schedule or Delivery Performance

For many years, construction, aerospace, and numerous service industries have used schedule or delivery performance incentives to motivate sellers to provide either early or on-time delivery of products and services.

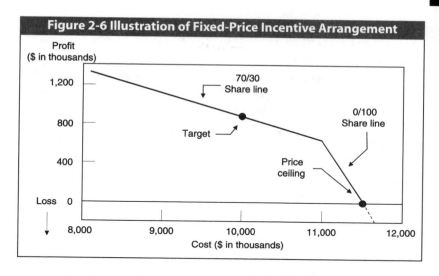

Figure 2-6 Illustration of Fixed-Price Incentive Arrangement

Liquidated damages, is a negative incentive (penalty) for late delivery. Typically, a liquidated damages clause stated in the contract terms and conditions designates how much money one party, usually the seller, must pay the other party, usually the buyer, for not meeting the contract schedule. Often the amount of liquidated damages payable is specified as an amount of money for a specific period of time (day, week, month). A key aspect of liquidated damages is that the penalty is to be based on the amount of damages incurred or compensable in nature, not an excessive or punitive amount.

A proven best practice for buyers is to require negative incentives (or penalties) for late delivery and late schedule performance. Likewise, a proven best practice for sellers is to limit their liability on liquidated damages by agreeing to a cap or maximum amount, and seeking positive incentives (or rewards) for early delivery and early schedule performance.

Incentives Based on Quality Performance

Quality performance incentives is one of the most common topics in government and commercial contracting. Surveys in both government and industry have revealed widespread service contracting problems, including deficient statements of work, poor contract administration, performance delays, and quality shortcomings.

When a contract is based on performance, all aspects of the contract are structured around the purpose of the work to be performed rather than the manner in which it is to be done. The buyer seeks to elicit the best performance the seller has to offer, at a reasonable price or cost, by stating its objectives and giving sellers both latitude in determining how to achieve them and incentives for achieving them. In source selection, for example, the buyer might publish a draft solicitation for comment, use quality-related evaluation factors, or both. The statement of work will provide performance standards rather than spelling out what the seller is to do. The contract normally contains a plan for quality assurance surveillance. And the contract typically includes positive and negative performance incentives.

Few people disagree with the concept that buyers, who collectively spend billions of dollars on services annually, should look to the performance-based approach, focusing more on results and less on detailed requirements. However, implementing performance-based contracting (using cost, schedule, and/or quality performance variables) is far easier said than done. The sound use of performance incentives is key to the success of the performance-based contracting approach.

Problems with Applying Objective Incentives

The objective-incentive schemes described have some merit, but they also involve some serious practical problems. First, they assume a level of buyer and seller competence that may not exist. Second, they assume effects that may not occur. Third, they create serious challenges for contract administration.

To negotiate objective incentives intelligently, the parties must have some knowledge of the range of possible costs for a project. They also must have some knowledge of the likely causes and probabilities of different cost outcomes. If both parties do not have sufficient information on these issues, they will not be able to structure an effective incentive formula.

It is important that the parties share their information. If one party has superior knowledge that it does not share with the other, it will be able to skew the formula in its favor during negotiation. If that happens, the whole point of the arrangement, which is to equitably balance the risks of performance, will be lost. The buyer is usually at a disadvantage with respect to the seller in this regard.

An objective incentive assumes that the seller can affect a performance outcome along the entire range of the independent variable. However, such may not be true. For instance, the seller may actually exercise control along only a short sector of the range of possible costs. Some possible cost outcomes may be entirely outside the seller's control because of factors such as market performance. In reality, the seller's project manager may have little control over important factors that may determine the cost outcome, such as overhead costs. In addition, short-term companywide factors, especially those involving overhead, may, on some contracts, make incurring additional cost rather than earning additional profit more advantageous for the seller.

In addition, objective cost incentives are complicated and costly to administer, with all the cost definition, measurement, allocation, and confirmation problems of CR contracts. The parties must be particularly careful to segregate the target cost effects of cost growth from those of cost overruns; otherwise, they may lose money for the wrong reasons. As a practical matter, segregating such costs is often quite difficult.

When using other performance incentives, the parties may find themselves disputing the causes of various performance outcomes. The seller may argue that schedule delays are a result of actions of the buyer. Quality problems, such as poor reliability, may have been caused by improper buyer operation rather than seller performance. The causes of performance failures may be difficult to determine.

One reason for using such contracts is to reduce the deleterious effects of risk on the behavior of the parties. Thus, if a pricing arrangement increases the likelihood of trouble, it should not be used. The decision to apply objective incentives should be made only after careful analysis.

Best Practices:
15 Actions to Improve Your Use of Contract Incentives

These best practices should be followed when using incentive contracts:

- Think creatively – Creativity is a critical aspect in the success of performance-based incentive contracting
- Avoid rewarding sellers for simply meeting contract requirements
- Recognize that developing clear, concise, objectively measurable performance incentives will be a challenge, and plan accordingly
- Create a proper balance of objective incentives - cost, schedule, and quality performance
- Ensure that performance incentives focus the seller's efforts on the buyer's desired objectives
- Make all forms of performance incentives challenging yet attainable
- Ensure that incentives motivate quality control and that the results of the seller's quality control efforts can be measured
- Consider tying on-time delivery to cost and or quality performance criteria
- Recognize that not everything can be measured objectively–consider using a combination of objectively measured standards and subjectively determined incentives
- Encourage open communication and ongoing involvement with potential sellers in developing the performance-based SOW and the incentive plan, both before and after issuing the formal request for proposals
- Consider including socioeconomic incentives (non-SOW-related) in the incentive plan
- Use clear, objective formulas for determining performance incentives
- Use a combination of positive and negative incentives
- Include incentives for discounts based on early payments
- Ensure that all incentives, both positive and negative, have limits

Subjective Incentives

Award Fee Plans

In an award fee plan, the parties negotiate an estimated cost, just as for cost-plus- fixed fee (CPFF) contracts. Then they negotiate an agreement on the amount of money to be included in an *award fee pool.* Finally, they agree on a set of criteria and procedures to be applied by the buyer in determining how well the seller has performed and how much fee the seller has earned. In some cases, the parties also negotiate a *base fee,* which is a fixed fee that the seller will earn no matter how its performance is evaluated.

The contract performance period is then divided into equal *award fee periods.* A part of the award fee pool is allocated to each period proportionate to the percentage of the work scheduled to be completed. All this information is included in the award fee plan, which becomes part of the contract. In some cases, the contract allows the buyer to change the award fee plan unilaterally before the start of a new award fee period.

During each award fee period, the buyer observes and documents the seller's performance achievements or failures. At the end of each period, the buyer evaluates the seller's performance according to the award fee plan and decides how much fee to award from the portion allocated to that period. Under some contracts, the seller has an opportunity to present its own evaluation of its performance and a specific request for award fee. The buyer then informs the seller how much of the available award fee it has earned and how its performance could be improved during ensuing award fee periods.

This arrangement invariably involves subjectivity on the part of the buyer; precisely how much depends on how the award fee plan is written.

Pros and Cons of the Award Fee Arrangement

The cost-plus-award fee (CPAF) contract is a cost-reimbursement contract, with all its requirements for cost definition, measurement, allocation, and confirmation. For the buyer, the CPAF contract requires the additional administrative investment associated with observing, documenting, and evaluating seller performance. However, this disadvantage may sometimes be overemphasized, because the buyer should already be performing many of these activities under a CR contract.

The disadvantages for the buyer are offset by the extraordinary power it obtains from the ability to make subjective determinations about how much fee the seller has earned. The buyer may have difficulty establishing objective criteria for satisfactory service performance.

The power of subjective fee determination tends to make sellers extraordinarily responsive to the buyer's demands. However, the buyer must be careful, because that very responsiveness can be the cause of cost overruns and unintended cost growth.

The buyer's advantages are almost entirely disadvantages from the viewpoint of the seller, because the seller will have placed itself within the power of the buyer to an exceptional degree. Subjectivity can approach arbitrariness or even cross the line. The seller may find itself dealing with a buyer that is impossible to please or that believes that the seller cannot earn all the award fee because no one can achieve "perfect" performance.

Other Special Incentives

There is a growing recognition by buyers and sellers worldwide, in both the public and private sectors, that contract incentives can be expanded and that they are indeed valuable tools to motivate the desired performance. Increasingly, when outsourcing, buyers are motivating sellers to subcontract with local companies, often with special rewards for subcontracting with designated small businesses.

Likewise, many sellers are providing buyers with special incentives for early payment, such as product or services discounts or additional specified services at no change.

Incentive Contracts

Cost-Plus-Incentive Fee Contracts

Cost-plus-incentive fee (CPIF) contracts allow overrun or underrun sharing of cost through a predetermined formula for fee adjustments that apply to incentives for cost category contracts. Within the basic concept of the buyer's paying all costs for a cost contract, the limits for a CPIF contract become those of maximum and minimum fees.

The necessary elements for a CPIF contract are maximum fee, minimum fee, target cost, target fee, and share ratio(s).

Fixed-Price Incentive Contracts

In a fixed-price incentive (FPI) contract, seller profit is linked to another aspect of performance: cost, schedule, quality, or a combination of all three. The objective is to give the seller a monetary incentive to optimize cost performance.

FPI contracts may be useful for initial production of complex new products or systems, although the parties may have difficulty agreeing on labor and material costs for such projects because of a lack of production experience. However, the cost uncertainty may not be great enough to warrant use of a CR contract.

Cost-Plus-Award Fee Contracts

Cost-plus-award fee (CPAF) contracts include subjective incentives, in which the profit a seller earns depends on how well the seller satisfies a buyer's subjective desires. This type of contract has been used for a long time in both government and commercial contracts worldwide. The U.S. Army Corps of Engineers developed an evaluated fee contract for use in construction during the early 1930s, based on its contracting experience during World War I. The U.S. National Aeronautics and Space Administration has used CPAF contracts to procure services since the 1950s. Other U.S. government agencies have also used these contracts extensively, including the Department of Energy and Department of Defense. A small but growing number of commercial companies now use award fees to motivate their suppliers to achieve exceptional performance.

Cost-plus-award fee contracts are used primarily to procure services, particularly those that involve an ongoing, long-term relationship between buyer and seller, such as maintenance and systems engineering support. Objective criteria for determining the acceptability of the performance of such services are inherently difficult to establish. The award fee arrangement is particularly well suited to such circumstances, at least from the buyer's point of view. However, this type of contract also is used to procure architecture and engineering, research and development, hardware and software systems design and development, construction, and many other services.

Time-and-Materials Contracts

In time-and-material (T&M) contracts, the parties negotiate hourly rates for specified types of labor and agree that the seller will be reimbursed for parts and materials at cost. Each hourly rate includes labor costs, overhead, and profit. The seller performs the work, documenting the types and quantities of labor used and the costs for parts and materials. When the work is finished, the seller bills the buyer for the number of labor hours at the agreed upon hourly rates and for the costs of materials and parts.

Time-and-materials contracts are most often used to procure equipment repair and maintenance services, when the cost to repair or overhaul a piece of equipment is uncertain. However, these contracts are also used to procure other support services.

Although T&M contracts appear to be straightforward, they may create some difficulties. This type of contract must be negotiated carefully, because each hourly rate includes a component for overhead costs, which include both *fixed* and *variable costs*. Fixed costs are the costs that will be incurred during a given period of operation, despite the number of work hours performed. To recover its fixed costs, the seller must estimate how many hours will be sold during the contract performance period and allocate a share to each hour. If the parties overestimate how many hours will be sold during the period of performance, the seller will not recover all its fixed costs. If the parties underestimate how many hours will be sold, the seller will enjoy a windfall profit.

Although the hourly labor rates are fixed, the number of hours delivered and the cost of materials and parts are not. Therefore, the buyer faces the problems of confirming the number of hours delivered and the cost of materials claimed by the seller. These problems are not as great as those under CR contracts, but they are not insignificant.

Figure 2-7 provides a range of contract types keyed to performance measurement and risk.

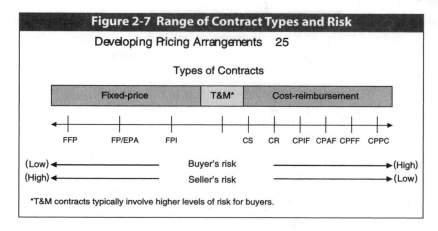

Figure 2-7 Range of Contract Types and Risk

Developing Pricing Arrangements 25

Types of Contracts

| Fixed-price | T&M* | Cost-reimbursement |

FFP   FP/EPA   FPI   CS   CR   CPIF CPAF CPFF CPPC

(Low) ◀———————————— Buyer's risk ————————————▶ (High)
(High) ◀——————————— Seller's risk ———————————▶ (Low)

*T&M contracts typically involve higher levels of risk for buyers.

Contract terms and conditions: Law and custom, company experience and policy, and project-specific analyses will determine what contract Ts and Cs the buyer will prefer. Governments and large companies usually have regulations or manuals that prescribe boilerplate clauses for the most common types of contracts.

Outputs

The outputs from the procurement planning process consists of the following items:

■ Acquisition plan or procurement management plan: This plan should describe how the remaining procurement processes (from solicitation planning through contract closeout) will be managed. The following are examples of questions to ask in developing the procurement management plan:
   ■ What types of contracts will be used?
   ■ If independent estimates will be needed as evaluation criteria, who will prepare them and when?
   ■ What actions can the project management team take on its own?
   ■ If standardized procurement documents are needed, where can they be found?
   ■ How will multiple providers be managed?
   ■ How will procurement be coordinated with other business aspects such as scheduling and performance reporting?

A procurement management plan may be formal or informal and highly detailed or broadly framed, based on business needs.

- *Performance Work Statement (PWS) or Statement of work(SOW):*
The PWS or SOW describes the buyer's requirements in sufficient detail to allow prospective sellers to determine whether they can provide the product, service, or solution. "Sufficient detail" may vary depending on the nature of the item, the needs of the buyer, or the expected contract form. The current trend is toward developing performance-based requirments that describe what is needed, not how to accomplish it.

Identifying and analyzing requirements should follow a systematic procedure. First, the buyer must determine the function to be performed by the required product or service and the relationship of that function to others. For example, if the buyer needs an item of hardware or software or needs a task performed, how does that item or task relate to other parts of the project? Second, the buyer must determine the specific types and levels of performance that must be attained. Third, the buyer may have to determine a specific design, that is, the physical form the item must take or the specific method or procedure by which the task must be performed.

These three categories of requirements—function, performance, and design—move from general to specific. Function is described by verbs that relate what the product or service must *do*. Performance and design are described by adjectives and adverbs that relate the *attributes* of the product or service, that is, *how well* the product or service must perform the function and the specific form that the product or service must take.

The requirements development team should be an Integrated Project Team and include the people who will use the product or service, if they are not already part of the business team. The process of developing the requirement must be rational and systematic, as it is iterative, achieving ever greater refinement of the buyer's ideas and descriptions with each iteration.

SELECTED INTERVIEW

Name: Rene G. Rendon

Job Title: Professor

Organization: Naval Postgraduate School

Location: Monterey, California

Major Responsibilities: Teach program management and contract management courses in MBA programs.

Background: 22 years Air Force acquisition management. Bachelor, master, and doctorate degrees in business administration.

QUESTIONS & ANSWERS:

Question: What do you consider to be proven best practices for Buyers when conducting procurement planning and development solicitations?

Answer: *Procurement Planning:* A thorough understanding of the market in terms of mature and emerging technologies and capabilities, and a thorough understanding of the customer's needs, desires, and expectations. Carefully fitting the market capabilities and customer's needs, desires and expectations is the key to successful procurement planning.

Solicitation Planning: Craft solicitations that are rigorous enough to ensure consistent, comparable responses, but flexible enough to allow considerations of contractor suggestions for more effective and efficient ways to meet the customer's needs, desires, and expectations.

Question: What actions do you suggest sellers take to ethically and appropriately influence buyer's requirements?

Answer: Sellers should be knowledgeable of the procurement ethics requirements (rules of the game) for discussing requirements with the buyers. If the sellers don't play by the rules, they should expect to be "thrown off the field" from the competition and sentenced to the "penalty box."

Question: What actions should sellers take to ensure they make intelligent Bid/No Bid Decisions on their critical deals?

Answer: Sellers should have a thorough understanding of risk management and use a designated risk management team to focus on effectively assessing risks and opportunities.

Sellers should conduct an extensive competitive analysis report to assess the competitive environment against the identified risks and opportunities.

Question: What do you consider to be the top five Seller best practices for developing a winning bid or proposal?

Answer: 1. Use an integrated team effort.

2. Use a solicitation compliance matrix to ensure compliance with the solicitation requirements.

3. Conduct a competitive analysis report to assess itself against its competitors.

4. Review past proposals that were successful and those that were not successful as a means of improving the proposal development process.

5. Use an external review team to evaluate the proposal before submission to the buyer.

Question: How can U.S. Government agencies truly streamline and improve their source selection process?

TWO

Answer: Use electronic source selection tools that will automate the paper process; educate and train source selection personnel to ensure they have the appropriate knowledge, skills and abilities to conduct best value source selections. Maintain a cadre of source selection experts to augment source selection teams.

Note: The subject interview solely expresses the informal opinions' of the interviewee, they do not necessarily represent the views or opinions of the organization, company, or agency which they are employed.

Buyer Step 2: Solicitation Planning

Figure 2-8 Buyer Step 2: Solicitation Planning

Input	Tools & Techniques	Output
• Procurement management plan • Statement of Work, Performance Work Statement, or Statement of Objectives • Other procurement planning output	• Standard forms • Expert judgment	• Procurement documents • Evaluation criteria • Statement of work updates • Due diligence

Inputs

The inputs to solicitation planning consists of the following items:

■ *Procurement management plan:* This plan, which describes how the procurement process will be conducted throughout contract management, should be reviewed at the start of solicitation planning.

■ *Statement of work (SOW), Performance Work Statement (PWS), or Statement of Objectives (SOO):* The SOW, PWS, or SOO is a key ingredient in solicitation planning and in the solicitation document to be developed.

■ *Other procurement planning output:* Other output, which may have been modified since procurement planning, should be reviewed. In particular, solicitation planning should be closely coordinated with the project schedule.

Tools and Techniques

Following are descriptions of the tools and techniques used for solicitation planning:

- *Standard forms:* These forms may include standardized versions of contracts, standardized descriptions of procurement items, or standardized versions of all or part of the needed bid documents. Organizations doing substantial amounts of procurement should have many of these documents standardized and automated.
- *Expert judgment:* As in procurement planning, expert judgment is a vital tool. Individuals with specialized knowledge or training, both in-house and outside the organization, should be consulted.

Outputs

Solicitation planning results in the following outputs:

- *Procurement documents:* Procurement documents, or solicitations, request proposals from prospective sellers. The terms bid and quotation are generally used when the source selection decision will be price driven (as when buying commercial items), whereas the term proposal or tender is generally used when nonfinancial considerations, such as technical skills or approach, are paramount (as when buying professional services). However, the terms are often used interchangeably and care should be taken not to make unwarranted assumptions about the implications of the term used. Types of procurement documents include the request for proposals (RFP), request for quotations (RFQ), request for tenders (RFT), request for information (RFI), invitation for bids (IFB), and invitation for negotiation (IFN).

   Procurement documents should be structured to facilitate accurate and complete responses from prospective sellers. They should always include the relevant SOW, a description of the desired form of response, and any required contract Ts and Cs (for example, a copy of a model contract's nondisclosure provisions). Some or all of the content and structure of procurement documents, particularly for those prepared by a government agency, may be defined by regulation.

   Procurement documents should be rigorous enough to ensure consistent, comparable responses but flexible enough to allow consideration of seller suggestions for better ways to satisfy the requirements.

- *Evaluation criteria:* Evaluation criteria are used to rate or score proposals. They may be objective (for example, "the proposed project manager must be a certified project management professional") or subjective (for example, "the proposed project manager must have documented previous experience with similar projects"). Evaluation criteria are often included as part of the procurement documents.

- *Statement of work updates:* Modifications to one or more SOWs may be identified during solicitation planning.

- *Due diligence:* Conduct one on one discussions between the buying organization and individual sellers/contractors, to learn more about the contractor and their capabilities and the buyer's requirements and capabilities.

SELECTED INTERVIEW

Name: William C. Pursch

Job Title: President

Organization: Pursch Associates

Location: Bradenton, Florida

Major Responsibilities: Consulting, Teaching, Reviewing Articles

Background: William C. Pursch, a Continuing Studies Faculty member with Villanova University, is president of Pursch Associates and professor emeritus and former department head of the Air Force Institute of Technology at Wright-Patterson Air Force Base, Ohio.

Dr. Pursch's background includes considerable experience in government purchasing. He has been a warranted contracting officer for the Department of Defense as well as a corporate purchasing specialist for Robbins and Myers, Inc. He has handled various logistical assignments in the fields of contracting management, inventory management, and materials management, including overseas assignments in Vietnam, Okinawa, and Germany. He has also consulted with federal agencies and with industry.

Dr. Pursch received his B.A. from Gettysburg College, an M.S. from the University of Southern California, and a Ph.D. from The Ohio State University. He is certified by NCMA as a Professional Contracts Manager.

QUESTIONS & ANSWERS:

Question: What do you consider to be proven best practices for Buyers when conducting procurement planning and development solicitations?

Answer: The more time spent in the Pre-Bid/Proposal phase to ensure accuracy in the Performance Work Statement, and source selection evaluation plan, the more dividends will be realized in the Post-Bid/Proposal Phase, especially in the Contract Administration and closeout activities.

Question: What do you consider to be the top five Seller best practices for developing a winning bid or proposal?

Answer: (1) Use a compliance matrix; (2) Prepare an Executive Summary; (3) Develop a risk and opportunity assessment; (4) Perform a complete analysis of the solicitation; (5) Offer to give an oral presentation of the proposal.

Question: Please share a brief personal success story regarding: Solicitations, Bids/Proposals, or Source Selection – Building a Winning Contract.

Answer: It is absolutely crucial to follow the source selection evaluation plan to the exact detail specified in the plan when evaluating the proposals and selecting the area within the competitive range. The development of the source selection evaluation plan starts with the Buyer's Solicitation Planning step.

I was the contracting officer on a multimillion dollar communications program in Europe for the U.S. Army. We set up a fairly detailed source selection evaluation plan and required the proposal to be delivered in three separate volumes addressing the Technical approach, the Managerial approach, and the Price. This information was included in the solicitation. It was also part of the source selection evaluation plan.

When the proposals arrived, we passed out the appropriate documents to the Technical panel, the Management panel, and the Cost panel. These panels were standing panels at the Agency used for many different procurement actions.

Following the usual procedures, we established the competitive range, conducted negotiations with each of the firms within the competitive range, made a selection, and announced the award of the contract, and offered a debriefing to the unsuccessful firms. Within three days after debriefing the unsuccessful firms, we were presented with a formal protest to the General Accounting Office, now the Government Accountability Office (GAO).

The basis for the protest was we had used a Cost Panel instead of a Price Panel and therefore "the entire source selection evaluation process was tainted with bias, irrationality, and ignorance." Fortunately all the firms had provided cost data even though we had specified price as a factor, including the protestant. Also, fortunately, I had a very sharp attorney (who was later destined to become a Judge on the Armed Services Board of Contract Appeals).

Together we prepared the Rule 4 File to send to the Comptroller General's Office for a decision. In the meantime, we suspended work on the Contract pending the review.

After what seemed like an eternity (it was only about 28 days) the Comptroller General announced that they could find no bias or irrationality in the evaluation process and they would not "substitute the protestant's opinion for that of the Contracting officer."

Note: The subject interview solely expresses the informal opinions' of the interviewee, they do not necessarily represent the views or opinions of the organization, company, or agency which they are employed.

Buyer Step 3: Solicitation Preparation

Figure 2-9 Buyer Step 3: Solicitation Preparation

Input	Tools & Techniques	Output
• Procurement documents • Qualified seller lists	• Seller focus groups, meetings, conferences, or web-based surveys • Advertising • Solicitation review(s) • Request for information (RFI) • Draft Request for Proposal (RFPs) • Understanding the seller's perspective	• Solicitation that leads to submission of quality bids or proposals from qualified sources

Solicitation consists of obtaining information (bids or proposals) from prospective sellers on how project needs can be met. Prospective sellers expend most of the effort in this process, normally at no direct cost to the buyer.

Inputs

The inputs to solicitation includes the following items:

- *Procurement documents:* Procurement documents, or solicitations, include RFPs, RFQs, ITBs, and so on.
- *Qualified seller lists:* Some buyers maintain lists or files with information on prospective sellers. These lists generally have information on relevant experience, past performance, and other characteristics of the prospective sellers.

  If such lists are not available, new sources must be developed. General information is widely available from library directories, Dun and Bradstreet Corporation, relevant local associations, trade catalogs, industry associations, and other similar organizations or publications. Detailed information on specific sources may require more extensive effort, such as site visits or contact with previous customers.

Tools and Techniques

Following are the tools and techniques used for solicitation:

- *Seller Focus Groups, Meetings, Conferences, or Web-based Serveys:* These are ways of gathering information from prospective sellers before they prepare their proposals. They may be conducted with one seller at a time or in groups in person, via video conference, teleconference, Net-meetings, or web-based surveys. The meetings ensure that all prospective sellers have a clear, common understanding of the procurement (both technical requirements and contract requirements). Responses to questions may be incorporated into the procurement documents as amendments. These buyer conducted/facilitated meetings where sellers give presentations and answer buyer questions can serve as powerful tools to help the buyer better understand the potential products and services available. Plus these sessions can provide valuable insights to best-in-class performance standards, measures, metrics, incentives, and solutions, which sellers can share with the interested buyer.
- *Advertising:* Existing lists of potential sellers can often be expanded by placing advertisements in general circulation publications, such as newspapers, or in specialty publications, such as professional journals. Some government jurisdictions require public advertising of certain types of procurement items; most

government jurisdictions require public advertising of subcontracts on a government contract typically via the internet.

- *Solicitation Reviews:* Depending upon the complexity, urgency, dollar amount, and numerous other factors, the buying organization will typically conduct an informal or formal review of the solicitation prior to its actual submission or release to the public/respective sellers. The solicitation review process will vary in range from simple to complex. A simple process may require just one or two people mere minutes or hours to review and approve the solicitation for submission. A highly complex, multiple review process, usually involves potentially numerous internal functional experts and/or consultants which may require weeks or months to conduct a comprehensive solicitation review.

- *Request for Information (RFI):* Often buying organizations realize they need much more input from prospective sellers, before they can effectively state their performance-based requirements. As a result, many buying organizations submit a RFI to gather more information before they prepare a RFP.

- *Draft Request for Proposal (RFP):* On many important outsourcing requirements, buyers will use a Draft RFP as a means to gather information from sellers, provide information to sellers, and improve their RFP by providing a draft RFP for review and comment. The key is to provide appropriate time to obtain feedback and incorporated needed changes.

- *Understanding the Seller's Perspective:* An informed and professional buying organization will seek to understand the procurement opportunity and risk from not only their buyer's perspective but, also from the seller's perspective. The seller's perspective, of Pre-Bid/Proposal phase involves identifying potentially successful contract opportunities and capturing and performing such contracts. A potentially successful contract is one that can be performed at a price that will enable the seller to meet the needs of the buyer and earn a reasonable profit or gain another benefit, such as future business. In this case, the seller must:

  - Identify contract opportunities such as revenue, basic gross profit, measured operating income, and future business
  - Determine the potential profit or other business potential of the contract, the cost to pursue and win it, the chances of winning, and the likelihood of successful contract performance
  - Define and assess the consequences of failure.

Output

The output from the solicitation preparation process is to receive quality bids or proposals, which are the written or oral offers to perform services or provide products to another party. Solicitations range from simple to highly complex.

Straight Talk: Suggestions for Significant Improvement

In both the public and private business sectors, buyers are usually in a rush to get something they need, and they often want it badly. As a result, buyers often get what they want – they get it bad (delivered late, over budget, does not meet their customer/user expectations, requires more service than expected, requires more upgrades than planned, and has a higher life-cycle cost than expected). Thus, the buyers first three steps discussed in this chapter must be properly staffed in both quality and quantity of resources with realistic schedules that should be mutually developed. Buyers should conduct market research, should seek and obtain seller's feedback via seller focus groups, meetings, conferences, or web-based surveys, use request for information, draft solicitations, and appropriate means using the appropriate communication technologies, including: webinars, teleconferences, videoconferences, etc. Further, buyers must stop vendor bashing suppliers and create real partnerships in order to maximize the opportunities for everyone involved in the Buying & Selling Life-Cycle.

Summary

This chapter has provided a detailed discussion of the buyers first three steps in the Pre-Bid/Proposal Phase of the Buying & Selling Life-Cycle: procurement planning, solicitation planning, and solicitation preparation. The chapter has provided a process approach with key inputs, proven tools and techniques, and desired outputs, with numerous best practices incorporated throughout the discussion. Plus, a brief discussion with suggestions for significant improvement was also provided. For the seller, these Pre-Bid/Proposal Phase activities typically incorporate two major steps, presales activities and bid/no-bid decision making. These steps will be discussed in much greater detail in the next chapter.

Questions to Consider

1. How effectively does your organization conduct procurement and solicitation planning?

2. Does your organization have the number of skilled resources needed to effectively conduct the procurement and solicitation planning steps?

3. How effectively does your buying organization obtain feedback from prospective sellers regarding pending solicitations?

4. How well does your buying organization review solicitations for clarity, accuracy, and concise prior to submission to potential sellers?

PRE-BID/ PROPOSAL PHASE: PRE-SALES ACTIVITIES & BID/NO BID DECISION

Introduction

The first two steps of the Pre-Bid Proposal Phase for the seller are Pre-Sales Activities and the Bid/No Bid Decision, see Figure 3-1, "The Buying & Selling Life-Cycle".

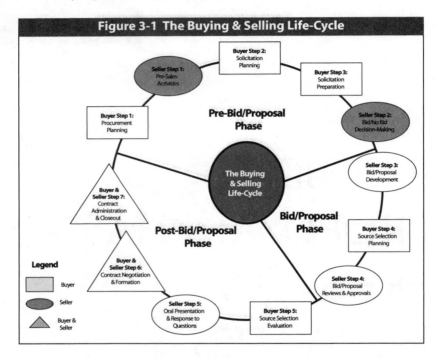

Figure 3-1 The Buying & Selling Life-Cycle

Seller Step 1: Pre-Sales Activities

The key objectives of the Pre-Sales Activities step are: 1) qualify the opportunity and risks, 2) gather competitive intelligence, 3) develop a Win Strategy, and 4) outline the opportunity.

The following graphic (Figure 3-2) summarizes the Inputs, Tools & Techniques, and Outputs covered in this chapter concerning the Pre-Sales Activities step of the Pre-Bid/Proposal Stage.

Figure 3-2 Seller Step 1: Pre-Sales Activities Process

Input	Tools & Techniques	Output
• Knowledge of your costomer • Knowledge of your company • Knowledge of your competitors	• Qualify Opportunity & Risk • Opportunity-Risk Assessment Grid • ORA Grid with Bid-No Bid Line • Elements of Opportunity • Elements of Risk • Opportunity Quantification Tool • Risk Quantification Tool • Gather Competitve Intelligence • Competitor Profile • Sources of Competitive Intelligence • Develop Win Strategy • Sweet Spot Sour Spot Analysis • Win Theme & Strategy Form • Customer Positioning Plan • Customer Contact Plan • Outline the Opportunity • Stakeholder Presentation Outline	• Qualified Opportunity • Competitor Profile • Win Strategy • Outline of Offer — Stakeholder Review Presentation

*This section is adapted from: "The Capture Management Life-Cycle: Winning More Business," by Gregory A. Garrett and Reginald J. Kipke, CCH, 2003.

Inputs

As with all processes and approaches, the value of making a great beginning cannot be understated. The three foundations or inputs of knowledge, see Figure 3-3, for success in the Pre-Sales Activities step are:

■ Knowledge of your customer
■ Knowledge of your competitors
■ Knowledge of your company

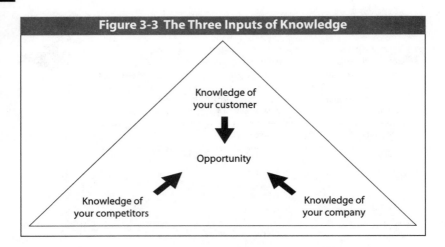

Figure 3-3 The Three Inputs of Knowledge

Knowledge of
your customer

Opportunity

Knowledge of
your competitors

Knowledge of
your company

The degree to which you master each of these will greatly impact your ability to spot potential opportunities and get a jump on your competitors.

SELECTED INTERVIEW

Name: Lee Ann Hunt, CPCM

Job Title: Director of Contracts

Organization: Intuitive Research and Technology Corporation

Location: Huntsville, AL

Major Responsibilities: Conducts integral role in developing proposal strategy, pricing and completion of final proposal package. Negotiates and manages prime and subcontract awards as well as modifications to existing award documents. Administers government and commercial contracts/subcontracts. Contract Administration includes but is not limited to ensuring all contract terms and conditions are met and are in accordance with legal requirements, customer specifications and government regulations and contract close-out. Subcontract Administration includes but is not limited to preparing for Certified Purchasing System Review (CPSR) Audit, writing, issuing and negotiation of awards and task orders. Responsible for Non-Disclosure Agreements (NDA), Teaming Agreements (TA), and consultant agreements. Participates in writing OCI Mitigation Plans. Works with Operations Manager to ensure Contractual Billing Procedures are followed. Contractual Point of Contact for all INTUITIVE efforts. Directs work efforts for Purchasing, Subcontracts, Pricing and Contract Administration.

Background: MBA , CPCM

Former jobs held: Administrative Manager of Fortune 200 Chemical plant; Accounting Manager, Business Manager, Contracts Manager

QUESTIONS & ANSWERS:

Question: What actions do you suggest sellers take to ethically and appropriately influence buyer's requirements?

Answer: Be responsive to all customer questions. Diligently work to build positive past performance references.

Question: What actions should sellers take to ensure they make intelligent Bid/No Bid Decisions on their critical deals?

Answer: Form a Business Development Integrated Project Team (IPT)

- Set an agenda for the Business Development IPT that solicits response from your Business Operations department as well as your lead technical employees.
- Stick to the agenda and business at hand. Discuss consequences of the following:
  - Bid and not awarded contract
  - Bid and awarded contract
  - Prime vs subcontractor role

Question: What do you consider to be the top five Seller best practices for developing a winning bid or proposal?

Answer: 1) Know your customer

2) Know your competitors' strengths and weaknesses

3) Know your company's strengths and weaknesses

4) Commit the total resources to compile a first-rate response

5) Proof, proof, proof!

Note: The subject interview solely expresses the informal opinions' of the interviewee, they do not necessarily represent the views or opinions of the organization, company, or agency which they are employed.

Tools and Techniques

Qualify the Opportunity and Risks

The first step of the Pre-Sales Activities step is to Qualify the Opportunity and Risks. Webster's defines opportunity as, "a set of circumstances providing a chance or possibility." Webster's defines risk as, "the possibility of danger, injury or loss." In other words, elements of opportunity are those characteristics which increase the probability of success and elements of risk are those characteristics which have the potential to negatively impact the result.

■ *Opportunity – Risk Assessment Grid:* There will often be more opportunities than you have resources to pursue, so you must prioritize and direct resources to those opportunities which have the highest probability of success and payback versus those which do not. Since you will need to compare opportunities to make choices, it is necessary to develop a methodology to assess and compare specific opportunities. This can be done using an x-y coordinate grid, see Figure 3-4, which plots opportunity on the "y-axis" and risk on the "x-axis." The grid has further been subdivided into quadrants in order to characterize different types of opportunities.

Quadrant A contains those opportunities which have a "high opportunity" value and are also "low risk." Quadrant A opportunities should be the highest priority as they have the highest probability of success with the best potential payback. In contrast, Quadrant D contains those opportunities which have "low opportunity" value yet have "high risk." Quadrant D opportunities are likely to be projects you should avoid and do not want to waste resources on pursuing as they have a low probability of success and a low potential payback.

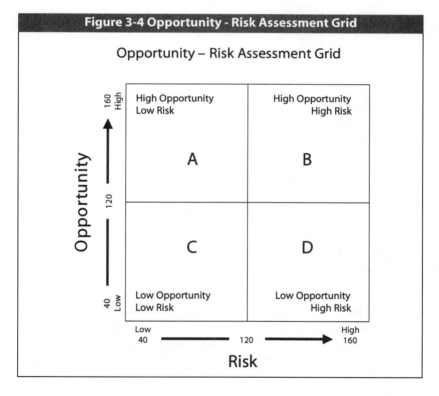

Figure 3-4 Opportunity - Risk Assessment Grid

- **ORA Grid with Bid – No Bid Line:** Quadrant B opportunities have a "low opportunity" value but are also "low risk," while Quadrant C opportunities are "high opportunity" value but also have "high risk." Opportunities in quadrants B and C should be considered marginal and you will want to focus on pursing those opportunities which fall into the upper left hand corner of each of quadrant, while avoiding those which fall into the lower right hand corner. Placing a "bid line" on the grid as shown below graphically, see Figure 3-5, illustrates this concept. Exactly where this line is placed on the grid will be based chiefly upon your company's resources and willingness to accept risk.

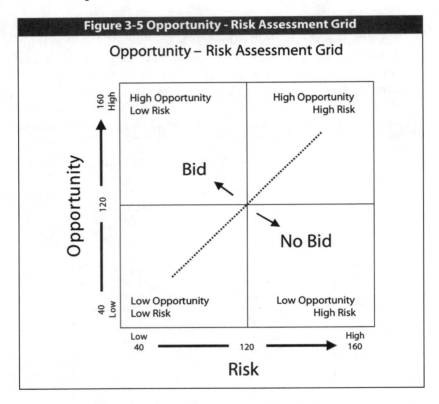

Figure 3-5 Opportunity - Risk Assessment Grid

In order to plot specific opportunities, we need to look at the specific elements or characteristics, which are typically used to assess opportunity and risk. While, the specifics might vary from company to company, the elements of opportunity and risk are common, which are shown on Table 3-1.

Table 3-1	
Elements of Opportunity	**Elements of Risk**
Corporate Direction Match	Customer Commitment
Competitive Environment	Corporate Competence
Revenue Value	External Obstacles
Potential Profitability	Opportunity Engagement
In-House Content	Solution Life Cycle Match
Future Business Potential	Period of Performance
Resources to Bid	Delivery Schedule
Probability to Success	Resource Coordination
Collateral Benefit	Non-Performance Penalties
Overall Strategic Value	Overall Feasibility

- Elements of Opportunity
  - *Corporate Direction Match*: refers to how consistent an opportunity is with your core business or corporate direction for new business. Companies have a much higher probability of winning and successfully delivering when an opportunity is consistent with their core business and strategic direction. One way to make this assessment is to honestly ask yourself "How perfect of an example is this opportunity in relation to the kind of new business your company is seeking?"
  - *Competitive Environment*: refers to whether you or your competitor is perceived by the customer as the solution leader and is favored as the solution supplier. Opportunities where the customer perceives your company as the leader and is the favored supplier (for reasons other than price) are highly desirable. Customer's may have this perception due to technology, reputation, past experience, industry commitment, and so on. Of course, the customer may perceive your competitor as the leader for the same reasons.
  - *Revenue Value*: refers to the dollar value of the opportunity. The intent is to distinguish "small" from "large" revenue opportunities. Obviously, this needs to be assessed in the context of the size of your company and the typical size and currency of new opportunities. Since exact pricing has yet to be developed, you must develop a best estimate and focus only on near-term revenues, such as those likely to be generated in the first year of contract delivery.
  - *Potential Profitability*: refers to the likely margins on the business given the competitive environment and what it

will take to win. Most companies have guidelines on profit-ability of new opportunities, which should serve as the basis to assess how "rich" or "poor" the margins are likely to be. Be sure to estimate this based on the near-term margins and do not include margins on future business.

- *In-House Content:* refers to the percentage of the products or services which will be provided by your company. Frequently, opportunities require some outside supplier product or service; however, ideally all or the vast majority of the products and services are from within your company. You will always have a higher probability of success with what you know best, which are products and services from your own company.

- *Future Business Potential:* refers to the degree to which an opportunity will impact additional business beyond the scope of that specific opportunity. For example, an opportunity may provide the means to gain a new account or protect an existing account. Consider the degree to which specific identifiable future business is dependent upon winning and successfully delivering this business.

- *Resources to Bid:* refers to the amount of resources required to bid and the impact the pursuit of this opportunity will have on other opportunities being pursued. Opportunities do not exist in a vacuum and all companies have resource constraints, so one needs to consider the "opportunity cost" of not pursuing or jeopardizing other opportunities. Conversely, you may have resources or assets that are idle, which you want to keep engaged and active to positively impact resource or asset utilization.

- *Probability of Success:* refers to the likelihood that you will win the business versus one of your competitors.

- *Collateral Benefit:* refers to the degree to which pursuit of an opportunity will improve the existing skill level or develop new skills that will benefit other opportunities or future business. Since additional work typically improves existing skill levels, consider the degree to which this opportunity will exceed the norm or have a wide-scale impact on a large population.

- *Overall Strategic Value:* refers to the overall need to win the opportunity as assessed by the sales manager or key account manager. This should be based upon consideration of all the of the opportunity elements, along with any other tangible or intangible aspects of the opportunity that are considered relevant.

- Elements of Risk
  - *Customer Commitment*: refers to the degree to which the customer has demonstrated a solid commitment to implement the solution offered in an opportunity. Typically this type of commitment is demonstrated through either budgeting for the implementation in a current or future business plan or identifying and assigning resources to support the implementation.
  - *Corporate Competence*: refers to your company's past experience or core competencies to deliver the solution required in an opportunity. The more experience your company has in projects similar to the opportunity, the lower the risk. Conversely, if a similar project has never been successfully completed by any company in the past, then there is a tremendous risk with this opportunity.
  - *External Obstacles*: refers to the degree to which roadblocks exist that are beyond the control of either your customer or company. A good example of this would be if your customer were a regulated utility who must obtain approval from a state or federal authority before they can implement the opportunity. Another example might be if your customer has yet to secure the capital needed to fund the implementation during a period of when capital is tightly constrained.
  - *Opportunity Engagement*: refers to the degree to which your company or your competitors were involved in establishing the customer's requirements. If you did not help your customer develop their requirements, chances are one of your competitor's did. The more involved your company is in establishing the requirements the more strengths your products and services will have and the more weaknesses your competitor's products and services will have.
  - *Solution Life Cycle Match*: refers to the degree to which your solution involves the use of existing mature products versus new products or leading edge technology. If your solution involves mature products available today, your risk of the solution working is very low. On the other hand, if your solution involves many new products which have yet to be released or are based on leading edge technology, you have a risk of encountering development delays or the products not working as planned.

- *Period of Performance*: refers to the length of the contract. The longer the contract the greater the chance of significant changes. Personnel, customer environment, and business climate are a few examples of changes which can introduce risk impacting the project.
- *Delivery Schedule*: refers to when delivery is required and who controls the schedule. The ideal situation is if the schedule is flexible and can be set by your company thus you can ensure you have adequate time to be successful. Conversely, if your customer has already fixed the delivery schedule and has also identified penalties for missing schedules you will be assuming a risk associated with missing deliveries. Keep in mind that while delivery schedules are typically an issue when too short, there can be situations where the delivery schedule is so far in the future that you may have risks ensuring the products you plan to deliver will still be in manufacture.
- *Resource Coordination*: refers to the number of internal groups in your company or external suppliers that must be engaged to deliver the solution. The larger the number of internal groups required, the more coordination that is required to ensure successful delivery and the higher the risk of having a disconnect and delivery problem. Coordination of outside suppliers introduces even more risk as you typically have more control over internal groups than external suppliers to resolve problems.
- *Non-Performance Penalties*: refers to the degree to which your customer has specified penalties for failure to deliver as promised. If your customer has not specified penalties or you can negotiate them with the customer then you can minimize the risks. If your customer has specified monetary or other penalties which are non-negotiable then this increases your risk.
- *Overall Feasibility*: refers to the degree of feasibility of the project as assessed by a knowledgeable representative of the group in your company accountable to deliver the solution. A major factor to consider in assessing feasibility is past experience with the customer on fulfilling their obligations or addressing unforeseen problems equitably. If the project is extremely complex and the customer has a poor track record of supporting complex projects there is a high risk of the project being successfully implemented.

Opportunity — Risk Assessment Tool

If we take each of the above elements of opportunity, we can use a four -point scale to assess each element, as shown below, see Form 3-1. Since all elements do not have equal import, we must also multiply this raw 1-to-4 score by a weight to develop a weighted score. These weighted scores can then be totaled to derive a Total Weighted Opportunity Score that can then be plotted on the Opportunity axis of the Opportunity-Risk Assessment Grid.

Form 3-1 Opportunity Quantification Tool						
Opportunity Element	Score				Weight	Weighted Score
	1	2	3	4		
Core Business / Corporate Direction	Counter to core business and corporate direction	Neutral to core business and corporate direction	Partially aligned to core business and corporate direction	Fully aligned to core business and corporate direction	6	
Competitive Environment	Competitor is clear leader and is favored by customer	Customer favors the competitor and is neutral to your company	No clear leader and customer has no supplier preference	Your company is clear leader and is favored by customer	5	
Revenue Value	Geater than $500K	Between $500K and $2.5M	Between $2.5M and $5M	Over $5M	4	
Potential Profitability	Profitabilty is Negative or Break Even	Profitability is between 0-50% of corporate requirements	Profitability is between 50-100% of corporate requirements	Profitability is over 100% of corporate requirements	4	
In-House Content	Less than 50% of content is from your company	Between 50-75% of content is from your company	Between 75-90% of content is from your company	Over 90% of content is from your company	4	
Future Business Potential	Little or no connection to future business	Possible link to future business	Likely link to future business	Assured or mandatory link to future business	3	
Resources to Bid	Will significantly drain resources working on other opportunities	Will drain some resources working on other opportunities	Will have little or no impact on resources working on other opportunities	Will use resources currently underutilized	3	
Probability of Success	Probability of success is near zero	Probability of success is less than 50%	Probability of success is over 50%	Success is almost certain	3	
Collateral Benefit	Little or no benefit to other projects or new company skills	Some benefit to either other projects or new company skills	Some benefit to both other projects and new company skills	Significant benefit to other projects or new company skills	3	
Overall Strategic Value	It is of low importance that your company win this business	It is somewhat important that your company win this business	It is of high importance that your company win this business	It is critical that your company win this business	5	

Case Study — IBM (Global Services)

IBM has a long and well deserved reputation for being very proactive with their customers. IBM has for many years taken great pride in their ability to understand their customers challenges and business needs, thereby developing products, services, and/or solutions to satisfy their customer's needs. IBM also has a well established business practice of evaluating both business opportunities and risks. IBM account executives and project managers always conduct a thorough opportunity and risk assessment for each deal.

To help mitigate business risks IBM seeks to not only understand their customer's business situation, but to influence the customer's selection process by which they purchase products and/or services. At IBM Global Services they have an old saying "No Blind-Bids," which means IBM wants to always know the customer's needs, the risks, and opportunities before a solicitation document (i.e. Invitation To Bid, Request for Proposal, etc.) is ever issued by a customer. At IBM, opportunity and risk assessment is a proven best practice and an essential part of their business processes.

Case Study — Boeing (Integrated Defense Systems)

As companies become more successful in dealing with challenges, risk management becomes a structured process that is performed continuously throughout the business life cycle. Such is the case at Boeing Integrated Defense Systems, where designing, manufacturing, and delivering aircraft can take years and a multi-billion dollar investment. Typically, Boeing evaluates the following risk categories and develops detailed risk mitigation strategies and actions to improve their business case by reducing or eliminating potential negative aspects.

Risk Categories at Boeing, include:

Financial: Up-front funding and payback period based upon number of planes sold

Market: Forecasting customer's expectations on cost, configuration, and amenities based on 30 to 40 year life of a plane.

Technical: Must forecast technology and its impact on cost, safety, reliability, and maintainability.

Production: Supply-Chain Management of a large number of subcontractors without impacting cost, schedule, quality, or safety.

If we use the same methodology for risk, as is shown below on Form 3-2, we can similarly develop Total Weighted Risk Score that can then be plotted on the Risk axis of the Opportunity-Risk Assessment Grid.

Form 3-2 Risk Quantification Tool						
Risk Element	Score				Weight	Weighted Score
	1	2	3	4		
Customer Commitment	Customer has assigned budget and personnel	Customer has assigned budget but not personnel	Customer has assigned personnel but not budget	Customer has not assigned personnel or budget	6	
Corporate Competence	Complete replication of past projects done by your company	More than 50% replication of past projects done by your company	Less than 50% replication of past projects done by your company	No replication of past projects done by your company	5	
External Obstacles	No obstacles exist which are outside control of customer	Some obstacles — customer is actively working to address each	Some obstacles customer has plan to address each	Significant obstacles, customer has no plan development to address each	4	
Opportunity Engagement	Your company developed requirements for the costomer	Your company guided customer in development of requirements	Your company provided comments after requirements were developed	Your company had no involvement in developing requirements	4	
Solution Life Cycle/ Match	All requirements can be met by mature, relesed products	Less than 30% of products will be pre-released or new products	Between 30-70% of products will be pre-released or new products	70% of products will be pre-released or new products	4	
Period of Performance	Contract is for less than 6 months	Contract is between 6 months and 1 year	Contracts is between 1 year and 3 years	Contracts is over 3 years	3	
Delivery Schedule	Delivery schedule is flexible and will be set by your company	Delivery schedule to be negotiated by customer and your company	Delivery schedule is fixed, but no penalties for missed dates	Delivery schedule is fixed and penalties exist for missed dates	3	
Resource Coordination	Need to coordinate less than 5 groups in your company	Need to coordinate 5 or more groups in your company	Need to coordiante company groups and up to 2 outside suppliers	Need to coordinate company groups and 3 or more outside suppliers	3	
Non-Performance Penalties	No penalties for non-performance	Penalties to be negotiated between customer and your company	Fixed monetary penalties for non-performance with a limit	Fixed monetary penalties for non-performance with no limet	3	
Overall Feasibility/ Risk	Project is feasible and risks are manageable	Project is feasible but risks require mitigation	Project has some elements which are questionable but risk can be mitigation	Project has questionable feasibility and very high risks	5	

You can adapt and modify the Opportunity and Risk Quantification Tools, Forms 3-1 and 3-2, based on the particulars of your business and past experience. The key to effective Opportunity and Risk Qualification is to ensure you have a consistent assessment methodology so opportunities can be compared and prioritized. Use of such a tool will prove invaluable towards improving sales representatives' productivity by directly them away from quadrant D opportunities (i.e., low opportunity-high risk) and focusing their energies on quadrant A opportunities (i.e., high opportunity low risk) and the high-end quadrant B and C opportunities (i.e., low opportunity-low risk and high opportunity-high risk above the bid line).

Gather Competitive Intelligence

Having done an initial qualification of the opportunity and risks, the next step in the Opportunity Profile stage is to Gather Competitive Intelligence. Basic information to be collected includes: 1) who are the competitors or competitive teams, 2) what is the solution you believe they will bid, 3) what are the strengths of the competitor or their solution, and 4) what are the weaknesses of the competitor or their solution.

- **Competitor Profile:** This information should be documented for future use and review by using a template such as the one below, Form 3-3.

Form 3-3 Competitor Profile				
Rank	Competitor or Competing Team	Solution Being Bid	Strengths of Competitor and Solution	Weaknesses of Competitor and Strengths
1				
2				
3				
4				
5				

- **Sources of Competitive Intelligence:** The term "Competitive Intelligence" is used to refer to information on competitors or competitive teams which is specific to an opportunity. This is in contrast to "Market Intelligence", which is general information on your competitors or competitive teams operating in the marketplace or industry. While, Market Intelligence should be not discarded as an input, the real value comes from understanding the competitors, which information can and should be collected from a variety of sources. This not only increases the amount of intelligence gathered, but will serve to validate information by confirming it from multiple sources. Care should be taken; however, to ensure that any and all competitive intelligence is gathered legally and ethically. For example, in addition to understanding your company's rules on soliciting information; it is equally important to understand your customer's rules regarding discussions with customer personnel and access to customer information that is part of the source selection process.

Table 3-2 shows typical sources of competitive intelligence:

Table 3-2
Sources of Competitive Intelligence
Public press releases
Public websites
Public brochures
Public advertisements
Articles in trade publications
Past bids by your company to this customer
Past bids by your company to similar customers
Customer list of companies requesting solicitation*
Customer conversations*
Customer events and meetings*
Trade or Industry Associations
Competitive research or analysis companies
*Which do not violate your companies or competitor's rules on disclosure

Develop a Win Strategy

■ **Win Strategy**: Having gathered Competitive Intelligence, the next step is to Develop a Win Strategy. A Win Strategy is a collection of messages or points designed to guide the customer's perception of you, your solution, and your competitors.

■ **Sweet Spot-Sour Spot Analysis:** Perhaps one of the best ways to graphically depict the elements of a win strategy is to use the concept of "Sweet Spot" and "Sour Spot" as presented by David G. Pugh, PhD. of the Lore International Institute in his article "A Bidder's Dozen: Golden Rules For Winning Work." Figure

3-6 "Sweet Spot – Sour Spot" model depicts the relationship of your company's strengths and weaknesses to the customer's needs and the strengths and weaknesses of our competitors. The "Sweet Spot" is where your company's strengths meet the customer's needs and coincide with your competitor's weaknesses. Conversely, the "Sour Spot" is where your competitor's strengths meet the customer's needs and coincide with your company's weaknesses.

The objective of a Win Strategy is to maximize the importance of your "Sweet Spot" to your customer and simultaneously minimize the importance of your "Sour Spot." This will require considerable time and effort, as your competitors will obviously be trying to do the exact opposite. Win Strategies that maximize the "Sweet Spot" are messages or points highlighting your strengths and amplify or "ghost" your competitor's weaknesses. Win Strategies that minimize your "Sour Spot" are messages or points mitigating your weaknesses and neutralize your competitor's strengths.

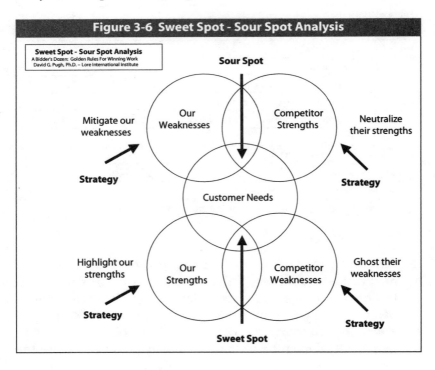

Figure 3-6 Sweet Spot - Sour Spot Analysis

Changing customer perceptions requires repetitive communication of a consistent message to numerous individuals in the customer organization. The most effective strategies are those that can be translated into straightforward "themes" or "phrases" which differentiate you from your competitor. These "themes" or "phrases" can then be delivered to your customer in sales calls, executive contacts, proposals, presentations, advertisements and all forms of communication over a period of time, thus changing perceptions.

Your strategies should also focus on the points which are the most significant to your customer in-terms of impact on their business problem or objective. The proverbial "80-20 Rule" is a good guide to use to determine significance. Typically 20% of the requirements account for 80% of the value, and conversely, the remaining 80% only account for 20% of the value. Ideally, you will want to position your "Sweet Spot" as being part of the 20% which creates 80% of the value, and your "Sour Spot" as being part of the other 80% which only has minimal impact (i.e., 20%).

One successful technique to developing win strategies is to gather a core team of individuals and hold a Strategy Session. During this session you will want to attempt to board and map the "Sweet Spot" and "Sour Spot" and develop strategies to address each. While this should be a small group it is important to include a knowledgeable individual from each of the following areas:

- Sales or marketing
- Manufacturing or supply chain
- Engineering or technical support
- Program management or product/service delivery
- Contracting or legal
- Finance or business management.

- ***Win Theme and Strategy Form:*** You will want to succinctly capture your Win Theme and Win Strategy for review with the Stakeholders and later as a guide for the Capture Team. Form 3-4 is an example of a Win Theme and Strategy form which can be used for this purpose.

Form 3-4
Win Themes and Strategies
Win Themes:
Strategies to maximize our strengths:
Strategies to minimize our weaknesses:
Strategies to neutralize competitor's strengths:
Strategies to ghost competitor's weaknesses:

■ ***Customer Positioning Plan:*** As part of executing your Win Strategy you will want to proactively communicate your messages to your customer through various channels in addition to your response or proposal. A key channel for communication is the relationship and regular contact between key customers and individuals in your company, referred to as Customer Positioning. As part of enhancing the impact of Customer Positioning, you will want to seize opportunities for potential customer contact by identifying major events or planned meetings and orchestrating the participation and messages to be communicated by key individuals from your company. It is vital to develop documented plans to address each of these.

Form 3-5, *Customer Positioning Planner* can be used to match key customers with the appropriate contact in your company to develop relationships. The planner allows you to show the name, title, and role of each key customer along with a primary and secondary contact from your company and the type and frequency of contact. Types of contact include phone calls, personal meetings, dinner or entertainment. Frequency of contact includes weekly, bi-weekly, monthly and as-needed. You will want to match "like-for-like", for example, you would likely want to match the CEO of your company as the primary contact with the CEO of your customer's company with your President as the secondary contact. This will allow you and the executives in your company to establish a regular schedule of contact with your key customers.

Form 3-5								
Customer Positioning Planner								

Customer Position	Customer Name	Role		Primary Contact	Secondary Contact	Frequency of Contact *		
		Decision Maker	Influencer			Phone Call	Personal Meeting	Dinner	Entertainment

(table: Form 3-5 — Customer Positioning Planner)

Customer Position	Customer Name	Decision Maker	Influencer	Primary Contact	Secondary Contact	Phone Call	Personal Meeting	Dinner	Entertainment

* Weekly, Bi-Weekly, Monthly, As-Needed

Form 3-6					
Customer Contact Planner					

Customer:			Prepared by:		Date:
Date	Event	Purpose	Objective(s)	Customer Participants	Your Company Participants

■ ***Customer Contact Plan:*** In addition, *Customer Contact Planner,* Form 3-6, can be used to manage contacts between key customers and individuals in your company at major events or planned meetings. This planner provides to space to identify each event, the date, purpose of the event, specific objective(s) you want to achieve at the event, customer participants and participants from your company. Examples of events you would want to manage include: trade shows, sporting events, briefings, seminars, etc. This will allow you and the executives in your company to keep track of the major events requiring participation in order to effectively establish and build relationships with your key customers.

Outline the Opportunity

Having Developed a Win Strategy, the next step is to Outline the Opportunity and develop material to review with Stakeholder's to solicit their buy-in to pursue the opportunity. While you will want to customize this to your company and your business, below is an outline of the basic information you will want to document into some type of presentation for review.

- **■ *Outline of Offer for Stakeholder Opportunity Review:*** The format and size of the presentation will vary depending upon such factors as the scope of the opportunity, the number and level of the stakeholders, and the resource commitment required. Whether you opt to standardize on viewgraphs or a written narrative format, the important thing is to document the opportunity in a form that can be shared and updated as the opportunity is pursued and more information is obtained. If using viewgraphs, be sure to match the size of the presentation to the opportunity. Presentations on smaller opportunities should be kept to one slide per category, while on larger ones may require one or more slides per subject to provide an adequate review.

  - **■ *Introduction*:** all Stakeholder Opportunity Reviews should start with a clear declaration and review of the Purpose, Agenda, Limit and Participants. This will ensure that everyone understands why they are there (i.e., the purpose), the topics that will be covered (i.e., the agenda), how much time is allotted for the meeting (i.e., the limit), and most importantly, who is in the meeting and their role (i.e., the participants). An easy way to remember this is to memorize the saying "be a PAL to Participants", where "P" is purpose, "A" is agenda, and "L" is limit.

    The Purpose of the stakeholder review, see Table 3-2 below, is typically: a) to review the opportunity, b) to make a bid/no bid decision, c) to solicit resource commitment, and 4) to establish escalation support. The Agenda is typically the topics covered, in sequence, along with the presenters who will cover each topic. The Limit is the time allotted to the meeting. The Participants are the stakeholders listed with their name, title and functional responsibility.

    Unless all of the stakeholders and everyone who will work on pursuit of the opportunity knows your customer thoroughly, you should prepare a Customer Profile. While stakeholders may have a general familiarity with your customer, you want to ensure that all the stakeholders have a common appreciation for the customer's business so they

THREE

can truly evaluate the opportunity and risks. Additionally, the customer profile will also be used as a reference document to introduce others to the opportunity.

- *Customer Profile*: should briefly cover three subjects: 1) Customer Business, 2) Your Presence, and 3) Competitor Presence. Customer Business refers to demographics of your customer's enterprise and would include such information as mission statement, market strategy, target markets, market share, annual revenues, number of employees or locations, and geography. Your Presence refers to your existing business with the customer, which is typically expressed in-terms of the quantities or values of past products and services purchased and the percentage of the customer's past purchases spent with our company. Competitor Presence refers to the existing business your customer has with competitors and is expressed in similar terms.

- *Opportunity Profile:* should briefly cover six subjects: 1) Problem, 2) Solution, 3) Contract, 4) Basic Scope, 5) Optional Scope, and 6) Key Dates. Problem refers to the business problem your customer is trying to solve or the objective they are trying to achieve which should be articulated as concisely and directly as possible. Solution refers to how you will potentially solve the customer's business problem including the major products and services you will use from your company and any outside products and services required. Contract refers to the anticipated type and term or length of the contract which is anticipated. Basic scope refers to the minimum or obligated geography or locations involved and the estimated value and/or quantities of major products and services. Optional scope refers to geography, locations, products or services, which the customer may or may not purchase. Key Dates refers to major milestones such as bid response date, anticipated contract signing date, first delivery date, and end of contract date.

- *Competitor Profile*: should briefly cover: 1) Competitors, 2) Solutions, 3) Strengths, and 4) Weaknesses. Competitors refers to the specific competitors or competitive teams, by name, pursuing this specific opportunity. Solution refers to the solution you anticipate each competitor or competitive team will offer to solve the customer's business problem. Strengths and Weaknesses refer to the specific strengths and weaknesses of the competitor or their solution. This information should have been captured during the Opportunity Profile stage and documented on the Competitor Profile form presented earlier.

- *Win Strategy*: should briefly cover: 1) Theme, 2) Sweet Spot, 3) Sour Spot, and 4) Positioning Plan. Theme refers to the overarching message(s) to be conveyed to the customer in all communications of "how and why" you solve the customer's problem the best. Sweet Spot and Sour Spot refers to the specific messages designed to maximize your Sweet Spot and minimize your Sour Spot as developed during the Opportunity Profile stage. Positioning Plan refers to the specific plans developed to communicate these messages to your customer, including such tactics as executive visits, briefings, tours, etc.

- *Issues/Concerns:* should briefly cover: 1) Product/Service gaps, 2) Availability gaps, 3) Resource gaps, and 4) Contract issues. Product/Service gaps refers to any major gap between your product/service to the requirements. Availability gaps refers to either the need to commit to requirements that your company has identified as a future capability but has yet to be funded for development or the need to deliver a product or service prior to the currently planned release schedule. Resource gaps refer to shortages or mis-matches in availability, skill set or funding for required resources for either the response or the delivery. Contract issues refers to terms, conditions or liabilities which are outside the norm for your company for an opportunity of this type.

- *Response Requirements*: should briefly cover: 1) Timeline, 2) People Resources, and 3) Other Resources. Timeline refers to the key milestones and dates required to develop an offer and deliverable document for the customer, whether it be in response to a customer solicitation or a proactive proposal. People Resources refers to the quantity and skill set of individuals required to develop the response. Other Resources refers to non-personnel resources required to develop the response and may include such items as lab equipment, travel and living, proposal production costs, and/or outside consultants. Together the People Resources and Other Resources represent the "resource commitment" you are asking the stakeholders to spend to pursue the opportunity.

- *Bid / No Bid Decision*: should briefly cover: 1) Stakeholder Commitment and 2) Action Items. Stakeholder Commitment refers to soliciting a clear commitment from the stakeholders that they: a) fully support development of the response, b) agree to promptly assign resources, c) agree to be a point of escalation to help resolve roadblocks, and d) agree to meet again to review and approve the response prior to submittal to the customer.

Case Study — NCR (Professional Services)

More than 10 years ago, NCR Professional Services formalized their Bid/No Bid Decision Making process, to include a tool which enabled them to assess both the opportunities and risks pertaining to a possible deal in a more objective and quantifiable manner. NCR calls their Bid/No Bid decision making support tool Project Opportunity and Risk Assessment (PORA). PORA allows NCR to identify opportunities and risks, assess probability, assess monetary impact, and determine the expected monetary value associated with the overall business scenario in timely, cost effective, and automated manner.

Outputs

At the completion of the Pre-Sales Activities step you should have:

- A Qualified Opportunity
- Competitor Profile
- Win Strategy
- Outline of Offer for Stakeholder Opportunity Review

SELECTED INTERVIEW

Name: Wayne E. Ferguson

Job Title: Manager, Contracts and Export Compliance Officer

Organization: CAE USA Inc.

Location: Tampa, FL

Major Responsibilities: Management and administration of all CAE USA contracts.

Background: B.S. in Management and MBA in Management, both from Wright State University, Dayton, OH. Former

USAF "Copper Cap" @ WPAFB, OH. Over 20 years experience both as a USAF civilian Procurement Contracting Officer and in industry.

QUESTIONS & ANSWERS:

Question: What actions do you suggest sellers take to ethically and appropriately influence buyer's requirements?

Answer: Have the "marketers" coordinate early with their contracts personnel and follow the "letter of the law" re: influence attempts. Establish an atmosphere of trust and mutual respect with the customer

Question: What actions should sellers take to ensure they make intelligent Bid/No Bid Decisions on their critical deals?

Answer: Do not "chase" every opportunity – look at those opportunities that match the seller's "core" business plans/competencies and stick with them. Have a formal Bid/No Bid process and follow it.

Question: What do you consider to be the top five Seller best practices for developing a winning bid or proposal?

Answer: 1) Read and follow the RFP requirements "to a T"
2) Get to know the buyer's and the users' real needs and attempt to roll these into the proposal
3) If one does not exist in the organization establish a formal proposal team and written processes/procedures for such team
4) Aim the proposal at the RFP requirements – do not include "fluff" in the proposal
5) Be timely in every action taken.

Note: The subject interview solely expresses the informal opinions' of the interviewee, they do not necessarily represent the views or opinions of the organization, company, or agency which they are employed.

THREE

Seller Step 2: Bid/No Bid Decision

Having completed the Pre-Sales Activities step, the next step of the Buying & Selling Life Cycle for the seller is to obtain a Bid/No Bid Decision. All of the inputs, tools and techniques, and outputs of this step are reflected below in Figure 3-7. The objectives or desired outputs of the Bid/No Bid Decision step are: Strategy Alignment, Resource Commitment, and Escalation Support, if the decision is to bid the opportunity. If the decision is to not bid, then the seller focuses its time and attention on conducting additional Pre-Sales Activities to identify better opportunities. The goal is to win business which will meet or exceed both the buyers and sellers business requirements.

Figure 3-7 Seller Step 2: Bid/No Bid Decision Process

Input	Tools & Techniques	Output
• Qualified Opportunity • Competitor Profile • Win Strategy • Outline of Offer — Stakeholder Review • Presentation • Introduction • Customer Profile • Opportunity Profile • Competitor Profile • Win Strategy • Issues & Concerns • Response Requirements • Bid/No Bid Decision	• Stakeholder Opportunity Review Presentation • Stakeholder Opportunity Review Outline • Tips for an Effective Stakeholder Review	• "Bid/No Bid" Decision • Alignment on Strategy • Resource Commitment • Escalation Support • Stakeholder Opportunity Review Package • Capture Core Team

Inputs

If you successfully completed all the steps described in the Pre-Sales Activities, you will have created all the inputs required for the next step Bid/Proposal Development. These are:

- A Qualified Opportunity
- Competitor Profile
- Win Strategy
- Outline of Offer for Stakeholder Opportunity Review.

If you do not have all these inputs, refer to the appropriate actions in the Pre-Sales Activities step to create the missing item(s).

Tools & Techniques

■ *Stakeholder Opportunity Review*: Countless opportunities are lost and resources are wasted due to failure to properly solicit and secure Stakeholder Buy-In. This is especially true given that the larger the company, the more complex your business, especially as technology and companies change more rapidly and customers change suppliers more frequently. Each of these factors changes the fundamental relationship between your company, your customer and your competitors. One cannot assume support based on a set of "fixed rules," one must solicit and positively confirm support since there is a set of "dynamic rules" which are constantly changing in order to stay one step ahead of the competition.

The most frequently asked questions regarding Stakeholders are: "who are the stakeholders" and "how do I identify them?" According to Kevin Forsberg, Ph.D. and Hall Mooz, in the best seller "Visualizing Project Management," a stakeholder is "any individual, group or organization that can affect, or be affected by, the project." Operationally, stakeholders are individuals who can make commitments on behalf of key groups or organizations within your company. For most opportunities, you will want representatives from the following groups or organizations:

■ Sales or marketing
■ Manufacturing or supply chain
■ Engineering or technical support
■ Program management or product/service delivery
■ Contracting or legal
■ Finance or business management
■ If product/service or availability issues, include a representative from Product Management or Research & Development.

Another frequently asked questions is "what level are the stakeholders?" It is essential to ensure you have stakeholders authorized to make commitments. However, you need to match the level to the size of the commitment required. While you don't want to waste the time of executives to review opportunities that could be approved by subordinates, you do want to ensure you have a commitment from someone with proper authority. Most companies have a "Schedule of Authorizations" or "Schedule of Approvals" which identifies the type and dollar value of commitment that can be made by individuals at various levels, which is an excellent guide for ascertaining the "right level" stakeholder. If due to schedule availability, you opt to not include stakeholder(s) who need to approve the final bid, you will have to account for this additional approval step in your Capture Project Plan work tasks and timeline.

■ ***Tips for an Effective Opportunity Stakeholder Review:*** A common mistake made, especially by large companies, is to minimize the number of stakeholders whose support is solicited. Frequently this is done to avoid or "go around" individuals who are known to be negative or difficult. Be careful in opting to exclude stakeholders. The individuals who have the biggest objections or concerns are exactly the people you need to get aligned with the solution and strategy. If you don't get these stakeholders "on board with the plan," you will likely encounter problems during the Bid Phase.

Another common mistake is for a sales representative to attempt to gain support from the CEO, President or a senior executive in their company and use this as "unconditional authority" to pursue an opportunity. While this approach is certainly easier and less time consuming on the sales representative, it is also a recipe for disaster. Despite a decree from a senior executive in your company identifying the opportunity as a "must win," you will need to solicit stakeholder support to obtain alignment on strategy, get resources committed, and established escalation support to resolve problems. On a related note, over time you should find that you have fewer and fewer "No Bids." This is generally a sign that your sales representatives have become better at qualifying opportunities and discarding those which are poor.

Like all group meetings, there is art to effectively managing a Stakeholder Review, especially if it involves senior executives in your company. Form 3-7 provides a checklist of tips to improve the effectiveness of your Stakeholder Opportunity Review.

Form 3-7
Checklist of Tips for an Effective Stakeholder Opportunity Review

Prior to the meeting:
- Pick a time for the meeting which maximizes stakeholder participation and provide adequate notification
- Confirm stakeholder participation and have stakeholders who cannot attend identify an authorized delegate
- Minimize the inclusion of individuals other than the stakeholders or presenters at the review
- Ensure presenters understand their material, the agenda and the time each has been allotted.

If the review will be via conference call
- Distribute presentation materials in advance of the meeting
- Take role of participants as they "beep in" to ensure there are no unauthorized participants
- If possible, use a unique bridge number for the review to reduce risk of uninvited participants
- Have participants put all speakerphones on "mute" to reduce background noise
- Have participants on cell or cordless phones with excessive noise drop-off and call-back on a different phone

During the meeting:
- Introduce yourself as the individual running the review
- Review the Purpose, Agenda and Limit for the review
- Introduce the stakeholders being sure to identify their role/accountability
- Keep track of time and "prod" presenters to move along if they are taking to long
- Do not try to solve problems on the call, identify them as action items and assign an owner to resolve
- Allow for adequate discussion, but do not permit endless debating or "grandstanding"
- Explain to stakeholders what you are asking them to commit to with their vote
- Perform a "roll call" of stakeholders where each stakeholder must vote "yes" or "no"
- If a stakeholder votes "no," have them explain why and make the issue an action item so they can vote "yes"

After the meeting:
- Update and redistribute the presentation with any material changes made during the review
- Document stakeholder participation and commitment as part of the updated presentation
- Share the updated presentation with those working on the opportunity to show stakeholder commitment

Outputs

At the completion of the Stakeholders Opportunity Review you want to have successfully obtained the following outputs.

Bid/No Bid Decision

The first objective, Conduct Bid/No Bid Decision, refers to presenting the facts to the stakeholders so they understand the opportunity and the risks. This should be done in an unbiased and objective manner. The future of your company depends upon consistently making the best decisions on how to prioritize opportunities and commit scarce resources. Don't try to "white-wash" problems and don't try to "over-sell" the opportunity. Not only will you lose personal credibility over time, you will potentially cause your company to waste resources that could have been spent on a better opportunity.

Alignment on Strategy

The second objective, Obtain Alignment on strategy, refers to ensuring all the stakeholders not only understand and agree to pursue the opportunity, but more importantly are in "alignment" on the solution proposed and the win strategy. Alignment is defined by Webster's as; "being in correct relative position to something else." This "alignment' is critical to ensuring everyone on the team is heading in the right direction, conveying the correct message (internally and to customers) and is not unintentionally creating problems or wasting resources on activities that are inconsistent with the win strategy.

Resource Commitment

The third objective, Get Resource Commitment, refers to ensuring all the stakeholders agree to provide the people and non-personnel resources needed to pursue the opportunity. Since many opportunities will operate on a fixed and short timeline, this commitment also means the resources will be provided when they are needed. It is always better to identify and highlight resource problems as early as possible in the process so there is time to develop a solution.

Escalation Support

The fourth objective, Escalation Support, refers to soliciting an agreement from stakeholders to actively help resolve roadblocks. This item is frequently overlooked and taken as a "given," which can lead to undue problems and stress during the Bid Phase. There will most assuredly be problems during the Bid Phase and you will need action taken quickly. Therefore, this is the best time to establish a rapport and expectation with the stakeholders that you will most likely call upon for assistance.

Stakeholder Opportunity Review Package

The Stakeholder Opportunity Review Package should be updated with any material changes that occurred during the review session, and should include recording Stakeholders participation on commitment and support. This package will serve as both an excellent introduction to new team members of the opportunity and should be used at the Capture Team Kickoff during the Bid Phase for this purpose.

Capture Core Team

As part of the initial resource commitment, the Stakeholders should assign individuals to a Capture Core Team to develop the Capture Project Plan. This team should include a Capture Manager, Proposal Manager, Sales Leader, Technical Leader, Delivery Leader, Pricing Leader and Contracts Leader. The roles & responsibilities of each of these individuals are discussed in-depth within the next chapter.

SELECTED INTERVIEW

Name: Rick Diehl

Job Title: Senior Contracts Manager

Organization: CSC Applied Technologies LLC

Location: Forth Worth, Texas

Major Responsibilities: Manages proposal preparation, contract negotiation and administration on assigned contracts for CSC Applied Technologies LLC in accordance with policies and procedures. Facilitates effective implementation of contract responsibilities within program objectives and requirements. Reviews and resolves applicable issues affecting company compliance and ensures satisfaction of legal requirements, company and customer objectives. Advises management on contractual rights and obligations; provides interpretation of terms and conditions.

Background: Undergraduate degree in Business Administration; Graduate degree: MBA

Thirty-seven (37) years of experience within Industry/Government in the areas of Acquisition/Contracting, pre-award, post-award, subcontract management, financial management, quality assurance, property assurance and manufacturing

---

processes and controls. Experience in Air Force Programmed Depot Maintenance (PDM) of various aircraft, new aircraft production and jet-engine overhaul.

Colonel, USAF, Retired

NCMA: CPCM – Fellow

QUESTIONS & ANSWERS:

Question: What actions do you suggest sellers take to ethically and appropriately influence buyer's requirements?

Answer: (a) Participate in pre-proposal conferences at every opportunity to voice opinions and ideas on how a solicitation should be structured, (b) take advantage of any Questions/Answers (Q&A) opportunities during the solicitation process that may influence buyer's requirements, (c) outside of a formal solicitation process, ask for an opportunity to brief potential customer to explain the product or service offered, (d) work on developing a trusting relationship with your customer, (e) look for opportunities to explain how your company operates and the ethical processes/procedures that guide the day to day operations, (f) look for opportunities to talk about your company products/services and why they are beneficial for the customers needs, (g) become a member of NCMA and take advantage of World Congress and other National Conferences where you may have an opportunity to be on a panel discussion with your customer, or otherwise have an opportunity to talk (ethically) to your customer during a conference atmosphere.

Question: What actions should sellers take to ensure they make intelligent Bid/No Bid Decisions on their critical deals?

Answer: (a) Determine if the opportunity fits the organizational sales strategy, (b) Assess if there is a clear chance of winning, (c) Assess the Bid & Proposal (B&P) financial status of company, (d) Determine your relationship with the customer, (e) Determine how your organization is better than the competition, (f) determine if the ROI is worth the bidding, (g) How acceptable are the terms and conditions, (h) determine the magnitude of the risks?

Question: What do you consider to be the top five Seller best practices for developing a winning bid or proposal?

Answer: (a) Follow all guidelines as specified in the RFP – fully understand Sections L & M, (b) fully understand the requirements of the RFP and what the customer wants – do not try to dictate to the customer what you think they want/need, (c) clearly define your processes and programs to meet the identified needs, (d) write and present proposal in positive, understandable terms, (e) know your competitors and outline the benefits of choosing your company – absolutely assure that all aspects of proposal are credible.

Note: The subject interview solely expresses the informal opinions' of the interviewee, they do not necessarily represent the views or opinions of the organization, company, or agency which they are employed.

Straight Talk: Suggestions for Significant Improvement

In both the public and private business sectors, sellers are often in zeal to bid and win a deal. As a result, many sellers do not take the time to properly conduct pre-bid/proposal activities especially assessing and analyzing risk. Thus, many sellers are too quick to develop a bid or proposal for an opportunity. Surprisingly, many companies win only 15% to 20% of the deals they bid/propose, thus spending a significant amount of money on bids/proposals that they often had little real chance of winning. Furthermore, many companies pursue the wrong deals, just because they believe they can win the deal. A company must realize just because you can win a deal, does not mean it should even bid the deal. Some deals are truly too high of a risk and there is little to no way to achieve excellence and profitability with integrity. For sellers it is tough to learn that sometimes no business is better than bad business. No company should adopt a strategy of "we bid everything" unless they are trying to go out of business as quickly as possible.

Summary

Before proceeding to the Bid/Proposal Phase, be sure to review the Inputs, Tools & Techniques, Outputs charts in this chapter and assess if you have successfully completed all the outputs identified. If you find gaps, go back and use the tools and techniques provided to complete the missing outputs.

Questions To Consider

1. How well does your organization qualify opportunities, gather competitive intelligence, develop win strategies, develop customer positioning plans, and obtain stakeholder buy-in to pursue opportunities?

2. How effectively does your organization walk away from poor opportunities?

3. Does your organization have documented processes or tools & techniques used to qualify opportunities, gather competitive intelligence, develop win strategies, develop customer positioning plans, and obtain stakeholder buy-in to pursue opportunities?

4. What actions has your organization taken to improve/develop opportunity qualification, competitive intelligence, win strategy, customer positioning planning or stakeholder buy-in skills for your sales managers, capture/proposal managers and contract managers?

5. How well does your organization document and share your opportunity qualification, competitive intelligence, win strategy, customer positioning planning and stakeholder buy-in lessons learned?

CHAPTER  4

BID/PROPOSAL PHASE: BID/ PROPOSAL DEVELOPMENT & REVIEWS/ APPROVALS

INTRODUCTION

The Bid/Proposal Phase for the seller is composed of two key steps, which are the Bid/Proposal Development and the Bid/Proposal Reviews and Approvals. These two steps should be completed in the sequence presented, as each step builds upon the preceding step. Similarly, the Bid/Proposal Phase builds upon the Pre-Bid/Proposal Phase, so you must be sure all outputs described in the previous chapter have been completed, see Figure 4-1, "The Buying & Selling Life-Cycle."

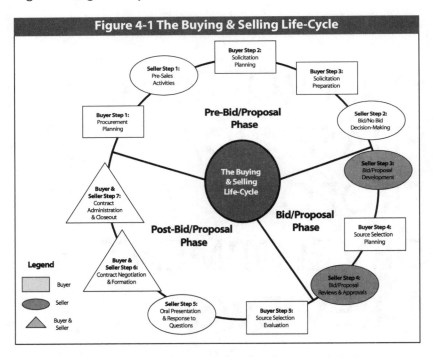

Figure 4-1 The Buying & Selling Life-Cycle

Seller Step 3: Bid/Proposal Development

The primary objective of the Bid/Proposal Development step is to finalize and execute the Capture Project Plan, including:

- Conduct a Capture Team Kickoff Meeting
- Develop the Customer Solution
- Develop Risk Mitigation Plans
- Develop Business Case(s)
- Develop the Proposal

The following graphic, Figure 4-2, shows the Inputs, Tools & Techniques, and Outputs of the Bid/Proposal Development step.

Figure 4-2, Seller Step 3: Bid/Proposal Development Process

Input	Tools & Techniques	Output
• Select a Capture Team	• Conduct a Capture Team Kickoff Meeting	• Customer Solution
• Draft a Preliminary Capture Project Plan	• Execute the Capture Project Plan	• Design
• Draft a Communication Plan	• Capture Team Status Meetings	• Pricing
• Review past lessons learned and best practices	• Action Item Register	• Delivery Plan
	• Stakeholder Status Report	• Risk Mitigation Plans
	• Stakeholder Status Review Outline	• Business Cases
	• Develop Solution	• Customer Proposal
	• Solution Architecture	• Executive Summary
	• Compliance Matrix	• Technical Response
	• Solution Linkage Matrix	• Delivery Response
	• Delivery Plan	• Pricing Response
	• Develop Risk Mitigation Plans	• Contractual Response
	• Sources of Risk	
	• Ways of Mitigating Risks	
	• Risk Mitigation Plan	
	• Risk Mitigation Plan Log	
	• Develop Business Case	
	• Business Case Scenarios	
	• Business Case Models	
	• Product/Service Profile	
	• Customer Business Case	
	• Common Business Case Terms	
	• Develop Proposal	
	• Attributes of Winning Proposals	

*This section is adapted from the book "The Capture Management Life-Cycle: Winning More Business," by Gregory A. Garrett and Reginald J. Kipke, CCH, 2003.

Inputs

The inputs for the Bid/Proposal Development step are: (1) Select a Capture Team, (2) Draft a Preliminary Proposal Capture Project Plan, (3) Draft a Communication Plan for the team, (4) Review Past Proposals Lessons Learned and Best Practices.

SELECTED INTERVIEW

Name: John A. (Jack) Bishop Jr.

Job Title: Director of Operations

Organization: Anteon Corporation, now General Dynamics Information Technology

Location: Albuquerque, NM

Major Responsibilities: Program Management, Contract Management & Administration, Business Development

Background: Education – MS/MBA, Abilene Christian University/Webster University. Experience – Contracting Division Chief/PCO, USAF/Air Force Research Laboratory and Contracts Director, Information Systems Group, Anteon Corporation, Fairfax, VA.

QUESTIONS & ANSWERS:

Question: What actions do you suggest sellers take to ethically and appropriately influence buyer's requirements?

Answer: a). Initiate dialog to assess buyer's "needs & wants" during open discussion. Use that information to provide solution insight, which has been prepared well in advance of these discussions as a result of thorough pre-planning.

b). Provide limited scope "white papers" either as a result of buyer request, or unsolicited.

c). Provide unsolicited proposals (limited scope) to entice buyer's actions.

Question: What actions should sellers take to ensure they make intelligent Bid/No Bid Decisions on their critical deals?

Answer: a). Perform thorough due diligence concerning the procurement using all appropriate means.

b). Authorize "capture managers" to recommend/ make bid/no-bid determinations at any time prior to bid submittal.

c). Ensure chasing the procurement is worth the B & P investment involved.

Question: What do you consider to be the top five Seller best practices for developing a winning bid or proposal?

Answer: a). Know the requirement cold.

b). Know buyer's needs & wants.

c). Don't skimp on bid and proposal costs.

d). Hire the right capture manager.

e). Manage cost, quality, schedule to the "nth" degree.

Question: Please share a brief personal success story re-garding: Solicitations, Bids/Proposals, or Source Selection - Building a Winning Contract.

Answer: First formal A-76 cost comparison at a specific Air Force Base. Bids already received from pro-spective vendors under a Two Step (pre-qualified technically) Invitation for Bid (IFB), and very near bid opening when Procuring Contracting Officer

(PCO) determined the government requirements for technical acceptability had not been met in accordance with regulations. The solicitation was cancelled. Pre-qualified vendors were notified of the circumstances, and when the solicitation would be reissued following government compliance with A-76 procurement specifics. This decision set the stage for all future cost comparisons by leveling the playing field in an era of uncertainty and mistrust on the part of industry toward the cost comparison process itself. Ultimately this procurement resulted in the outsourcing of the function to industry.

Note: The subject interview solely expresses the informal opinions' of the interviewee, they do not necessarily represent the views or opinions of the organization, company, or agency which they are employed.

TOOLS & TECHNIQUES

■ ***Conduct Capture Team Kickoff Meeting***: Perhaps the single biggest factor in developing a winning bid is having a team of resources who are aligned and dedicated to the same goal. This alignment and dedication does not occur by itself. It requires planning and cultivation on the part of the Capture Manager and the Core Capture Team.

The first step is to assemble the team and conduct a Capture Team Kickoff. If all team members are in the same location, or if travel is appropriate, you should conduct this session face-to-face. While, a face-to-face session is desirable, the kickoff can be conducted equally effectively by conference bridge or an intranet sharing application, such as NetMeeting. It is essential to maximize participation, so even if the session is held face-to-face, you will also want to use a conference bridge or an intranet sharing application for anyone who can not be there in person.

The following Capture Team Kickoff Checklist, Form 4-1, presents the recommended topics, sequence, and presenters for the session. You will note that for most topics on the agenda there is a reference document that was developed during the Pre-Bid Phase, which means there should be no special pre-sentation materials required for the session.

	Form 4-1		
	Capture Team Kickoff Checklist		
Checklist	**Agenda Topics**	**Reference Documents**	**Discussion Leader**
❏	**Introduction** • Purpose, Agenda, Limit • Introduce Team Members		Capture Manager
❏	**Review Opportunity** • Customer Profile • Opportunity Profile • Competitor Profile • Win Theme & Strategies • Issues/Concerns	• Stakeholder Opportunity Review Package	Sales Leader
❏	**Validate Capture Plan** • Work Tasks • Resources • Timeline • Communication Plans	• Work Breakdown Structure (WBS) • Organization Breakdown Structure (OBS) • Responsibility Assignment Matrix (RAM) • Team Leader Roles & Responsibilities • Task List Schedule Customer Positioning & Contact Plans • Project Communication Plan • Change Request Plan • Alert-Jeopardy-Escalation Plan	Capture Manager
❏	**Review Proposal Development Plans** • Development Process • Production Requirements • Layout & Assignments • Proposal Reviews	• Proposal Development Checklist • Proposal Production Checklist • Proposal Layout with Assignments • Pink Team & Red Team Checklists	Proposal Manager
❏	**Action Items and Next Steps** • Action Items • Meeting Schedule	• Action Item Register	Capture Manager

As with all meetings, you will want to start by reviewing the purpose, agenda and limit for the meeting and introduce all participants. You will then want the Sales Leader to review the customer, opportunity, competitor profiles, win themes and strategies, and issues/concerns. The Stakeholder Opportunity Review Package should be used as the presentation materials. Not only will this eliminate the need for a separate presentation, it will additionally serve to communicate to the team the Stakeholders support for the opportunity.

The next topic should be to validate the capture project plan, which will include reviewing the deliverables, work tasks, resources, team structure, timeline and communications plans. The objective during this portion of the session is to get feedback on the plans, so prepare yourself for criticism and don't take any of the feedback personally. It is recommended that the Capture Manager lead this discussion as it will serve to establish their role as leader of the capture team. It also provides the opportunity for the Sales Leader to endorse this role at the close of their presentation.

The next topic should be a review of the proposal development plans by the Proposal Manager. This should include a review of the Proposal Development Process, Proposal Production Requirements, and Proposal Layout with Volume & Section Assignments, all of which should have been developed during the Capture Project Plan stage. If not all of the Section Assignments have yet to be made, you can complete this during the kickoff session, assign it as an action item to the Volume Owners, or complete this at the next team meeting. If there are still open questions concerning either Proposal Development or Proposal Production, assign them as action items with an owner and due date. You may also opt to review the objective and format for Proposal Reviews at a later team meeting to save time.

The last topic on the agenda should be to review any action items developed during the session, as well as, establish a schedule for team meetings.

Finalize and Execute the Capture Project Plan

■ **Capture Team Status Meetings**: While each subteam (i.e., Technical, Delivery, Pricing, Contractual) will meet on their own to complete work tasks and resolve open items, you should establish a schedule of regular status meetings with the entire team. Regular status meetings are essential to ensuring the team is aligned and on-track by collecting status on work tasks and action items, as well as, providing a forum to exchange information with the team.

The frequency of the regular status meetings should be gauged to the length of the bid development stage and how close you are to completion. As a rule of thumb, meet daily during the last 3-4 weeks, two to three times per week when

4-10 weeks from completion, and once per week if 10 weeks or more from completion. You will want to meet more frequently if you have a large team that is not well aligned or when a large, complex opportunity has many open items or changes.

The key with regular status meetings is to keep them focused and brief. Status meetings are not working meetings or forums to resolve open items, they are a forum to share information and collect status on work completed. The more frequently you meet, the shorter the meetings should be as there is less to report since the last meeting. Daily meetings should strive to be no more than 30 minutes, whereas, once per week meetings should strive to be no more than 60 minutes.

Form 4-1 provides a recommended agenda for Regular Status Meetings which shows the recommended topics, sequence, time, reference documents and discussion leader. Start the meeting by doing a roll-call of participants, followed by a poll for new agenda items and any team announcements. Have each core team member provide a brief update on work tasks focusing on work started, work completed, problems needing assistance, and issues that should become new action items. This should be followed by a review of the Action Item Register to collect status on open items, after which, you can discuss new agenda items the team identified. Finally, close with reminders regarding upcoming events and a reminder regarding the next status meeting.

- ■ ***Action Item Register:*** One of the biggest challenges during bid development is to effectively and efficiently resolve open items. Open items may be the result of new information, a change, an unforeseen event, a work task that is running behind, or an unanswered question identified in the capture project plan. There is an old expression "bad news does not get better with age," and the same is true of open items – the longer they remain unresolved, the bigger the potential negative impact. The key to resolving open items is to identify them early as action items for resolution.
  - ■ *Action Items:* There are four parts which compose a solid action item and increase the probability of resolution. The first part is a clear and concise definition of the open item which is the issue or problem. The second part is a clear and concise definition of the expected outcome or result.

The third part is an owner, identified by name, who agrees to resolve the action item. The fourth part is a due date by which the action item must be resolved.

■ *Action Item Register:* For each action item, document the issue, required action, owner and due date on an Action Item Register, see Form 4-2. Note an action item as having an "open" status, which will later change to "closed" once resolved. Each action item should be assigned a unique tracking number for easy reference, and the status should be noted as either "open" or "closed." Action items should also be assigned a severity level; such as "high," "medium" or "low" impact, so they can be prioritized for resolution and escalation if not resolved.

Form 4-2							
Action Item Register							
Status	No.	Issue	Action Required	Owner	Due Date	Severity	Progress

During each status meeting review the Action Item Register to ascertain progress toward closure of each item. Each owner should report on the actions they have taken and a prognosis on resolution. Make sure owners understand that if items do not get resolved by the due date or there is no prognosis of resolution by the owner it will result in an Alert-Jeopardy-Escalation being issued. This will serve as an incentive for owners to resolve open items, and ensure there are no surprises later if an Alert-Jeopardy-Escalation is used.

■ *Alert-Jeopardy-Escalation:* Alert-Jeopardy-Escalation is a means to raise the visibility of an issue and ask for help when an open item has not been resolved. In fact, there will be some open items which can only be closed by an Escalation, in which case an Escalation must be issued early to provide stakeholders time to take action. By identifying action items and regularly reviewing the Action Item Register, you and the team can identify the need for an Alert-Jeopardy-Escalation in a timely manner, thus maximizing the time available and increasing the probability for resolution.

■ *Customer Questions or Missing Information:* You will frequently need to ask your customer questions or find you are missing information needed to develop your bid. Be sure you ask questions as early as possible so it does not delay work tasks or lead to last minute changes. Do not delay a work task on the critical path due to a question or missing information. Instead, you should make an assumption based on input from the Sales Leader and appropriate team members and document it in your response. If a competitive solicitation where all questions are shared with all bidders, you should review questions carefully to ensure they do not telegraph your strategy or weaknesses to your competitors.

■ *Change Requests:* There is a common saying that proves true in life and especially proves true in the pursuit of opportunities: "the only constant is change." While change is inevitable, ensure the team understands that changes should not be incorporated into work tasks until a change request has been approved. The inclusion of unapproved changes can easily result in mismatches during handoffs, which jeopardizes the integrity of the solution and will likely result in the need for re-work. Do not delay work tasks on the critical path due to potential or pending change requests, rather, engage the core team leaders and decide on a course of action.

■ **Stakeholders Status Report:** An important aspect of ensuring continued stakeholder support is to keep them informed on progress. This can be done informally through a broadcast voice mail or a regular email sent to all stakeholders, which is fine for smaller opportunities of a short duration. On large, complex or long duration opportunities, you will want to use a more formal means to report progress, such as a regular status report or a Stakeholder Status Review.

Form 4-3 is an example of a status report which can be used on a regular basis to update stakeholders on progress. Note that it has blanks to identify the capture manager, due date of response, customer, opportunity tracking number, opportunity name, date of this report, date of last report and date of next report. It also provides a space for an assessment regarding the solution, proposal, and budget using a simple "Red," "Yellow" or "Green" indicator. This provides a means to advise Stakeholders if things are on-track (i.e., green), somewhat off-track (i.e., yellow) or completely off-track (i.e., red). There are also spaces provided to briefly highlight work tasks completed since the last report, work tasks due before the next report and any outstanding jeopardies or escalations.

Form 4-3											
Stakeholder Status Report											
Capture Management:							Due Date:				
Customer:							Tracking #:				
Opportunity:											
Report Date:				Last Report:				Next Report:			
Solution Assessment	Red	Yellow	Green	Proposal Assessment	Red	Yellow	Green	Budget Assessment	Red	Yellow	Green
Work tasks completed since last report											
Work tasks due before next report											

- ***Stakeholder Status Review Outline:*** If there is a lengthy time between the Stakeholder Opportunity Review and Stakeholder Approval Review you may want to hold a Stakeholder Status Review. The purpose of this review is to keep stakeholders informed on the status of the work (both completed and remaining), changes (involving customer, opportunity, competitors or win strategy), and issues (including jeopardies and escalations and potential issues). Form 4-4 is a recommended outline for a stakeholder status review showing the topics and sequence of material to review.

Form 4-4		
Stakeholder Status Review Outline		
Category	**Subject**	**Suggested Topics or Contents**
Introduction	Purpose	Purpose is typically to 1) Review Status, 2) Review Changes, 3) Review Issues.
	Agenda	Agenda is typically the topics covered, in sequence, with presentors
	Limit	Identify time alloted for meeting
	Participants	List of stakeholders with name, title, and functional responsibility
Status	Work Completed	Update on response timeline showing status of work completed
	Work Remaining	Update on response timeline showing status of work remaining
Changes	Customer Profile Update	Update on changes in customer business, your presence, or competitor presence
	Opportunity Update	Update on changes in problem, solution, contract, basic scope, optional scope or key dates
	Competitor Update	Update on changes in competitors, solutions, strengths or weakenesses
	Win Strategy Update	Update on changes in win theme, sweet spot, sour spot or positioning plan
Issues	Jeopardies	Review of Jeopardies and Escalations
	Potential Issues	Review potential problem areas or areas of concern
Closing	Next Review	Set date for next review or stakeholder meeting
	Action Items	Review of Action Items created during review

Develop the Solution

As the capture team develops the solution, including design, pricing and delivery plan, it is critical that the team remain tightly linked to ensure holistic compliance of the solution. Holistic compliance means that the technical, delivery, pricing and contractual aspects of the solution are consistent and linked with each other, see Figure 4-3, to: 1) solve the customer's problem or objective, and 2) satisfy company requirements for profitability and risk.

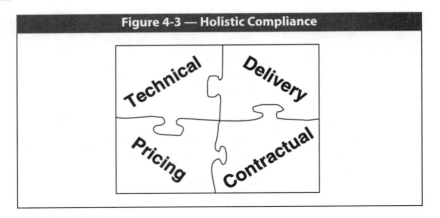

Figure 4-3 — Holistic Compliance

- ***Solution Architecture***: Typically, you will be on a short time-frame when responding to a customer solicitation, hence it will be necessary for work activities to occur concurrently. You will want a way to communicate the solution to the team in a summary form. One technique that is effective at achieving both ends, is to create a Solution Architecture document.

    A Solution Architecture document is typically composed of one or more pictures or diagrams which show the solution, usually with a "before" and "after" view. This is augmented by a list of the products (e.g., hardware, software, version, release) and services which compose the solution. This document can serve as the basis for the detailed design and pricing to occur concurrently with development of the technical/delivery response. Additionally, this documentation can be used as an introduction for new team members, as well as, to review the solution later during the Stakeholder Approval stage.

- ***Compliance Matrix:*** When responding to customer solicitations, it is not uncommon to have customer requirements that cannot be fully met, and there is even the potential to have some that cannot be met at all. This is chiefly due to the fact that most customers solicit input from multiple suppliers and create a solicitation document by taking the best input from each supplier. A common technique used to identify where you have gaps in your ability to meet customer requirements is through the use of a Compliance Matrix, as shown below in Form 4-5. A compliance matrix lists all the solicitation reference and functional requirements, along with an indication of whether your compliance is "full," "partial," or "none" and provides space for an explanation for "partial" compliance.

Frequently, your customer will ask you to include a Compliance Matrix within your response. Even if it is not required for submittal to your customer, you should complete a compliance matrix as part of your risk mitigation planning to understand gaps and potential risk areas.

Form 4-5					
Compliance Matrix					
Solicitation Reference	Functional Requirement	Compliance			Explanation
		Full	Partial	None	

- ***Solution Linkage Matrix:*** Another common problem is ensuring linkage of the design, description and pricing of the solution. This can easily occur when you have different team members performing separate roles, especially when a lot of changes exist. A Solution Linkage Matrix, such as the one shown in Form 4-6, is a simple tool that can help ensure the solution designed is compliant and matches the solution described and the solution priced. Start by listing the solicitation references, functional requirements and your solution product or service which satisfies the requirement. Then identify the accountable team member for the design, description (i.e., response), pricing and overall linkage. Typically, the overall linkage will be provided by either the Technical or Delivery Team leader.

Form 4-6						
Solution Linkage Matrix						
Solicitation Reference	Functional Requirement	Solution Product/Service	Individual Accountable for Solution			
			Design	Description	Pricing	Overall Linkage

■ ***Delivery Plan:*** As part of developing the solution, you will also need to develop a Delivery Plan that answers the who, what, when, where, how and how much to deliver to your customer. Typical elements to consider in a delivery plan include: program management, site inspections, engineering, ordering, manufacturing, transportation, warehousing, staging, installation, testing, acceptance, training, documentation, and Operations, Administration & Maintenance (OA&M). Gauge the extent and detail of the Delivery Plan to the scope of the solution being offered and priced. For example, if the solution being offered includes "minimum delivery," your Delivery Plan may only need to address ordering, manufacturing, transportation and acceptance.

Develop Risk Mitigation Plans

■ ***Sources of Risk:*** As you develop the solution and your response, you will find that there is uncertainty regarding future events, which represent risks. Table 4-1 presents examples of common Sources of Risk.

Table 4-1			
Sources of Risk			
Technical Risks	**Delivery Risks**		**Financial Risks**
Hardware Design Errors	Material Availability	Reliability	Changes in COGS
Software Design Errors	Personnel Availability	Maintainability	Changes in SG&A Expenses
Testing / Modeling	Personnel Skills	Operations & Support Equipment Availability	Changes in Interest Rates
Integration / Interface	Safety		Changes in Exchange Rates
Safety	Security	Transportation	Pricing Errors
Requirement Changes	Environmental Impact	Training Availability	Customer Financial Stability
Fault Detection	Communication Problems	Documentation Accuracy	Supplier Financial Stability
Operating Environment	Labor Strikes	Zoning-Regulatory Approval	**Contractual Risks**
Unproven Technology	Requirement Changes	Degree of Concurency	Terms & Conditions
System Compexity	Subcontractor Stability	Number of Critical Path Items	Supplier Contracts

■ ***Ways of Mitigating Risk:*** Risk is mitigated through one of four fundamental strategies: 1) avoid the risk, 2) transfer the risk, 3) share the risk, or 4) reserve the risk. Avoid the risk means you avoid the scenario that can cause risk, such as staying away from requirements you cannot satisfy. Transfer the risk means you shift the risk to another, such as buying hazard insurance or hiring a subcontractor under a turnkey contract. Share the risk means you spread the risk, such as having a partner or other related projects to assume some of the risk. Reserve the risk means you establish a reserve of funds to cover all or a portion of the risk, kind of like self- insurance.

Table 4-2 is a summary of various "Ways of Mitigating or Avoiding Risks" developed by John R. Schuyler, which can serve as a good generator of ideas.

Table 4-2	
Ways of Mitigating or Avoiding Risk	
Portfolio Risks	**Operational Risks**
Share risks by having partners	Hire contractors under turnkey contracts
Spread risks over time	Tailor risk-sharing contract clauses
Participate in many ventures	Use safety margins; overbuild and overspecify designs
Group complementary risks into portfolios	Have backup and redundant equipment
Seek lower-risk ventures	Increase training
Specialize and concentrate in a single, well-known area	Operate with redirect and bail-out options
Increase the company's capitalization	Conduct tests, pilot programs, and trials
Commodity Prices	**Analysis Risks (Reducing Evaluation Error)**
Hedge or fix in the futures markets	Use better techniques (I.e., decision analysis)
Use long- or short-term sales (price and volume) contracts	Seek additional information
Tailor contracts for risk sharing	Monitor key and indicator variables
Interest Rate and Exchange Rate	Validate models
Use swaps, floors, ceilings, collars, and other hedging instruments	Include evaluation practices along with project post-reviews
Restructure the balance sheet	Develop redundant models with alternative approaches and people
Denominate or index certain transactions in a foreign currency	Involve multiple disciplines, and communicate cross-discipline
Environmental Hazards	Provide better training and tools
Buy insurance	
Increase safety margins	**Source:** Schuyler, John R. Decision Analysis in Projects: Summary and Recommendations. PM Network, October 1995.
Develop and test an incident response program	

When considering a mitigation strategy, you will need to understand both the probability that an event will occur, as well as the impact should the event occur. For risks with a high probability of occurrence and a high impact, consider an "avoid" strategy. For risks with a low probability of occurrence and a high impact, consider a "transfer" strategy. For risks with a high probability of occurrence but a low impact, consider a "share" strategy. For risks with a low probability of occurrence and a low impact, consider a "reserve" strategy. These guidelines are summarized on the following grid, Figure 4-4.

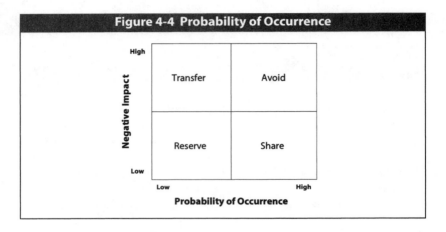

Figure 4-4 Probability of Occurrence

- ***Risk Mitigation Plan:*** For each risk identified, you will want to develop and document a Risk Mitigation Plan, which can be completed using Form 4-7. The Risk Mitigation Plan provides a space to identify the opportunity, opportunity tracking #, risk name (i.e., what you refer to the risk as), an assigned risk number, name of person that developed the plan, their title and date prepared. There is a space to indicate the type of risk (i.e., technical, delivery, pricing, contractual) and a brief description of the risk along with it's probability and impact. There is a space to show the mitigation strategy used (i.e., avoid, transfer, share, reserve) along with a brief description of the specific strategy. Finally, there is a place to identify who owns implementation of the mitigation plan and their title.

Form 4-7 Risk Mitigation Plan			
Opportunity:		Tracking #:	
Risk Name:		Risk #:	
Developed by:	Title:		Date:
Type Risk ☐ Technical	☐ Delivery	☐ Pricing	☐ Contractual
Briefly describe the risk it's probability and it's impact:			
Mitigation Strategy ☐ Avoid	☐ Transfer	☐ Share	☐ Reserve
Briefly describe the migitation strategy:			
Mitigation Plan Owner:		Title:	

- **Risk Mitigation Planning Log:** As you may identify a number of risks, you will want a means to track them and summarize them for the stakeholders. Form 4-8 is a template of a Risk Mitigation Planning Log which can be used for this purpose. It provides a space to list each risk, the risk number, the type of risk, who is developing the mitigation, the date (once it is developed) and the strategy used.

Form 4-8											
Risk Mitigation Planning Log											
		Type Risk						Strategy			
Risk Number	Risk Name	Technical	Delivery	Pricing	Contractual	Mitigation Plan Developed By	Date	Avoid	Transfer	Share	Reserve

Develop Business Case

You will need to develop two business cases. One will be an internal business case showing your company's revenues and costs associated with the opportunity, which will be required to secure authority to bid. The other will be a customer business case to be included in your response to show the costs and benefits your customer will incur and realize by implementing your solution. Commercial customers purchase solutions to either generate revenues or reduce expenses, so your customer will need a business case to justify the expenditure within their company. It is to your benefit to prepare a customer business case to ensure all the benefits are identified, the costs are not overstated, and to show your customer that you understand their business problem.

■ *Business Case Scenarios:* For both business cases you will need to develop a clear set of assumptions regarding the size of the opportunity and the timing of the delivery. You should already have developed most of the information that is needed as you developed the solution (i.e., design, pricing, delivery plan); however, you may need additional assumptions to produce a Worst Case, Most Likely Case and Best Case scenario Business Case. The Worst Case scenario, assuming you have a winning bid, is the minimum solution your customer will choose to implement. The Best Case scenario is the maximum solution your customer will choose to implement. The Most Likely Case scenario is between the two and represents how much of the solution the customer is most likely to implement. Factors to consider in each scenario include:

  ■ Single versus multiple supplier awards,
  ■ Minimum or maximum purchase requirements,
  ■ Factors which could delay or accelerate the speed of delivery,
  ■ Factors which could shorten or extend the life of the solution, and
  ■ Factors which could increase or decrease the size of the problem.

■ *Business Case Models:* You can simplify the work required to create each scenario by using business case models. It is likely that your overall solution can be broken down into a model solution composed of the typical products/services which would be delivered to solve one instance of the problem for your customer. You may find that there are several sizes or types of problems to be resolved, so several solution models may be required. Using these solution models, identify how many instances of each of the problems exist and how many solution models you expect to deliver per year under a set of assumptions for each scenario.

Table 4-3 shows how to develop these estimates using one problem, which occurs 8,000 times over five years, and one solution model. In the Worst Case Scenario, which might represent the minimum purchase under a multiple supplier award, you assume solving 25% of the problems each year, in years one through three, for a total of 1,500 solution models. In the Best Case Scenario, which might be the maximum delivery under a single award, assumes solving 50% in year 1 and increasing to solve 90% in year 5, for a total of 5,350 solution models. The Most Likely Case Scenario, which might be a modest delivery under a multiple supplier award, assumes 35% in year 1 and increasing to 55% in the last three years, for a total of 3,850 solution models. You can make the model more realistic by introducing different size problems, multiple solution models, or different assumptions about the number of problems under each scenario.

Table 4-3						
Business Case Models						
	Year					
Item	1	2	3	4	5	Total
# of Problems	1,500	2,500	2,000	1,000	1,000	8,000
Worst Case Scenario						
% of problems solved	25%	25%	25%	0%	0%	
# of solutons delivered	375.00	625.00	500.00	0	0	1,500
Most Likely Case Scenario						
% of problems solved	35%	45%	55%	55%	55%	
# of solutons delivered	525	1125	1100	550	550	3,850
Best Case Scenario						
% of problems solved	50%	60%	70%	80%	90%	
# of solutons delivered	750	1500	1400	800	900	5,350

■ *Product / Service Profile:* You may find that your company does not have 100% of the solution to offer and that you need to source product or service from a 3rd party. The use of third parties introduces risk of their performance, which should be reserved by including a mark-up or margin on their products and services. The amount of third party versus in-house products and services will significantly impact profitability and price competitiveness of your solution. When you develop your solution models, determine the in-house versus 3rd party product and service amount in each model. You can then use the units per year to populate a summary, see Form 4-9, which shows the % of in-house versus 3rd party product and service for each scenario.

Form 4-9				
Product / Service Profile				
Product / Service	Year One	Year Two	Year Three	Total
In-House Product				
3rd Party Product				
Product Subtotal				
% In-House Product				
In-House Service				
3rd Party Service				
Service Subtotal				
% In-House Service				
In-House P & S Total				
3rd Party P & S Total				
Product & Service Total				
% In-House				
% Product				

■ *Customer Business Case:* The customer business case can be developed using the same problem and solution models. For costs, use your price for each solution model times the number of models delivered. For benefits, determine the revenue increase or cost savings associated with solving each instance of each size problem and multiply by the number of problems solved. Alternatively, you may find it is easier to estimate the benefits by looking at the revenue increase or cost savings associated with the aggregate number of problems solved. Look at the following factors to estimate your customer's benefits:

- Increased revenues from new products or services
- Increased revenues from a larger volume of products or services
- Increased revenues from introducing products or services earlier
- Reduced personnel or contractor costs
- Reduced space, utilities, or support hardware/software
- Reduced insurance, interest or cash flow requirements
- Depreciation/amortization on capital assets

- ***Common Business Case Terms:*** While the business cases should be developed by someone on the Pricing Team with financial training, Table 4-4 provides the definitions of the common business case terms you will encounter.

Table 4-4	
Common Business Case Terms	
Item	**Definition**
Gross Sales	Total revenues at invoice value before any discounts or allowances
Discounts, Allowances and Returns	Price discounts, returned merchandise
Net Sales	Gross Sales minus Discounts, Allowances and Returns
Variable Costs	Costs associated with production that change directly with the amount of production, e.g., the direct material or labor required to complete the build or manufacturing of a product
Fixed Costs	Operating expenses that are incurred to provide facilities and organization that are kept in readiness to do business without regard to actual volumes of production and sales. Examples of fixed costs consist of rent, property taxes, and interest expense
Cost of Goods Sold (COGS)	Direct costs of producing finished goods for sale
Gross Profit Margin	Net Sales minus Cost of Goods Sold. Also called Gross Margin, Gross Profit or Gross Loss
Gross Profit Margin % or Ratio	Gross Profit Margin $ divided by Net Sales
Contribution Margin	Net Sales minus Variable Costs. Also called called Marginal Income. It is the amount of money available to cover fixed costs and generate profits.
Contribution Margin % or Ratio	Contribution Margin divided by Net Sales
Selling, General & Administrative (SG&A) Expenses	Administrative costs of running business
Depreciation	Amount of expense charged against earnings by a company to write off the cost of a plant or machine over its useful live, giving consideration to wear and tear, obsolescence, and salvage value
Amortization	Process of spreading the cost of an intangible asset over the expected useful life of the asset.
Operating Expenses	SG&A plus Depreciation and Amortization
EBITDA	Earnings Before Interest, Taxes, Depreciation and Amortization, but after all product / service, sales and overhead (SG&A) costs are accounted for. Sometimes referred to as Operating Profit.
EBITDARM	Acronym for Earnings Before Interest, Taxes, Depreciation, Amortization, Rent and Management fees.
Discounted Cash Flow (DCF)	Combined present value of cash flow and tangible assets minus present value of liabilities
Discount Rate	Interest rate used in calculating present value

Develop Proposal

Having developed the solution, you need to explain the solution to your customer through a well written response or proposal. You have already developed several inputs to define the "who," "what," and "how" to what needs to be written, as well as the "why" in the form of messages to convey. The Proposal Layout with Volume & Section Assignments define who is responsible to write each of the responses. The Proposal Development Checklist defines the mechanics of how you will develop your assigned sections and share them. The Win Themes and Strategies defines the overarching message to convey in the response and specific strategies to maximize your strengths, minimize your weaknesses, neutralize the competitor's strengths, and ghost the competitor's weaknesses.

- *Attributes of Winning Proposals:* Before team members start writing responses, you should share with them the following attributes of a proposal, see Table 4-5. This listing was designed with ease of evaluation in mind and was developed by David G. Pugh, Ph.D. of the Lore International Institute to help them develop the right mindset.

Table 4-5	
Attributes of a proposal designed with ease of evaluation in mind	
A Powerful Executive Summary	Powerful Proposal Design
Audience Designed	Double Exposure on a Single Page
1/3 Visuals, 2/3 Text, Ample White Space	Double or Message Column
Separately Bound	Themed and Captioned
Customer Focused	Emphatically written
Strategy Driven	Active Voice and Personal Pronouns
Benefits Rich (Answers Why us? And So what?)	Effective Organization
Source: A Bidder's Dozen: Golden Rules for Winning Work, David G. Pugh, Ph.D. - Lore International Institute	

Outputs

The outputs of the Bid Development stage are a well developed Customer Solution, including the design, pricing and delivery plan, Risk Mitigation Plans, and Business Cases both internal distribution and customer presentation. Also developed should be a winning Customer Proposal, generally composed of an Executive Summary, Technical Response, Delivery Response, Pricing Response and Contractual Response.

SELECTED INTERVIEW

Name: Gregory C. Landon

Job Title: Supervisory Contract Specialist

Organization: U.S. Army Communications-Electronic Life Cycle Management Command

Location: Fort Monmouth, New Jersey

Major Responsibilities: Supervise teams of contracting officers and specialists who award and administer intelligence, electronics warfare and sensor (IEWS) and communications weapons systems contracts for the US Army, and other military customers. Also serve as a customer representative of the acquisition center to IEWS customers, and serve as joint partner for Fort Monmouth communications and electronics for Lockheed-Martin Corporation.

Background: BA in East Asian History, Amherst College cum laude – 1971, MA in Procurement Management, Webster University – 1976, Member National Contract Management Association since 1976, Member Army Acquisition Corps – 1992, Level III Certified in Contracting, Defense Acquisition – 1994, Army Management Staff College (class president) – 1997.

Since 1974, served as a contract specialist or supervisory contract specialist in various major subordinate command posts in the US Army Materiel Command (AMC). Served in twelve commands at four geographical locations as a contract specialist, contract negotiator, contracting officer, and supervisory contract specialist.

QUESTIONS & ANSWERS:

Question: What actions do you suggest sellers take to ethically and appropriately influence buyer's requirements?

Answer: The time for requirements influence is early in the requirements generation process, the earlier the better. This has always been so. Today's acquisition techniques tend to shorten that time in many cases, as the old model of Government funded phased development from mock-up concepts through engineering development is now commonly discarded for accelerated programs that capitalize on technologies generated elsewhere. The request for proposal may ask for seller input to unnecessary requirements, but the chances for outcomes favorable to a particular seller based on hoped for changes are much reduced by this stage. Most seller input should take place by the close of the draft solicitation process.

Sellers need to take care of avoiding conflicts of interest that could develop even early in the requirements generation process. Sellers need to avoid the hiring of personnel, or indirectly the hiring of such personnel through subcontractors, to support programs, for which those personnel have, or have had, requirements generation roles for such. The hiring process for program support personnel needs to distinguish between expertise and inside information.

Question: What actions should sellers take to ensure they make intelligent Bid/No Bid Decisions on their critical deals?

Answer: Sellers need to have a realistic plan to ultimately make money on a contract converting from the bid, whether that be attaining an expected profit on the instant contract, or from future legitimate business that is likely to ensue. Most Government buyers today are in the mode of performance work statements rather than detailed product specifications. The old paradigm of bidding low and mining the design flaws in the drawing package through the changes processes is mostly gone now. Don't expect to "get well" later.

Sellers need to understand the solicitation. Whether the contract is large and complex or small and relatively simple, too many contracts run into trouble under failed assumptions. Ask questions in writing, preferably in the pre-solicitation process, if there is one, but during the solicitation if need be, prior to preparing offers. And when asking those questions follow proper channels specified by the contracting officers.

Question: What do you consider to be the top five Seller best practices for developing a winning bid or proposal?

Answer: 1) The seller knows his company's strengths at all times, and develops those strengths in anticipation of likely customer requirements. Business development is focused.

2) The seller knows the competition and how it may stack up against them. All information related thereto must be achieved through legitimate means.

3) The seller keeps constantly abreast of their Government customers needs related to company interests through the various appropriate information channels provided.

4) The seller knows the appropriate channels to the buyer for each stage of the process of solicitation generation and offer preparation. They typically narrow as the process matures, but every stage demands attention to proper relationships. Develop trust and deserve it.

5) The seller pays close attention to the entire solicitation, but, pays even closer attention to the criteria provided for source selection, the relative importance of those various criteria, and the in-

structions provided therein for the preparation of their offer. Those are the rules of all offerors, and a selection of a winner must follow from them.

Question: Please share a brief personal success story regarding: Solicitations, Bid/Proposals, or Source Selection – Building a Winning Contract.

Answer: The earliest experiences, whether very good or bad, seem to stand out the most. An experience of mine from 1978 had a good result which,

Nevertheless, taught me much.

I had a rather large competitive solicitation for a satellite ground station for the US Army. Four large aerospace companies competed energetically for this two step sealed bid award. While the two steps logically divided the selection process into the technical acceptability and price portions, the separation did not necessarily simplify the process overall. Each portion of the process was a significant competition in itself, the sealed bid process at the end being the payoff.

The major lesson that I learned is to keep all offerors/bidders consistently aware of the process rules. Do not tell something to one and something else to another. But in any case, make sure they know. Another lesson was to be responsive to offerors/bidders as expeditiously as possible. Every potential offeror/bidder is important, as are their questions. All questions from each of them, however trivial, need to be categorized and answered somehow. During the sealed bid phase the clock can be very demanding in meeting this requirement, especially if there are competing demands on the buyer's time. In my own case I had a large negotiated competition for an engineering development at the same time. Prioritizing essential tasks is a must in such circumstances.

> In the cited example the bid opening was fruitful and a winner was easily determined. Even the losers were complimentary of the process. This outcome was not inevitable.
>
> **Note:** The subject interview solely expresses the informal opinions' of the interviewee, they do not necessarily represent the views or opinions of the organization, company, or agency which they are employed.

Seller Step 4: Bid/Proposal Review & Approval

The objectives of the Bid/Proposal Reviews & Approval step is to:

- Certify the solution is sound and compliant,
- Ensure proposal is accurate and complete.

Below is a graphic, Figure 4-5, showing the Inputs, Tools & Techniques, and Outputs of the Bid/Proposal Reviews & Approval step.

Figure 4-5 Seller Step 4: Bid/Proposal Reviews & Approval Process

Input	Tools & Techniques	Output
• Customer Solution	• General Actions	• Customer Solution Certified as "Sound" and Compliant
• Design	• Why proposals lose evaluation points	• Design
• Pricing	• Pink Team Reviews	• Pricing
• Delivery Plan	• Pink Team Question Checklist	• Delivery
• Risk Mitigation Plans	• Proposal Deficiency Form	• Risk Mitigation Plans
• Business Cases	• Proposal Deficiency Log	• Business Cases
• Customer Bid or Proposal	• Red Team Reviews	• Customer Proposal Reviewed and Certified as Accurate & Complete
• Executive Summary	• Red Team Question Checklist	• Executive Summary
• Technical Response	• Red Team Evaluation Form	• Technical Response
• Delivery Response	• Red Team Scoring Form	• Delivery Response
• Pricing Response	• Red Team Do's and Don'ts	• Pricing Response
• Contractual Response	• Obtain Offer Certifications	• Contractual Response
	• Offer Certification Form	

Inputs

The inputs to the Bid/Proposal Reviews & Approval:

- Customer Solution (including the design, pricing and delivery plan)
- Risk Mitigation Plans
- Business Cases, both internal and customer
- Customer Bid or Proposal

Tools & Techniques

General Actions

- **Why proposals lose evaluation points:** Before describing the steps of the Bid Reviews stage, it is important to first understand why proposals lose evaluation points. You will want to look in your proposal for the following signs provided in Table 4-6. These "pitfalls" were developed by the National Contract Management Association (NCMA).

Table 4-6
Why Proposals Lose Evaluation Points
Questionable or inadequate understanding of requirements or needs
Incomplete response to the solicitation; critical sections left out of the proposal
Noncompliance with specifications; misinterpretation of the specificications
Insufficient resources (time, funds, personnel, etc.) to accomplish the required services or tasks
Insufficient information about the resources required for satisfactory performance under the contract
Poor proposal organization; obstacles in correlating proposal content to the solicitation or requirements
Failure to show relevance of past experience to the proposed project
Unsubstaintiated or unconvincing rationale for proposed approaches or soutions
Wordiness. Mindboggling wordiness.
Repeating requirements without discussing how they will be performed
Source: Building a Contract: Solicitations/Bids and Proposals — A Team Effort? National Contract Management Association

Conduct Pink Team Reviews

The first step in the Bid Reviews stage is to conduct Pink Team Reviews. The objective of Pink Team Reviews is to ensure the proposal is complete and accurate. Due to the size of the response, the timing of when it is available for review, and the size of the opportunity, team, and content in each response, you will likely have multiple Pink Team Reviews. For example, it is not unusual to have one Pink Team for the Technical-Delivery response, a separate Pink Team for the Pricing-Contractual response, and a third Pink Team for the Executive Summary.

The participants in the Pink Team Reviews are the individuals who wrote the responses, while the reviewers are other team members, team leaders, a Sales Leader, Proposal Manager and Capture Manager. Ideally, Pink Team Reviews should be conducted face-to-face; however, a review can be equally as effective with the use of technology, such as NetMeeting, videoconferencing, and teleconferencing, but it must be properly prepared. For small responses with few authors, you may choose to not conduct "live" Pink Team Reviews session, opting instead to distribute the responses and have reviewers forward their comments directly to the author by a specified deadline. This approach can also be used for larger responses as the means to conduct a Pink Team Review of the Executive Summary.

Be sure to distribute responses to the reviewers prior to the actual review session. This will allow for a shorter review session, while maintaining the quality of the review. The Pink Team Reviews should be managed by the Proposal Manager. Also, it is important to ensure reviewers understand the purpose, format, time and location for the Pink Team Reviews.

Pink Team Question Checklist: On the following page, Form 4-9 is a Pink Team Question Checklist, which reviewers can use as a guide for questions that should be consider during Pink Team Reviews. The Pink Team Review provides general questions to consider in reviewing all responses for organization, appearance, accuracy and graphics. There are also specific questions to consider for the Executive Summary, Technical-Delivery response, and the Pricing-Contractual response.

Form 4-9	
Pink Team Review - Questions Checklist	
Is the proposal complete and accurate?	**X**
GENERAL — **Organization** — Is the proposal organized in a logical manner?	☐
Does it have a clear table of contents? Is is logical?	☐
Does the internal organization follow the table of contents?	☐
Is the proposal a consistent document that appears to have been written by one person?	☐
Appearance — How does the overall proposal look? Does it look professional?	☐
Is it inviting to read? Is the proposal easy to follow?	☐
Is the style consistent? Is the format consistent?	☐
Is the proposal free of serious mistakes or typographical errors?	☐
Accuracy — Is the solution presentation credible?	☐
Are the facts correct? Is the data accurate?	☐
Are the claims believable? Are the claims proven?	☐
Is every claim supported? Is there an appropriate amount of supporting data?	☐
Graphics — Are there enough graphics? Are there too many? Are they appropriate?	☐
Are they well-designed, to truly present information and key concepts at a glance?	☐
Are they creative as well as accurate?	☐
Are they correctly referenced in the text?	☐
EXECUTIVE SUMMARY — Does it give a sense of the overall proposal?	☐
Does it present the customer problem/objective and the solution?	☐
Is it an effective presentation of your company?	☐
Is it sensitive to the customer's needs & requirements?	☐
Does it sufficiently and clearly convey the win theme and strategies?	☐
Was it worthwhile reading?	☐
TECHNICAL / DELIVERY — Is the customer problem or objective stated and analyzed?	☐
Does the proposed solution solve the problem or attain the objective?	☐
Is it clear? Too much detail? Not enough detail?	☐
Is this the best solution? Why? Are there alternative solutions?	☐
Are all customer specified questions answered?	☐
Are there any conflicting responses?	☐
Do the responses support the solution?	☐
Are all responses satisfactory to the team and properly represent your company?	☐
Is the delivery response complete and realistic?	☐
Will the delivery response satisfy the customer's requirements?	☐
PRICING / CONTRACTUAL — Do all of the numbers add up?	☐
Are the detailed pricing pages consistent with the summary pricing pages?	☐
Has anything been "double counted?" Has anything been left out?	☐
Is there a logical flow of information that follows an outline?	☐
Are the terms and conditions explicit?	☐
Are all appropriate terms and conditions included? Are any missing?	☐

FOUR

■ **Proposal Deficiency Form**: In order to ensure feedback is properly captured for the authors, you will want to document deficiencies using a Proposal Deficiency Form, see Form 4-10. This form provides space to identify the proposal, proposal manager, deficiency owner (i.e., the author), who identified the deficiency, volume, section, solicitation reference, page number, brief description of the deficiency, and recommended action. There is also space to assign a deficiency number, as well as space to capture how and when the deficiency was resolved.

Form 4-10		
Proposal Deficiency Form		
Proposal:	Volume:	Deficiency Number:
Proposal Manager:	Section:	
Deficiency Owner:	Solicitation Reference:	
Identified By:	Page Number:	Date Resolved:
Deficiency		
Recommended Action:		
How Resolved:		

■ **Proposal Deficiency Log:** In order to ensure all deficiencies are closed, you should create a summary of all deficiencies by their volume/section, which can then be used as a checklist by that volume/section owner. You can also use the Proposal Deficiency Log to collect and document all deficiencies in lieu of using an individual form for each deficiency. The Proposal Deficiency Log, see Form 4-11, provides space to identify the opportunity, proposal, volume/section, volume/section owner, deficiency number, solicitation reference, page number, deficiency, recommended action, deficiency owner, who identified the deficiency and the date a deficiency was resolved.

Form 4-11							
Proposal Deficiency Log							
Opportunity:				Proposal:			
Volume/Section:				Volume/Section Owner:			
Deficiency Number	Solicitation Reference	Page Number	Deficiency	Recommended Action	Deficiency Owner	Identified By

Red Team Reviews

The second step in the Bid Reviews stage is to conduct Red Team Reviews. The objective of Red Team Reviews is to ensure the proposal makes sense and that it solves the customer's business problem. If resources and time permits, you can also have reviewers evaluate and score the responses as though they are the customer. Similar to the Pink Team Review, you will likely have one Red Team for the Technical-Contractual response, one for the Pricing-Contractual response and one for the Executive Summary.

Red Team reviewers should be individuals who are familiar with the customer's requirements, as well as the subject matter within the response; however, they should not be individuals who were a part of the response team. As an example, peers or supervisors of the individuals who wrote the response are good candidates for Red Team reviewers. You will want to have reviewers "mirror" the customers by evaluating each section. As an example, you may want to have stakeholders review the Executive Summary. In addition to the responses, be sure reviewers have access to the solicitation, win themes and strategies, and relevant reference material in order to help them during their review.

- *Red Team Question Checklist:* Form 4-12 is a *Red Team Question Checklist* that reviewers can use as a guide for questions that must be considered during Red Team Reviews. This checklist provides general questions to consider in reviewing all responses for organization and emphasis, win theme and strategies, compliance and responsiveness, appearance and presentation, consistency and brevity, and visuals.

Form 4-12	
Red Team Review - Questions Checklist	
Does the proposal make sense and solve the customer's problem?	X

		X
Organization and Emphasis	Do the content and organization of the response follow the content and organization of the customer request?	❑
	Are all of the main ideas up front?	❑
	Has the content of each section been previewed at the beginning?	❑
	Summarized content at the end?	❑
	Are the paragraphs logical and easy to follow?	❑
	Does each paragraph have only one main idea?	❑
Win Theme and Strategies	Does the response effectively present the value of your company' solution?	❑
	Is it persuasive? Does it sell?	❑
	Does it follow the overall win theme ?	❑
	Are the win strategies reflected throughout the document?	❑
	Does the response emphasize your company's strengths?	❑
	Does the response mitigate your company's weaknesses?	❑
	Does the response ghost the competition's weaknesses?	❑
Compliance and Responsiveness	Does the solution solve the customer's problem or attain the objective?	❑
	Have all the customer's questions been answered?	❑
	Has every part of every question been answered?	❑
	Does the response address every customer request requirement?	❑
	Do the answers echo the customer's language?	❑
	Is the writing clear and to the point? What would make it clearer?	❑
	Do all the sentences make sense?	❑
	Are any statements vague or confusing or misleading?	❑
Appearance and Presentation	Is the response document professional?	❑
	Does it reflect the proper image of your company?	❑
	Do the pages have a clean, professional appearance?	❑
	Are all of the names and dates right?	❑
	Do all of the cross-references have the correct page numbers?	❑
	Are all of the figures numbered consecutively?	❑
Consistency and Brevity	Do the writing styles match? Does the response seem as though one person wrote it?	❑
	Were consistent terms and abbreviations used?	❑
	Are your numbers consistent?	❑
	Have extraneous words, sentences, paragraphs, visuals, facts, or data been eliminated?	❑
	Has all of the boilerplate been customized for this customer and their requirements?	❑
	Do any brochures or information sheets reflect a different format, give extraneous information, or appear to be placed in the document merely to add bulk?	❑
Visuals	Do visuals and text complement each other?	❑
	Are any visuals unnecessary?	❑
	Does the text make them redundant?	❑
	Are visuals appropriate for the technical level of the readers?	❑
	Are visuals simple, uncluttered?	❑
	Does each one have a clear message?	❑
	Do visuals stand by themselves?	❑
	Was each visual introduced before it appears?	❑
	Do the key visuals reflect the strategy?	❑
	Do they illustrate the major benefits for the customer emphasized in the bid?	❑

■ **Red Team Evaluation Form**: You will want to document feedback from the Red Team reviewers for the authors. You can use the Proposal Deficiency Form and Proposal Deficiency Log from the Pink Team Reviews to capture specific feedback. In addition, you should have the reviewers provide an overall evaluation of each volume by using the below Proposal Evaluation, Form 4-13. This form identifies the opportunity, volume, and evaluator as well as asks the reviewer to assign a score of 1-to-5 for each category on the Red Team Question Checklist. Reviewers can then total the scores to provide an overall rating of each volume.

Form 4-13						
Proposal Evaluation Form						
Opportunity:						
Volume:	Evaluator:					
Evaluation Factor/Subfactor	Excellent	Good	Average	Poor	Terrible	Score
	5	4	3	2	1	Assigned
Organization and Emphasis	❑	❑	❑	❑	❑	
Win Themes and Strategies	❑	❑	❑	❑	❑	
Compliance and Responsiveness	❑	❑	❑	❑	❑	
Appearance and Presentation	❑	❑	❑	❑	❑	
Consistency and Brevity	❑	❑	❑	❑	❑	
Visuals	❑	❑	❑	❑	❑	
Totals	❑	❑	❑	❑	❑	

■ **Red Team Scoring Form**: If you have the specific criteria your customer will use to evaluate the response, you may opt to have reviewers score the responses as if they were the customer using the Proposal Scoring Form 4-14. First, this form identifies the opportunity, volume and evaluator. Next, you will need to populate it with the factors for the evaluation, maximum score, weighting (if any), and the weighted maximum score. Reviewers can then use the form to assign an evaluated score and weighted evaluated score.

Form 4-14					
Proposal Scoring Form					
Opportunity:					
Volume:		Evaluator:			
Evaluation Factor/Subfactor	**Maximum Score**	**Weight**	**Weighted Maximum Score**	**Evaluated Score**	**Weighted Evaluated Score**
Factor One					
Factor Two					
Factor Three					
Factor Four					
Factor Five					
Factor Six					
Factor Seven					
Factor Eight					
Factor Nine					
Factor Ten					
Totals					

- ***Red Team Dos and Don'ts:*** Table 4-7 is a compilation of recommended things to do and not to do in order to improve the effectiveness of Red Teams.

Table 4-7
RED TEAM DOs AND DON'Ts

Dos	Do organize and plan the proposal review process early in the proposal preparation.
	Do select the proposal review method that will do the most to increase win probability.
	Do consider using a running red team for a proposal that is to be written on a very tight schedule.
	Do consider dual red teams for major, must-win proposals.
	Do use a majority of outsiders and proposal professionals on red teams.
	Do make an early review of the proposal (sometimes called a "pink team") to ensure proper proposal structure and approach methodologies.
	Do have the proposal complete (including executive summaries, section/subsection introductions, and graphics) prior to red team review.
	Do hard edit a proposal prior to red team review.
	Do provide red team members with copies of both the solicitation and a comprehensive solicitation-to-proposal compliance matrix well before the proposal review.
	Do keep the red team members collocated during the proposal review.
	Do be specific in making comments and recommendations - general statements are usually useless.
	Do combine red team comments into a single volume.
	Do present proposal strengths and well-written areas during the red team debrief to the proposal team.
	Do remember that the proposal manager has total authority to accept or reject red team recommendations.
Don'ts	Don't select any red team member who is not fully committed to work full time on the review and to stay and participate in making recommended fixes.
	Don't use a formal red team review if the review process delay will hurt the proposal effort.
	Don't ask a red team to score a proposal against the evaluation factors unless the proposal is complete.
	Don't ask the red team to pick between multiple approaches or solutions.
	Don't present minor issues during the red team debrief —concentrate the presentation on important issues.

Source: Focus on Basics — Using Red Teams Effectively, David H. Herond, Journal of the Association of Project Management Professionals, Fall 2000

Obtain Offer Certifications

■ *Offer Certification Form*: The third step of the Bid Reviews stage is to Obtain Offer Certifications using Form 4-15 below before proceeding to Stakeholder Approval and submittal of the response to the customer. The purpose of the Offer Certification is to ensure accountability by having each Team Leader sign that their portion of the solution is "sound" (i.e., is doable and is the appropriate solution for your company to offer), complies with all stated customer requirements, and verifies that the response has been reviewed and deemed accurate and complete. Additionally, the Sales Leader and Capture Manager should concur that they have reviewed the entire solution and responses and verify the package meets the same criteria.

Form 4-15		
Offer Certification Form		
Certifications		
Technical	Solution is certified as being Technically Sound and compliant with all stated customer requirements / Technical Response has been reviewed and is certified as being accurate and complete	
Technical	Signature:	Name:
Technical		Title:	Date:
Delivery	Solution is certified as being Delivery Sound and compliant with all stated customer requirements / Delivery Response has been reviewed and is certified as being accurate and complete	
Delivery	Signature:	Name:
Delivery		Title:	Date:
Pricing	Solution is certified as being Financial Sound and all pricing is certified as complete and accurate / Pricing Response has been reviewed and is certified as being accurate and complete	
Pricing	Signature:	Name:
Pricing		Title:	Date:
Contracts	Solution is certified as being Contractual Sound and includes all appropriate Terms & Conditions / Contractual Response has been reviewed and is certified as being accurate and complete	
Contracts	Signature:	Name:
Contracts		Title:	Date:
Concurrences		
	Solution is concurred as being compliant with all stated customer requirements / Entire response has been reviewed and is concurred as being accurate and complete	
Sales Leader	Signature:	Name:
Sales Leader		Title:	Date:
Capture Manager	Signature:	Name:
Capture Manager		Title:	Date:

Stakeholder Approval Review

Earlier in the process you identified stakeholders who were part of a Stakeholder Opportunity Review to approve development of an offer. In this last stage of the Bid Phase you will reassemble these same stakeholders and solicit their approval to submit the bid to the customer. If you held a Stakeholder Opportunity Review, and issued Stakeholder Status Reports or held Stakeholder Status Reviews, the stakeholders will be very familiar with the opportunity and you should not have an issue with obtaining approval.

Form 4-16 is an outline of the topics to review with the stakeholders and recommended presenters. The Capture Manager should start by reviewing the purpose, agenda and limit for the session, introduce all the stakeholders, and then provide a review of the timeline. The Sales Leader should review any changes in the customer profile, opportunity profile, competitor profile or win strategy since the last stakeholder meeting. This should be followed by a review of the solution by the Technical or Delivery Leader, although it could be provided by the Sales Leader if he/she is comfortable with the material. The Capture Manager should then review Risk Mitigation Plans, who is followed by the Pricing Leader to review the Business Case. Once all material is reviewed and questions answered, the Capture Manager should poll the stakeholders.

Form 4-16			
Outline for Stakeholder Approval Review			
Category	**Subject**	**Suggested Topics or Contents**	**Presenter**
Introduction	Purpose	Purpose is typically to: 1) Review Changes, 2) Review Solution, Risks and Financials and 3) Obtain Authority to Bid.	Capture Manager
	Agenda	Agenda is typically the topics covered, in sequence, with presentors	
	Limit	Identify time alloted for meeting	
	Participants	List of stakeholders with name, title, and functional responsibility	
Status	Timeline update	Update on response timeline showing status	
Changes	Customer Profile Update	Update on changes in customer business, your presence, or competitor presence	Sales Leader
	Opportunity Update	Update on changes in problem, solution, contract, basic scope, optional scope or key dates	
	Competitor Update	Update on changes in competitors, solutions, strengths or weakenesses	
	Win Strategy Update	Update on changes in win theme, sweet spot, sour spot or positioning plan	
Solution	Solution	Review of solution showing before and after along with products and services offered	Technical or Delivery Leader
Risks	Risk Mitigation Plans	Review Risk Mitigation Plans	Capture Manager
Financials	Business Case	Review Business Case Assumptions, Inputs and Analysis	Pricing Leader
Authority to Bid	Stakeholder Commitment	Ensure stakeholder's understand they: 1) agree solution is Technically Sound, Delivery Sound, Financially Sound, and Contractually Sound and 2) they grant Authority to Bid	Capture Manager

Refer back to the "Tips for an Effective Stakeholder Opportunity Review" in Chapter 3, as these same tips are appropriate for the Stakeholder Approval Review. Similar to the Stakeholder Opportunity Review, you should issue an update of the review package following the session while documenting stakeholder participation and approval, along with any material changes or important points from the session.

Depending upon the size of the opportunity and potential liabilities you may need additional approval from a senior executive, such as the company President or CEO, and potentially even the Board of Directors. This is an important safeguard in companies to ensure offers to enter into contracts with significant obligations are only done so by individuals with the authority to bind the company. This information is generally identified in a Schedule of Authorizations or Approvals which should be available from the CFO or General Counsel of your company.

This approval will typically require an executive briefing document and approval package, which should have been identified as a work task in the Capture Project Plan. Details on the format of this package should be available from the Pricing Leader or the CFO, business management or contracting stakeholder. These same individuals should be able to explain who should secure the approval and the time required.

Outputs

The outputs of the Bid/Proposal Reviews and Approval Step is the Authority to Bid which grants permission for the bid or proposal to be delivered to the customer. Stakeholder approval is documented in the updated Stakeholder Approval Review package along with the appropriate signed approval documents as required by your company's Schedule of Authorizations or Approvals.

SELECTED INTERVIEW

Name: John E. Stuart

Job Title: Senior Program Manager – Subcontracts

Organization: Lockheed Martin

Location: Arlington, Virginia

Major Responsibilities: Lead the Aviation Domain Subcontract Team on the $24 Billion Deepwater program for the recapitalization of U.S. Coast Guard (USCG) Aviation and Surface assets. Responsible for the acquisition planning, subcontract placement, and performance (schedule, cost and technical) management of new fixed wing maritime patrol aircraft, development of Vertical Take-off & Landing (VTOL) Unmanned Aircraft Vehicle (UAV), re-engine and modernization of legacy helicopters and aircraft, and selection and acquisition of airborne sensors.

Background: A seasoned program, contracts and procurement executive with MBA, Professional Certifications, and proven track record in U.S. Government, international and commercial contracting, program management, subcontract and supply chain management, pricing, and business development. Work experience in Government and private sector includes R&D, production, systems integration and support of major weapons systems and component hardware involving aircraft and space technologies. 25 years Aerospace contract formation, subcontract management, pricing, negotiation, review & approval, and administration; 22 years Director and Manager level – directing, controlling, policy & procedures formulation and execution, resource management and allocation; 14 years International and commercial; 12 years Technical, engineering and program management.

MBA (Honors) Management and Finance – U of Missouri; BA Political Science and International Economics – U of Colorado; Executive Program Management – Defense Systems Management College; Air War College – USAF Air

University; Education with Industry – Air Force Institute of Technology; Fellow and Certified Professional Contracts Manager – National Contract Management Association; Professional Designation in Contract management – Air Force Institute of Technology.

QUESTIONS & ANSWERS:

Question: What do you consider to be proven best practices for Buyers when conducting procurement planning and developing solicitations?

Answer: Develop a robust and deliberate specification and technical requirements generation process – know and define what your buying, how and why

- Establish a well defined and understood acquisition life cycle model with realistic event/milestone schedules — don't squeeze generation and review process and sellers response times to make-up for poor scheduling and planning management
- Institute a rigorous budgeting, cost estimating and funding process to support and validate cost of meeting programs requirements — avoid sticker shock and cash flow problems

You can't bargain for a donkey expecting a racehorse!

Question: What actions do you suggest sellers take to ethically and appropriately influence buyer's requirements?

Answer: A true balancing act with consequences for falling short – sellers need to establish and develop buyer confidence in their judgment, play by the rules and regulations, and refrain from back-door selling. Equally important are understanding roles and behavior in competitive and sole source environments. A key premise must be seller's knowledge of buyer's requirements and needs have been obtained legally and from the public domain. To be effective and provide value add, sellers need to understand buyer's "customer" requirements, schedules and funding. Using acceptable marketing, business development, review and comment opportunities sellers can identify cost and risks drivers in requirements, technical approach and maturity, and provide business case analysis which are overcome or lessened by their solution.

Question: What actions should sellers take to ensure they make intelligent Bid/No Bid Decisions on their critical deals?

Answer: Establish a rigorous and independent assessment process with specific review points and defined exit/continuation criteria in parallel with the proposal process. The Bid/No Bid decision must be viewed as a continuous assessment process. Key elements that the independent review must initially assess are the competitive field, customer preferences and desires, and price to win (PTW). When proposal solution is sufficiently mature, develop an Independent Cost Estimate (ICE) for examination against PTW. Throughout process there must be a robust risk identification and mitigation process. Final Bid/No Bid should be made prior to proposal submittal and include assessment of capability to resource, execute and meet financials should award be made. *Check cards and know when to fold or hold...*

Question: What do you consider to be the top five Seller best practices for developing a winning bid or proposal?

Answer: Create a strong Business Development organization, providing marketplace analysis and validated buyer/customer requirements, needs, schedules and funding.

Build a formal and established bid and proposal process managed by a core organization.

Assign best people to leadership positions on team.

Ensure an adequately staff team with required resources and expertise.

Establish rigorous "pink/red" team review process.

Substance over verbiage – all is revealed in fact-finding.

Question: How can U.S. Government agencies truly stream-line and improve their source selection process?

Answer: Start with good procurement package with clear and meaningful selection criteria and priorities – *Let the sellers know what you want and what's important.* Make timely and continuous "competitive range determinations" – *carrying unnecessary baggage is costly and time consuming for both buyer and seller.* Just like industry best practice of having an established process and core group for developing winning proposal – USG needs to have a formal source selection process managed by a professional core group – *quell SS reinvention with each new procurement*

Question: What do you consider to be some of the source selection best practices typically used in the commercial business sector?

Answer: Use of clear and concise specifications and requirements with unambiguous selection criteria. Develop and work with a reliable and known supplier base. Sample marketplace and technology maturity base using RFI and survey techniques, and screen marginal suppliers or sources not able to meet requirements.

Establish core "buying IPTs" using proven and repetitive source selection process

Note: The subject interview solely expresses the informal opinions' of the interviewee, they do not necessarily represent the views or opinions of the organization, company, or agency which they are employed.

Straight Talk: Suggestions for Significant Improvement

In both the public and private business sectors, the sellers bid/proposal phase efforts should be guided by their risk assessment and their business case. Sellers should be focused on three key aspects: can we win, should we win, and how to win while achieving profitability with integrity. Developing and effectively communicating your win theme to the buyer is essential. Further, selecting the right people both internally and externally to review your bid or proposal is very important to maximize your opportunities and minimize your risks. All too often, these bid or proposal reviews are merely a rubber stamp, which only adds time and money, yet offers little real value to the bid or proposal.

Summary

Having successfully completed the Bid/Proposal Phase, the seller can submit their offer to the customer and proceed to the Post-Bid/Proposal Phase. Review this chapter, as well as the previous chapter, to ensure you have completed all the outputs identified as this material will be needed during the Post-Bid/Proposal Phase.

By following the steps outlined in this chapter, you should have developed a solid solution to the customer's business problem, which is good business for both you and your customer. More importantly, you will have done this while optimizing scarce resources, having a well defined strategy and process to manage work tasks, manage change, minimize re-work, and maximize the probability of success.

Questions to Consider

1   How well does your organization kickoff capture teams, develop bids, review bids, and obtain stakeholder approval to submit bids?

2.   How effectively does your organization submit proposals which are win-win for your customer and you?

3.   Does your organization have documented processes or tools & techniques used to kickoff capture teams, develop bids, review bids, and obtain stakeholder approval to submit bids?

4.   What actions has your organization taken to improve/develop capture team kickoff, bid/proposal development, bid/proposal reviews and approval skills for your Sales managers, capture/proposal managers and contract managers?

5.   How well does your organization document and share your capture team kickoff, bid/proposal development, bid/proposal reviews and approvals lessons learned?

CHAPTER

BID/PROPOSAL PHASE: SOURCE SELECTION PLANNING & EVALUATION

INTRODUCTION

In this chapter, we shall examine source selection planning as the buyer's process of preparing to conduct evaluations of one or more bids or proposals. Next, we will review the bids or proposals evaluation process, which is designed to determine if a qualified seller(s) exists that can provide timely delivery of quality products, services, and/or solutions at a fair and reasonable price. Then we will briefly discuss the process of oral presentations by sellers and their responses to buyer's questions during the source selection evaluation process, see Figure 5-1 "The Buying & Selling Life-Cycle."

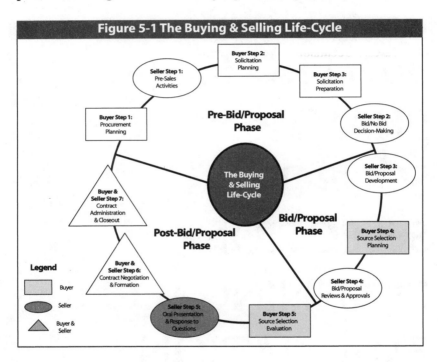

Figure 5-1 The Buying & Selling Life-Cycle

The nature of the source selection planning process, the techniques for getting information, the procedures used in evaluation, and the decision-making methods vary from procurement to procurement, buyer to buyer, and industry to industry. Figure 5-2 illustrates some of the key inputs, tools & techniques, and desired outputs of the source selection planning process.

Figure 5-2 Buyer Step 4: Source Selection Planning Process

Input	Tools & Techniques	Output
• Bids or Proposals	• Bidder's conference	• Source selection
• Evaluation criteria	• Weighting system	plan
• Evaluation standards	• Screening system	
• Source selection staffing	• Independent estimates	
	• Source selection process	

Source selection planning entails: preparing to receive bids or proposals, preparing to apply evaluation criteria, and determining standards to select a seller(s). This process tends to be a complicated one because:

■ Price may be the primary determinant for an off-the-shelf item, but the lowest proposed price may not be the lowest cost if the seller proves unable to deliver the product in a timely manner

■ Proposals are often separated into technical (approach) and commercial (price) sections with each evaluated separately

■ Multiple sources may be required for critical products

Bids or Proposals may be simple, requiring only one person to evaluate the sources and select the best alternative; they may be complex, requiring a panel of experts. In fact, some proposal evaluations may require a consultant's assistance. But no matter the level of complexity, the following process should be followed:

Inputs

The inputs to a source selection planning consist of the following items:

■ *Bids or Proposals:* The buyer will ultimately select a seller(s) from among the bids or proposals submitted in response to a solicitation.

■ *Evaluation criteria:* In the source selection planning process, the buyer prepares to evaluate sources of goods and services and decide which one or more has the greatest potential for successful performance. Accomplishing this task requires applying evaluation criteria to assess the attributes offered by potential sellers (see the "Evaluation Criteria" section presented later in this chapter for detailed information).

■ *Evaluation standards:* An evaluation standard is a gauge used to measure a potential source to determine its value (see the "Evaluation Standards" section later in this chapter for detailed information).

■ *Source Selection Staffing:* It is critical to ensure the Buyer has the right people (staffing) dedicated to supporting the source selection planning and evaluate both quality and quantity of potential source in order to succeed.

Tools and Techniques

The following tools and techniques are used for source selection planning:

■ *Bidder's Conference:* A meeting conducted by the buyer, either face-to-face or via teleconference/Netmeeting, to discuss the Draft Request for Proposal (RFP) and obtain seller feedback on the source selection process, and/or RFP as previously discussed in Chapter 2.

■ *Weighting system:* After selecting the attributes to be used for evaluation, as well as establishing evaluation standards, the next task is to determine the importance of each attribute relative to the others (see the "Weighting System" section later in this chapter for specific information).

Assume that a prospective buyer of a product decides that price and quality are the greatest attributes of interest and that quality is more than twice as important as price. Accordingly, the buyer assigns quality a fixed weight of 0.70 and price a fixed weight of 0.30. However, after receiving the proposals, the buyer discovers that the quality differences among the proposed products are small but that the differences in price are relatively large. Under these circumstances, the assigned fixed weights could result in the buyer paying a premium for a relatively small quality gain. When comparing the actual ranges of variance, the buyer may decide that price is more important than quality in making the final decision.

■ *Screening system:* A screening system is used to process the information regarding potential sources. The buyer must read and analyze the information, apply the appropriate standards, and assign scores that express how well or how poorly each proposal measures up. Depending on the amount of information to be analyzed and the technical complexity of the requirement(s), this work might be performed by a purchasing agent or a panel of experts.

If the procurement is complex enough to warrant establishing a panel of experts, the evaluators on the panel should include someone from the buyer's organization who will ultimately use the product or service and someone from the buyer's purchasing office. Additional advice may also be needed from accountants and attorneys. In some cases, the buyer may need to hire consultants to provide technical assistance. All evaluators should be thoroughly familiar with the specification, statement of work, and evaluation criteria.

Before the evaluation begins, the buyer must decide how the evaluators will present their findings, to whom, and what kind of documentation they will prepare. The process should be kept as simple as possible. To ensure the confidentiality of information received from competing sources, many organizations require that the evaluators communicate with the sources under consideration only through the purchasing department.

- *Independent estimates:* Using consultants or outside experts to help in this process is common and can be of great value.
- *Source Selection Process:* The process a buyer uses for source selection will vary based upon numerous factors. Figure 5-3 illustrates the two most common methods.

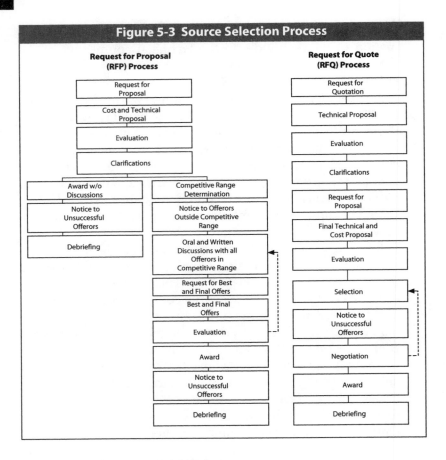

Figure 5-3 Source Selection Process

Request for Proposal (RFP) Process

- Request for Proposal
- Cost and Technical Proposal
- Evaluation
- Clarifications
- Award w/o Discussions → Notice to Unsuccessful Offerors → Debriefing
- Competitive Range Determination
- Notice to Offerors Outside Competitive Range
- Oral and Written Discussions with all Offerors in Competitive Range
- Request for Best and Final Offers
- Best and Final Offers
- Evaluation
- Award
- Notice to Unsuccessful Offerors
- Debriefing

Request for Quote (RFQ) Process

- Request for Quotation
- Technical Proposal
- Evaluation
- Clarifications
- Request for Proposal
- Final Technical and Cost Proposal
- Evaluation
- Selection
- Notice to Unsuccessful Offerors
- Negotiation
- Award
- Debriefing

Case Study: Eastman Kodak Company

Eastman Kodak Company has lead the market in the United States in four major consumer digital photography segments: digital cameras, snapshot photo printers, retail photo kiosks, and online picture sharing sites. In the late 1990s, worldwide purchasing at Kodak moved from a highly decentralized structure to a highly centralized structure. The change resulted in a new chief purchasing officer (CPO) and a mandate from the CEO to reduce procurement costs by $1 billion. One initiative to achieve this target was a change to the sourcing process. The objectives of the change management team were to:

■ Provide a structure to enable optimal results from the sourcing effort

- Identify the basic activities and deliverables of the sourcing process
- Identify when to use the sourcing process
- Clarify the benefits of using the sourcing process

The sourcing process was designed for all applications while using cross-functional project teams, and consisted of a formalized, consistent eight-phase process with gates and reviews to ensure project success and stakeholder buy-in. The eight phases of the sourcing process are:

Phase 0: Opportunity Identification

Phase 1: Project Definition

Phase 2: Supplier Qualification and Selection

Phase 3: Transition Readiness

Phase 4: Supplier Transition

Phase 5: Pre-Production Verification

Phase 6: Shipping Approval

Phase 7: Continuous Improvement

Phase 8: Discontinuance

Gatekeeping meetings provide a chance for stakeholders and sponsors to formally review the issues and agree to progress to the next phase. The key questions at each gate are:

Gate Zero: Is the business case complete?

Gate One: Is the business requirements document complete?

Gate Two: Was the supplier selection process followed?

Gate Three: Is the transition plan complete?

Gate Four: Is the supplier ready for the transition?

Gate Five: Are the pre-production samples acceptable?

Gate Six: Has the supplier agreed to the production schedule, forecast, and inventories?

Gate Seven: Is the supplier quality process underway?

Gate Eight: Is due diligence with the supplier complete?

The biggest benefit of the sourcing process is that the process itself builds sponsor and stakeholder buy-in. At the end of the process, there is little or no argument over the results because the stakeholders were a part of the entire process including updates to the business case at each phase and even signed off at each gate. Other benefits of the centralized and formalized sourcing process include:

- Linking multiple processes used by worldwide purchasing such as supplier quality, diversity, strategy, and e-commerce
- Adding consistency and integrity to the purchasing processes resulting in better decisions
- Applying formal methods to key purchasing decisions and ensuring consistency between worldwide purchasing and internal clients

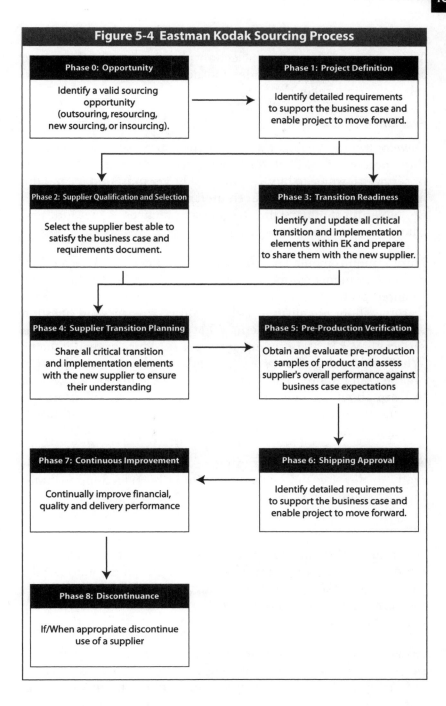

Figure 5-4 Eastman Kodak Sourcing Process

Phase 0: Opportunity

Identify a valid sourcing opportunity (outsouring, resourcing, new sourcing, or insourcing).

Phase 1: Project Definition

Identify detailed requirements to support the business case and enable project to move forward.

Phase 2: Supplier Qualification and Selection

Select the supplier best able to satisfy the business case and requirements document.

Phase 3: Transition Readiness

Identify and update all critical transition and implementation elements within EK and prepare to share them with the new supplier.

Phase 4: Supplier Transition Planning

Share all critical transition and implementation elements with the new supplier to ensure their understanding

Phase 5: Pre-Production Verification

Obtain and evaluate pre-production samples of product and assess supplier's overall performance against business case expectations

Phase 7: Continuous Improvement

Continually improve financial, quality and delivery performance

Phase 6: Shipping Approval

Identify detailed requirements to support the business case and enable project to move forward.

Phase 8: Discontinuance

If/When appropriate discontinue use of a supplier

Outputs

The outputs of the source selection planning step is the source selection plan, which includes the people, budget, and time to select the right seller(s).

Evaluation Criteria

Developing the evaluation criteria for source selection requires three prerequisites. First, the buyer must understand what goods or services it wants to buy. Second, the buyer must understand the industry that will provide the required goods or services. And third, the buyer must understand the market practices of that industry. Market research provides this information.

During requirements analysis and development of the specification or statement of work, the buyer gains an understanding of the required products or services. Understanding the industry means learning about the attributes of the goods or services in question and the firms that make them: What features do those goods or services have? What processes are used to produce or render them? What kinds and quantities of labor and capital are required? What are the cash requirements? Understanding the market allows you to learn about the behavior of buyers and sellers: What are the pricing practices of the market, and what is the range of prices charged? What are the usual terms and conditions of sale?

After gaining an understanding of these issues, the buyer is ready to develop the evaluation criteria by selecting attributes for evaluation.

Attributes

A consumer shopping for an automobile does not evaluate an automobile, per se, but rather selected attributes of the automobile, such as acceleration, speed, handling, comfort, safety, price, fuel mileage, capacity, appearance, and so forth. The evaluation of the automobile is the sum of the evaluations of its attributes.

An automobile has many attributes, but not all are worthwhile subjects of evaluation. The attributes of interest are those that the consumer thinks are important for satisfaction. The attributes that one consumer thinks are important may be inconsequential to another consumer.

In most procurement, multiple criteria will be required for success-ful performance for several reason. First, buyers usually have more than one objective; for example, many buyers look for both good quality and low price. Second, attributes essential for one objec-tive may be different from those essential for others; for example, in buying an automobile, the attributes essential for comfort have little to do with those essential for quick acceleration.

To complicate matters further, some criteria will likely be incom-patible with others. The attributes essential to high quality may be inconsistent with low price; high performance, for example, may be incompatible with low operating cost. Thus, for any one source to have the maximum desired value of every essential attribute—for example, highest quality combined with lowest price—may be impossible. If so, the buyer must make trade-offs among the various attributes when deciding which source is best. These are considerations that make source selection a problem in *multiple attribute decision making*, which requires special decision analysis techniques.

Source selection attributes fall into three general categories relating to a source's (as an entity) products, services and prices offered. Thus, the buyer must have criteria for each category that reflect the buyer's ideas about what is valuable. The criteria concerning the sources themselves, as entities, are the *management criteria*; the criteria concerning the products or services offered are the *technical criteria*; and the criteria concerning the prices of the products or services are the *price criteria*.

Management Criteria

In the contracting process, the buyer enters a relationship with a seller, and each party exchanges promises about what it will do for the other in the future. Thus, when comparing sources, the buyer must determine which entity would make the best partner. Management criteria relate to this set of attributes.

The specific attributes that will make for a good partner and the relative emphasis the buyer should place on them will depend on the buyer's contractual objectives and the practices in the industry and marketplace. Nevertheless, certain categories of at-tributes should always be considered, such as reputation for good performance, technical capability, qualifications of key managerial personnel, capabilities of facilities and equipment, capacity, financial strength, labor relations, and location.

Technical Criteria

In response to the buyer's solicitation, each potential source will likely offer the buyer something that is somewhat different or offer the same product or service as the other sources, but propose to use different production or performance procedures. If these differences are significant enough to affect the source's prospects for success, the buyer must compare them to determine their relative merits. The buyer must develop criteria to evaluate *what* each source will do or deliver and *how* each source will proceed with the work—in other words, determine product or service quality and procedural effectiveness. These attributes are called technical criteria.

The precise nature of the technical criteria will depend on the specification or statement of work. If the solicitation specifies all aspects of product design or service performance, the buyer will not have to develop further criteria to evaluate what the source will do or deliver. However, the buyer may want to evaluate proposed production plans, policies, procedures, and techniques to decide which source is most likely to do the best job. However, if the buyer specifies only function or performance, it also must evaluate each proposal to determine the proposed product or service that will satisfy the requirement and determine which one will do it best. The buyer's criteria should reflect the significant attributes of function or performance.

Price Criteria

Besides evaluating management and technical attributes, the buyer must evaluate the reasonableness of each proposed price, in terms of realism and competitiveness.

- *Realism:* Regarding whether a proposed price is too low, realism is determined by evaluating consistency among a potential source's management, technical, and price proposals. The question is whether a source's proposed price entails too much risk given what the source's qualifications are as a company, what it has promised to do, and what methods it has proposed to use. Risk affects behavior, often in undesirable ways. If a price is too low, entailing too much risk, the seller may fail to achieve project objectives. Therefore, each proposal must be analyzed to determine whether the proposed price allows for sufficient resources to do the job. The technique used to evaluate realism is cost analysis.

In the short term, the prices of commercial goods and services are not necessarily determined entirely by the cost of their manufacture or performance. Thus, a source may offer something for sale at prices set below cost for various sound business reasons. Still, the buyer must investigate if a price seems too low; otherwise, the risk of poor performance may become a reality

■ *Competitiveness:* Competitiveness refers to whether a proposed price is too high compared with what is available in the marketplace. Competitiveness is evaluated by comparing each proposed price to the others and to other pricing information. The technique used to evaluate competitiveness is price analysis.

Qualitative vs. Quantitative Evaluation Criteria

The source selection evaluation criteria describe a level of value that must be met. Some values may be stated *quantitatively*, such as size, weight, speed, mean-time-between-failure, mean-time-to-repair, and price. Other values must be stated *qualitatively*, using words rather than numbers (unless the buyer is willing to go to great efforts to develop quantitative expressions of them). Examples include attractiveness, experience, and comfort.

Theorists of decision making sometimes refer to qualitative criteria as "fuzzy" criteria, and they have developed various ways to convert qualitative judgments to quantitative expressions. One example is the scale used to evaluate the taste of food samples. Quantitative criteria are generally easier to use, but qualitative criteria are frequently unavoidable.

Evaluation Standards

Three types of evaluation standards—*absolute, minimum,* and *relative*—express values. The main difference between these three types of standards is the amount of information required to establish them and the kind of information they provide to the buyer.

Absolute Standards

Absolute standards include both the maximum and the minimum acceptable values. When a buyer uses an absolute standard during evaluation, the performance of the source being rated is compared to the standards to determine the absolute value of its performance. For example, assume an absolute standard for price that ranges from no cost (best value) to $5 million (worst value). A potential source's proposed price of $4.5 million can be compared to the standards to determine its absolute value.

If the buyer's utility for price is a straight-line function, a source whose proposed price is $4.5 million could earn 10 out of 100 value points, a source whose price is $4 million could earn 20 points, and a source whose price is $2 million could earn 60 points. Each point score tells the buyer absolutely how good or bad the price is relative to the buyer's standard of value and relative to the other potential sources.

The problem with an absolute standard is that the buyer needs a great deal of information to develop an absolute range of values. The buyer must know the highest preference level as well as the lowest. The evaluation result may not be worth the effort of developing this information.

Minimum Standards

A minimum, or ratio, standard requires only that the buyer know the minimum acceptable level of performance. Each potential source is compared to that minimum, and the source with the highest level of acceptable performance receives the highest score, 100 on a scale of 0 to 100. Sources that do not meet the minimum standard are eliminated. All other sources are scored in comparison to the best.

Assume that the highest acceptable price for a product or service is $5 million. Assume that of all potential sources, the one with a price of $2 million is considered the best. That source receives a score of 100 points. A source whose price is $4 million could receive a score of 33 points, and one whose price is $4.5 million could receive a score of 17 points.

The advantage of the minimum standard over the absolute standard is that the buyer needs less information. The obvious disadvantage is that the evaluation scores will not tell the buyer absolutely how good or bad each alternative is.

Relative Standards

A relative standard entails direct comparison of each potential source to the each other in order to determine the best and the worst sources. The best source receives the maximum number of points, 100 on a scale of 0 to 100. The worst receives no points. Having established the best and the worst alternatives, the buyer can construct a graph to determine the scores of the sources that fall between them. Those scores also can be determined mathematically.

Using a relative scale to score the same prices as described in the example used for minimum standards, the $2 million price would receive 100 points, the $4.5 million price would receive no points, and the $4 million price would receive 20 points.

The relative standard requires the least amount of advance information on the part of the buyer. Scores developed on a relative standard tell the buyer how good or bad each source is relative to the others, but not how good or bad they are absolutely. Nevertheless, this information will be sufficient for many source selections.

Weighting System

The evaluation of each source will be the sum of the evaluations of its individual attributes. The scores initially assigned to attributes during the evaluation will not reflect differences in importance among the attributes. The scores will be *raw* (unweighted). The decision to add the raw scores together to determine the value of the source is tantamount to a decision that each attribute is equally important. But such may not be the case. If some attributes are more important than others, the buyer must assign a weight to each.

Assume that a consumer decides that the relevant attributes in an automobile are acceleration, maximum speed, attractiveness, price, and fuel mileage. If any of these attributes is more important than the others, the raw scores must be weighted before adding the scores. The weights will reflect the consumer's trade-off decisions among the various attributes and will affect the final determination of which automobile is the best.

The buyer may establish either *fixed weights* or *variable weights*. Fixed weights are established before receiving the proposals and do not change. Variable weights are established only after determining the raw scores. Variable weights allow for making trade-offs when comparing the ranges of actual performance among the alternatives.

SELECTED INTERVIEW

Name: Rex Elliott

Job Title: Procurement Analyst/Contracting Officer

Organization: Program Procurement Division, NASA/Goddard Space Flight Center

Location: Greenbelt, MD

Major Responsibilities: Training & employee development for procurement workforce, workforce succession planning, professional certification, contracting officer warrants, employee awards, contract terminations.

Background: Master of Arts in Public Policy, 1983–Rutgers University; Bachelor of Public Administration, 1981–Seattle University. 1983 Class of Presidential Management Interns. 20 years of procurement operations experience (contracting with/for major system development, construction, R&D, institutional services, information technology, cooperative agreements, educational institutions, small businesses, large businesses, etc.) 3 years of procurement staff work (human capital management, legislation reviews, contract terminations, policy analysis, file reviews, training seminars, etc.).

QUESTIONS & ANSWERS:

Question: What do you consider to be proven best practices for Buyers when conducting procurement planning and developing solicitations?

Answer: Start early. Conduct market research with an eye toward the specific issues you're likely to face (e.g. sole source justifications, set-aside considerations, etc.), and document the results. Develop a milestone schedule with clear delineation of who is responsible for completing which tasks. Show others on the procurement team how to do their jobs (without actually doing things for them). Have lots of tools/checklists/relevant templates available to help.

Question: What actions should sellers take to ensure they make intelligent Bid/No Bid Decisions on their critical deals?

Answer: Be prepared for the Government to slip the schedule (particularly if there is expected to be lots of competition). Know the marketplace/competition. Target only a select few of the business opportunities (rather than blanketing the place with mediocre proposals). Don't be surprised when a joint venture gets approved by SBA for competing on a particular procurement (it isn't the procuring agency's fault that you didn't know). Be prepared to no-bid when it's clear the Government doesn't know what it's doing. Most of the problems we get into are due to poorly defined requirements, so be watchful for this.

Question: What do you consider to be the top five Seller best practices for developing a winning bid or proposal?

Answer: Focus on only the competitions you're likely to be most competitive on. Do not assume the Government personnel evaluating your proposal know anything about you, your capabilities, or even the capabilities of industry in general. Ask questions and make requests early—you'll really tick off the Government if you wait till the last minute. Focus on making your proposal the best it can be (rather than on restricting the pool of your competitors to the smallest it can be). If you don't have confidence in your ability to propose against all of your competitors, you should not expect the Government to have confidence in your ability to perform. Think in terms of discriminators (what really distinguishes your firm from your competitors). Do not whine, especially not to members of Congress.

Question: How can U.S. Government agencies truly streamline and improve their source selection process?

Answer: Unless the agencies structure their procurement workforces around specific commodity types (where they develop expertise in only one or a few types of buying), they're going to have learning curves on most of their procurements. And, as long as these agencies' management teams are so averse to protests, they will be very conservative about conducting and documenting very thorough proposal evaluations. This often conflicts with the goals of streamlining, or doing things efficiently. That said, the only obvious choices for getting more streamlined source selections are: 1) develop a procurement workforce that's more knowledgeable about the specific industries and procurement strategies/techniques/pricing structures, etc. that are specific to those industries, or 2) reduce the perceived risk of protest by: a) assuring the Government personnel that the firms involved have no interest in protesting, b) reducing the possibility of a firm filing a protest in the first place, or c) increasing the negative consequences for firms filing frivolous protests.

Question: What do you consider to be some of the source selection best practices typically used in the commercial business sector?

Answer: I'm a fan of oral proposals. They're usually quicker and result in better quality information being exchanged. I also like to see RFPs that are lean enough to focus on only the likely discriminators in a source selection (too many ask for information that won't affect the source selection). I'm also a fan of selecting on the initial proposals, since that usually results in a selection decision that's easier to make. One technique I'd like to see done more in the construction world is what I call "Two Step Best Value" source selection. That's where everybody sends in a cost proposal, but only the 3 or so cheapest offerors are invited in to present their technical proposals. I think it results in better source selections than sealed-bidding produces. Industry has always had the flexibility to do things this way, but I've rarely seen the Government do this.

Question: Please share a brief personal success story regarding: Solicitations, Bids/Proposals, or Source Selection – Building a Winning Contract.

Answer: Under the flexibilities allowed by FAR 13.5, Commercial Test Program, I conducted two of the "Two Step Best Value" source selections for fixed-price construction of facilities requirements. One of the competitions resulted in a low bid selection (same result as if it had been sealed bidding), but we did not select the low bidder on the second one. Instead, we selected the next lowest offeror because it had better past performance and a better management plan. I didn't get a protest, but the selected contractor performed excellently, and avoided some problems that I believe would have resulted if we'd had to select the low bidder.

I also participated on a $143M task order selection (using GSA's Millenia contract) for high performance (super) computing. We made a best value selection in record time (67 days from release of solicitation to selection). GSA did most of the

> logistical work on the competition, but it was still a privilege to be part of something that big that worked so well.
>
> **Note:** The subject interview solely expresses the informal opinions' of the interviewee, they do not necessarily represent the views or opinions of the organization, company, or agency which they are employed.

Post-Bid/Proposal Phase

Buyer Step 5: Source Selection Evaluation

Source selection evaluation is about successfully implementing your source selection plan to identify the right seller(s) to provide in a timely manner the desired products, services, and/or solutions at fair and reasonable prices.

Figure 5-5 Buyer Step 5: Source Selection Evaluation Process

Input	Tools & Techniques	Output
• Bids or Proposals • Source Selection Plan • Evaluation Criteria • Evaluation Standards • Weighting System • Screening System • Source Selection Process • People • Training	• Opportunity and Risk Management (ORM) model • Past Performance Evaluation Database • Source Selection Best Practices Checklist • Total Cost of Ownership (TCO) Evaluation • Source Selection Decision Making Guidelines • Evaluation of Oral Presentations by sellers	• Selected seller(s) who will provide timely delivery of quality products, services, and/or solutions at a fair & reasonable price

Inputs

■ *Bids or Proposals:* In order to conduct source selection evaluation you must have one or more proposals. Typically, most buyers will seek at least two or three bids or proposals from qualified or even pre-qualified sellers.

- *Source Selection Plan (SSP):* As previously discussed, the SSP should include the following key elements: evaluation criteria, evaluation standards, weighting system, screening system, and source selection process.
- *People:* The buyer must ensure the appropriate quality and quantity of human resources are available to support the source selection evaluation process.
- *Training:* The buyer must ensure the people involved in source selection evaluation are properly trained to conduct and document the evaluation process fairly, cost-effectively, and efficiently. If novices or trainees are used in the source selection evaluation process, then a coach or experienced mentor should be assigned to guide the trainees through the process and verify quality of work.

Tools & Techniques

The following are a few of the many proven tools and techniques to help business professionals involved in the complex selection process to conduct their evaluation process more effectively and efficiently.

Opportunity & Risk Management (ORM) Model

Opportunity and risk management is an important element of both contract management and project management, because every project contains elements of uncertainty, such as varying amounts of funding, changes in contract delivery date(s), changes in technical requirements, and increases or decreases in quantity. Opportunity and risk management should be thought of as a part of project management methodology. In general, outsourcing business opportunities is becoming increasingly larger and more complex. In today's systems environment, it is not uncommon for business solutions to consist of numerous product and service components from inside, as well as outside an organization. This complexity brings with it new business opportunities and risks. Buyers, like sellers, should regularly assess the opportunities and risks prior to contract award and throughout the project life-cycle.

What is Opportunity?

Opportunity is the measure of the probability of an event, a positive desired change occurring, and the desired impact of that event.

What is Risk?

Risk is the measure of the probability of an event, an unwanted change occurring, and the associated effect of that event. In other words, risk consists of three components:

- A risk event (an unwanted change)
- The probability of occurrence (uncertainty)
- The significance of the impact (the amount at stake)

What is Opportunity and Risk Management (ORM)?

The primary goal of opportunity and risk management (ORM) is to continually seek ways to maximize opportunities and mitigate risks. ORM is an iterative process approach to managing those opportunities and risks that may occur during the course of business and could affect the success or failure of the project. Once identified, the probability of each event's occurrence and its potential effect on the project are analyzed and prioritized or ranked from highest to lowest. Beginning with the highest prioritized events and working down, the project team determines what options or strategies are available and chooses the best strategy to maximize opportunities and to reduce or prevent the identified risks from occurring. This information is the basis for the ORM plan, which should be continually used and updated during the project life-cycle.

Integrating ORM into Project Management

Some business managers rely solely on their intuitive reasoning (ability to guess correctly) as their basis for decision making. But in today's complex systems environment, an astute business manager understands the importance of using a highly skilled project team to identify both opportunity and risk events, assess the possible impacts, and develop appropriate strategies to increase opportunities and reduce risks. A project work breakdown structure (WBS) is an effective means of relating project tasks to possible opportunities and risks.

To integrate opportunity and risk management (ORM) successfully into project management, the project manager must ensure that an ORM plan is included as part of the overall business management planning process. It is vital that ORM become a mindset for all business professionals, especially sales managers, purchasing managers, contract managers, and project managers.

THE OPPORTUNITY & RISK MANAGEMENT (ORM) MODEL

The ORM Model (Figure 5-6) is an ongoing process model that has two major pieces: opportunity/risk assessment and opportunity/risk action plans. Opportunity/risk assessment is composed of three steps: identify opportunities and risk, analyze them, and prioritize them. Opportunity/risk action plans are also composed of three steps: develop strategies for the opportunity and risk action plans, implement opportunity and risk action plans into the project management plan, and evaluate project results. The following diagram illustrates the suggested six-step opportunity and risk management (ORM) model.

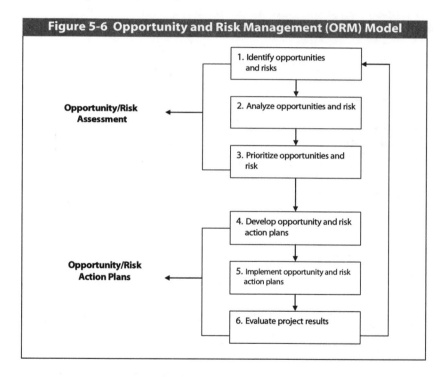

Figure 5-6 Opportunity and Risk Management (ORM) Model

Past Performance Evaluation

Buyers should always include past performance as an evaluation criteria/factor in their request for proposal (RFP) and subsequent source selection process. The weighting of the importance of past performance will vary based upon numerous factors. Seller's with no similar past performance should not be assigned a negative rating nor should they receive a positive rating, because they have no poor past performance. The key factors to consider regarding each seller's past performance is the relevancy of the work and the currency of the past performance. Clearly, a seller that has recently completed highly similar work and done so very well (on-time, within budget), and met or exceeded customer requirements, should receive an excellent past performance rating.

Today, most sophisticated buyers maintain a past performance database, which is typically electronically stored with key-word searchable data files, on each of their key suppliers. It is important that buyers maintain current, accurate, and (as complete as possible) past performance records on each of their key sellers to aide in cost-effective and efficient source selection.

Source Selection — 7 Best Practices Checklist

Form 5-1 contains a checklist of seven proven effective source selection best practices.

Form 5-1	
Checklist	**Source Selection 7 Best Practices**
❑	Cycle-time Targets — the buyer establishes a target of 90 days or less from issuance of the RFP to contract award
❑	Greater Pre-Solicitation Efforts — the buyer actively encourages more definitive procurement planning, bidders conferences with prospective sellers, and circulation of draft RFPs to prospective sellers
❑	Proposal Page Limitations — the buyer provides that pages in proposals over a specified number will not be read, but will be returned to the seller
❑	Reduced Number of Evaluation Factors — the buyer uses only essential evaluation factors
❑	Small Source Selection Teams — the buyer uses a small number of evaluators, each reading all of their specialization/section (technical, management, past performance, or cost) of the proposals
❑	Oral Presentations — the buyer requires the sellers to make oral presentations to the source selection team in the early stages of evaluation of the proposals
❑	Limiting the Competitive Range — the buyer requires rigorous exclusion of marginal sellers from the competitive range

Total Cost of Ownership (TCO) Evaluation – Total Cost of Ownership (TCO) is the latest buzzword, formerly known as Life Cycle Cost (LCC). No matter what you call it, TCO or LCC, there is a real, compelling need for buying organizations to spend some time and effort evaluating the potential product, service, and/or solution throughout its life-cycle, from initial procurement through operational use, including support/maintenance/upgrades, to the end of the product/service life.

Source Selection Decision Making Guidelines

The key to source selection is ultimately identifying the most qualified individual, within the buying organization, to serve as the lead decision maker (LDM) or Source Selection Authority (SSA). The LDM or SSA should be based upon general business knowledge, experience within the industry, expertise in contract management and supply-chain management, demonstrated leadership, and business integrity.

The LDA shall use the evaluation criteria/factors, standards, weighting system, and screening system established in the source selection plan that should be contained within the solicitation document. The LDA shall consider any rankings and ratings prepared by the source selection evaluation team/board/committee. The LDA should seek clear differentiators between proposals or bids that are consistent with the evaluation criteria and weightings established in the solicitation. Unlike, U.S. Government source selections the final decision of the LDM or SSA should not be subject to bid protests.

Evaluation of Oral Presentations

As previously discussed, oral presentations can serve as a powerful and effective tools for both buyers and sellers. Buyers should require sellers to provide oral presentations, as needed, especially for large, complex, and critical systems and/or professional outsourced services. Buyers should pre-determine the weighting and key evaluation criteria factors for the basis of the evaluation of all oral presentations provided by the sellers.

Output

The key output of the Bid/Proposal Phase – Buyer Step 5: Source Selection Evaluation Process, is the selection of a seller(s) who will provide timely delivery of quality products, services, and/or solutions at a fair and reasonable price.

Seller Step 5: Oral Presentations & Response to Questions

When a Request for Proposal (RFP) is announced, those seeking the contract typical prepare a large, comprehensive written proposal;

however, preparing a single written proposal involves a long, costly process. Reliable studies have shown that, due to the complexity of today's proposals, selection board members generally do not understand 75 percent of what they read in a proposal. Because of the challenges associated with written proposals, government agencies are placing more emphasis on untraditional methods for awarding contracts.

While a comprehensive written proposal is still often expected, an additional method, the oral presentation, is quickly becoming a standard feature of the evaluation process in both the public and private business sectors. In contrast to written proposals, oral proposals more effectively convey the contractor's technical approach, management experience, and past performance. Oral presentations also reduce procurement lead time and administrative costs for both buyers and sellers, see Figure 5-7.

Figure 5-7 Seller Step 5: Oral Presentations & Response to Questions Process

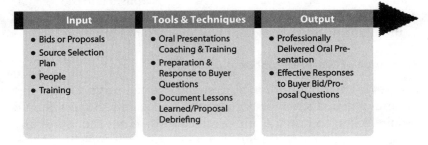

Input	Tools & Techniques	Output
• Bids or Proposals • Source Selection Plan • People • Training	• Oral Presentations Coaching & Training • Preparation & Response to Buyer Questions • Document Lessons Learned/Proposal Debriefing	• Professionally Delivered Oral Presentation • Effective Responses to Buyer Bid/Proposal Questions

Inputs

All of the key inputs listed below were discussed earlier in this chapter:

■ Bids or Proposals
■ Source Selection Plan
■ People
■ Training

Tools & Techniques

Oral Presentations — Coaching & Training

The bottom line for business development is that oral presentations (orals) of the evaluation process matters and will probably determine the outcome of the entire contract. In response to the importance of the oral proposal, organizations have begun to invest in orals coaching to effectively prepare the orals team.

Organizations realize that the orals team represents the company and can project a positive or negative image based on the perceived cohesiveness and competency of the team. Thus, sellers who want to win contracts engage an orals coach. As a general rule, teams who have an orals coach win more contracts than teams without such guidance. Some sellers choose an internal orals coach to direct their proposal team. Though this may reduce costs in the short term, an internal coach usually lacks experience, objectivity, and full expertise with the oral proposal process.

Today, more organizations hire external orals coaches. These external coaches have extensive experience, understand what it takes to win contracts, and have a proven track record of teaching effective presentation skills. They know how to direct the intense orals coaching process on selecting team members, developing individual presentation skills, creating a cohesive team, highlighting discriminators, and continually practicing until the presentation is flawless.

Recommendations regarding the use of an orals coach is available in *Orals Coaching: The Secret Weapon for Winning Contracts*, by the Association for Proposal Management Professionals (APMP) Journal, Spring/Summer issue 2004. The article states that "No matter what type of orals coach is hired, the coach should have the experience and capacity needed to: (1) deliver the needed content and instruction and (2) understand and use a tailored coaching process."

The Needed Content and Instruction

An orals coach should have a tool box of knowledge, skills, and abilities to coach the orals team. Generally, each orals coach has certain specialties and interests. A coach should be selected because of his/her match with the requirements of the specific orals team and proposal requirements. The following list describes the significant areas of expertise that an orals coach can use to effectively train an orals team.

Form 5-2	
Orals Coaching Content	
Speaking and Presentation Skills	Speech Writing and Script Preparation
Content Development and Organization	Group Practice Coaching
Customer Profiling and Analysis	Preparation of Charts and Graphics
Leadership Development	One-on-One Coaching
Video Taping and Analysis	Question and Answer Preparation
Credibility and Presence Development	Rapport Building Skills
Team Cohesion	

The Orals Coaching Process

An orals coach needs to use a process that guides the coaching. Using a process prevents mistakes and ensures important aspects are not overlooked. Having a process also suggests that the orals coach knows what he/she is doing and knows what it takes to make a winning orals team. An orals coach should consider the organization's expectations and the specific needs of the orals team when crafting an orals coaching process. The usual orals coaching timeframe is 4-6 weeks of full-time effort. Form 5-3 shows the orals coaching process.

Form 5-3
Orals Coaching Process
Quick study of the situation (RFP, customer needs, history of contract, any special circumstances)
Assessment of individual and team capability
Development of presenters into a cohesive team
Video taping each presenter to determine initial strengths and weaknesses
Identification and emphasis of key discriminators
Designing a coaching plan and schedule
Monitoring the design of all charts and visuals
Coaching for presentation at pink team
Conducting extensive team and one-on-one coaching with video feedback
Preparing for red team
Polishing presentations using video feedback
Finalizing plans for delivery to the source selection board

Preparation & Response to Questions

It is essential that the seller have the right people available to quickly and effectively address any specific buyer questions.

Document Lessons Learned/Proposal Debriefing

After being removed from the competition or receiving notice of award to another company, the seller should immediately request in writing from the buyer to conduct a debriefing. The debriefing is usually scheduled at the mutual convenience of both parties. Proposal debriefings can and should be requested even if the seller is awarded a contract.

The debriefing should provide the following information at a minimum, which should be documented in the meeting minutes:

- The significant weakness or deficiencies found in the proposal,
- The overall evaluation of price and/or cost and the technical ratings,
- The overall ranking of offerors, and

- Answers to questions relevant to the buyer's conduct of the competition and source selection.

At the conclusion of the debriefing, the seller's contracts team should issue the minutes to the seller's management and members of the capture team, records depository, and/or the competitive intelligence organization, for future lessons learned and win-loss analysis package for future opportunities.

Outputs

The key outputs of the Oral Presentations and Response to Questions process are those two items presented professionally, cost-effectively, and accurately, thereby enhancing the seller's likelihood of being selected for contract award.

Straight Talk: Suggestions for Significant Improvement

The private business sector tends to do their source selection planning and evaluation very quickly and cost-effectively, especially in comparison to the U.S. Federal Government's acquisition of major systems.

The U.S. Federal Government tries to make their acquisition process as fair to all sellers as humanly possible, since they are dealing with the U.S. taxpayer's money. As a result of the U.S. Federal Government's zeal to be viewed as a fair and honest buyer, they often drive up the costs dramatically and take far longer to acquire the products, services, and/or solutions needed due to laws, regulations, and policies designed to achieve transparency, objectivity, and fairness. A classic example is the U.S. Federal Government's bid protest process, which allows any interested party to file a protest after a contract award. This process is intended to correct any possible wrong doings by the Government or another contractor. However, in the vast majority of bid protest cases, the Government Contracting Officer's final decision is upheld. Thus, most bid protest cases do not add any real value to the winning contractor, nor the Government. In fact, most bid protests often result in significant delays of the start and subsequent performance of the needed work, as well as higher costs to the U.S. taxpayer.

Yet, the biggest cost is truly unknown and has never really been quantified by the U.S. Government or industry. You see the biggest cost is the additional documentation and reviews the U.S. Government's buying organization must go through to "cover your assets" (CYA), due to the constant fear of a bid protest. Thus, the U.S. Government Buying organizations spend an incredible amount of time and taxpayers dollars to thoroughly document every action to ensure they will win any possible bid protest. Thus, we suggest the U.S. Federal Government consider either eliminating the bid protest process entirely or making it applicable to only a limited number of key acquisitions, either way saving the U.S. Government, industry, and the U.S. taxpayers potentially billions of dollars annually.

Summary

So in retrospect, this chapter reviewed two of the Buyer's key steps to source selection planning and evaluation. For each step, we have identified and discussed the key inputs, proven effective tools & techniques, and desired outputs. In the next chapter, we shall tackle the art and science of contract negotiation and formation.

Questions to Consider

1. How effectively does your buying organization plan and prepare for large and complex source selections?

2. What actions has your buying organization taken to streamline source selections?

3. Does your selling organization provide oral presentations of your proposals?

4. Does your selling organization properly train team members to provide best-in-class oral presentations?

CHAPTER  6

POST-BID/ PROPOSAL PHASE: CONTRACT NEGOTIATION & FORMATION

INTRODUCTION

Many people consider themselves to be good negotiators. However, most people do not obtain consistent high performance results in their negotiations, especially when buying or selling large complex deals involving multiple products, services, and integrated business solutions. Most contract negotiators do not spend enough time planning and properly preparing, because they are often in a rush to get a deal which they believe they need badly. As we like to say, if you want it bad, then you will probably get it bad! In this chapter we provide a proven effective process approach to achieve more consistent high performance results in contract negotiations via better planning, preparation, and communication, see Figure 6-1, "The Buying & Selling Life-Cycle."

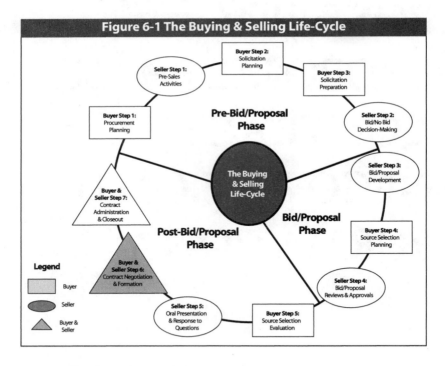

Figure 6-1 The Buying & Selling Life-Cycle

Case Study: Deutsche Lufthansa AG

Founded in 1926, Lufthansa had 92,300 employees and generated revenue of $18.1 billion in 2005. Together with United, US Airways, Air Canada, and 15 other major airlines, Lufthansa is part of the Star Alliance, the world's largest global service network, operating nearly 15,500 daily flights and serving approximately 390 billion passengers every year.

Recent crises arising from 9/11, the war in Iraq, and the outbreak of SARS in Asia have hit the airline industry. The resulting crises management programs required drastic and immediate cost reductions, which could not be implemented simply by "squeezing the lemon" one more time. Until these events, Lufthansa Purchasing had focused primarily on demanding cost reductions from its suppliers. As a response to the crises, the focus of purchasing had to change to include cost-reduction potential inside the company. This put the purchasers into a new role as critical partners with their internal customers. Making cost drivers transparent, formulating need-based specifications, and looking for more flexible and cost-efficient business models fundamentally changed the purchaser's job in times of crisis.

Overcoming past crises has shown Lufthansa Purchasing how increased spending discipline can free up internal value-creation potential. Now purchasing has to transfer such "crisis-proof" levers and behavioral patterns into its daily routines. Table 6-1 gives an illustrative example of the fundamental difference between the problem-oriented and the traditional request-oriented purchasing pattern.

Buyers Turn into Professional Negotiation Designers

As the problem-oriented purchasing pattern questions, the single elements of each request, it increases the number of possible solutions. More sellers compete to become candidates for a contract, which enables the buyer as a negotiation designer to use market forces more effectively, i.e., to let market forces decide the optimal price-performance-ratio.

This requires strict procedure and a well-structured preparation of the bidding phase, which clarifies the evaluation criteria for alternative solutions offered by the sellers.

Table 6-1		
Request-oriented purchasing pattern TODAY	→	**Problem-oriented purchasing pattern FUTURE**
Specify need		Understand economic problem
↓ Database management and server system		↓ Securing and retrieval of customer data
Determine technical specifications		Deriving value drivers & decision criteria
↓ Hardware and software solution		↓ Costs, security, scalability, access speed, etc.
Identify possible suppliers		Determine problem-oriented specification
↓ Supplier 1, supplier 2, supplier 3, etc.		↓ Efficient, safe and need-driven data management
Send out Request-for-Quotes		Expand solution space with alternatives
↓ Specified performance, prices for server capacity, etc.		↓ Service instead of investment and operation (pay-per-customer)
Discuss & Pre-select suppliers		Monetary evaluation of differences
↓ Server capacity, security, service levels, etc.		↓ Bonus for service levels, scalability, etc.
Personal final negotiation & award of contract		Project-specific negotiation design with clear rules
↓ Consideration of qualitative and quantitative aspects		↓ Optimal use of solutions space

Source: PRACTIX Change Management in Purchasing - Best Practices from Germany's No. 1 Airline Deutsche Lufthansa AG, CAP, July 2006

Buyer & Seller Step 6: Contract Negotiation & Formation

Contract negotiation is the process by which two or more competent parties reach an agreement to buy or sell products and/or services. Contract negotiations may be conducted formally or informally and may involve many people or just two – a representative for the Buyer and a representative for the Seller. Contract negotiation may take a few minutes or may involve many discussions over days, months, or years. The desired result of the contract negotiation process is a contract. Contract formation is the process of putting together the essential elements of the contract and any special items unique to a particular business agreement, see Figure 6-2.

Figure 6-2 Buyer & Seller, Step 6: Contract Negotiation & Formation Process

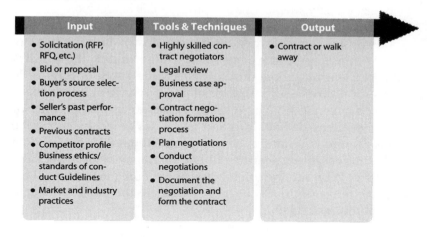

Input	Tools & Techniques	Output
• Solicitation (RFP, RFQ, etc.) • Bid or proposal • Buyer's source selection process • Seller's past performance • Previous contracts • Competitor profile Business ethics/ standards of conduct Guidelines • Market and industry practices	• Highly skilled contract negotiators • Legal review • Business case approval • Contract negotiation formation process • Plan negotiations • Conduct negotiations • Document the negotiation and form the contract	• Contract or walk away

From: Contract Negotiations: Skills, Tools, & Best Practices, by Gregory A. Garrett, CCH, 2005.

Key Inputs

(The following section is a modified extract from the book Contract Negotiations: Skills, Tools, & Best Practices, by Gregory A. Garrett, CCH, 2005)

The key inputs to negotiations and contract formation consists of the following items:

■ *Solicitation:* The solicitation is either an oral or written request for an offer (Request for Proposal (RFP), Request for Quote (RFQ), Invitation for Bid (IFB), and so on) prepared by the buyer and provided to one or more potential sellers.

■ *Bid or proposal:* The bid or proposal is either an oral or written offer by potential sellers to provide products or services to the buyer, usually in response to a solicitation. It also includes all supporting documentation, such as delivery plans, assumptions, and cost/price models.

■ *Buyer's source selection process:* Source selection is the process by which a buyer selects a seller or source of supply for products or services. Buyers typically apply evaluation criteria to select the best seller to meet their needs.

■ *Source Selection Evaluation Criteria:* Developing the evaluation criteria for source selection requires three prerequisites. First, the buyer must understand what goods or services it wants to buy. Second, the buyer must understand the industry that will provide the required goods or services. And third, the buyer must understand the market practices of that industry. Market research provides this information.

During requirements analysis and development of the specification or statement of work, the buyer gains an understanding of the required products or services. Understanding the industry means learning about the attributes of the goods or services in question and the firms that make them: What features do those goods or services have? What processes are used to produce or render them? What kinds and quantities of labor and capital are required? What are the cash requirements? Understanding the market means learning about the behavior of buyers and sellers. What are the pricing practices of the market, and what is the range of prices charged? What are the usual terms and conditions of sale?

After gaining an understanding of these issues, the buyer is ready to develop the evaluation criteria by selecting attributes for evaluation.

■ *Source Selection Attributes:* A consumer shopping for an automobile does not evaluate an automobile, per se, but rather selected attributes of the automobile, such as acceleration, speed, handling, comfort, safety, price, fuel mileage, capacity, appearance, and so forth. The evaluation of the automobile is the sum of the evaluations of its attributes. An automobile has many attributes, but not all are worthwhile subjects of evaluation. The attributes of interest are those that the consumer thinks are important for satisfaction. The attributes that one consumer thinks are important may be inconsequential to another.

In most procurements, multiple criteria will be required for successful performance, for the following reasons: First, buyers usually have more than one objective; for example, many buyers look for both good quality and low price. Second, attributes essential for one objective may be different from those essential for others; for example, in buying an automobile, the attributes essential for comfort have little to do with those essential for quick acceleration.

To complicate matters further, some criteria will likely be incompatible with others. The attributes essential to high quality may be inconsistent with low price; high performance, for example, may be incompatible with low operating cost. Thus, for any one source to have the maximum desired value of every essential attribute—for example, highest quality combined with lowest price—may be impossible. If so, the buyer must make trade-offs among attributes when deciding which source is best. These are considerations that make source selection a problem in *multiple attribute decision making*, which requires special decision analysis techniques.

- *Seller's past performance:* The past performance of a seller is often a critical aspect of contract negotiation. Has the seller delivered previous products and services on time? Has the seller provided high-quality products and services?
  Past performance can be seen as a separate evaluation factor or as a subfactor under technical excellence or management capability. Using the past performance history also reduces the emphasis on merely being able to write a good proposal.

- *Previous contracts:* Has the seller provided products or services to this buyer in the past? If so, what did the previous contract say? How was it negotiated? Who negotiated it?

- *Competitor Profile:* The competitor profile, developed during the Pre-Bid Phase provides a written summary of the seller's competitors and their respective strengths and weaknesses compared to the seller's.

- *Business ethics/Standards of Conduct Guidelines:* Ethics is especially important, in light of numerous recent cases of corporate greed, corruption, and violations of state, federal or international laws. Every company should have mandatory business ethics policies, procedures, and well-defined standards of conduct. Even the appearance of conflicts of interests should be avoided. All business activities should be conducted in a professional and ethical manner.

- *Market and industry practices:* Knowing what the competitors are offering (most-favored pricing, warranties, product discounts, volume discounts, and so on) is essential for a successful outcome to negotiation.

Tools and Techniques

The following tools and techniques are used for negotiations and contract formation:

- *Contract negotiation process:* The contract negotiation process is discussed in detail later in this chapter.

- *Highly skilled negotiators:* Conducting contract negotiation is a complex activity that requires a broad range of skills. Providing negotiators with the best available training in contract negotiation is vital. Top negotiators help their organizations save money and make higher profits.

Case Study: General Electric (GE)

One successful business negotiation strategy is to give something of value away, in order to sell something of even greater value. General Electric (GE) Commercial Finance unit not only understands the strategy of giving something of value away, in order to sell something of greater value – they have mastered it! In fact, GE's famed Six Sigma management consultant experts, Black-belts, are now frequently going out to customer business locations to perform their rigorous statistical analyses of business operations and find ways to cut costs and improve performance results for free. Why you might ask? The answer is simple: the valuable GE Six Sigma consulting services buys a great deal of customer loyalty.

GE has found the free Six Sigma consulting services program has increased the odds that the small to mid-size firms, to which GE is lending money, will not only stay in business long enough to pay back the loans, but will be much more likely to grow in the future, thus need more capital. GE has provided their valuable Six Sigma Black-belt consulting services to hundreds of firms worldwide, from Red Robin Gourmet Burgers, a Denver, CO based restaurant chain to Komori, a Japanese maker of printing presses. Clearly, GE's Six Sigma Black-belts help create a true Buyer-Seller win-win situation.

Case Study: Northrop/Grumman

For more than 25 years, Northrop/Grumman has had an excellent reputation in building or developing highly skilled contract negotiators and negotiation teams. Northrop/Grumman has traditionally ensured their sales managers, contract managers, and contract administrators receive appropriate and timely negotiation training, via in-house professional seminars, university-based courses, and attendance at educational conferences and seminars. In addition, Northrop/Grumman has for many years developed and maintained a seasoned and highly-skilled major negotiations team, which is tasked to tackle the largest and most important contract negotiations.

The Contract Negotiation Process

The contract negotiation process is composed of three phases planning negotiations, conducting negotiations, and documenting the negotiations. Table 6-2 describes an effective, logical approach to plan, conduct, and document contract negotiations based on the proven best practices of world-class organizations.

Table 6-2 — Contract Negotiation Process

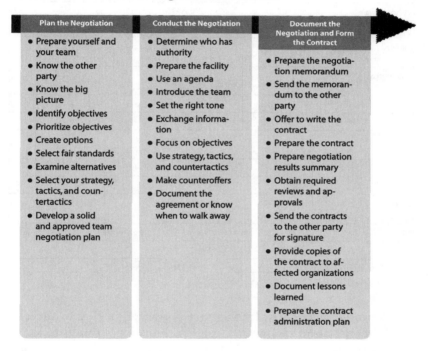

Plan the Negotiation	Conduct the Negotiation	Document the Negotiation and Form the Contract
• Prepare yourself and your team • Know the other party • Know the big picture • Identify objectives • Prioritize objectives • Create options • Select fair standards • Examine alternatives • Select your strategy, tactics, and countertactics • Develop a solid and approved team negotiation plan	• Determine who has authority • Prepare the facility • Use an agenda • Introduce the team • Set the right tone • Exchange information • Focus on objectives • Use strategy, tactics, and countertactics • Make counteroffers • Document the agreement or know when to walk away	• Prepare the negotiation memorandum • Send the memorandum to the other party • Offer to write the contract • Prepare the contract • Prepare negotiation results summary • Obtain required reviews and approvals • Send the contracts to the other party for signature • Provide copies of the contract to affected organizations • Document lessons learned • Prepare the contract administration plan

Plan the Negotiation

The following ten actions should be performed to properly plan the negotiation:

1. *Prepare yourself and your team:* Ensure that the lead negotiator knows his or her personal and professional strengths, weaknesses, and tendencies as well as those of other team members. Many self-assessment tools are available to help with this task, including the Myers-Briggs Type Indicator® assessment. These tools can provide helpful insight on how an individual may react in a situation because of personal or professional tendencies. Preparing a list of the strengths and weaknesses of team

members can be an important first step in negotiation planning (see Form 6-1).

Form 6-1	
Team Members Strengths, Weaknesses and Interests	
Team Member	**Team Member**
Name	Name
Job Title	Job Title
Phone No.	Phone No.
Fax No.	Fax No.
E-Mail:	E-Mail:
Strengths 1	Strengths 1
2	2
3	3
Weaknesses 1	Weaknesses 1
2	2
3	3
Interests 1	Interests 1
2	2
3	3

Date Prepared:_____   Lead Negotiator:_____

2. *Know the other party:* Intelligence gathering is vital to successful negotiation planning. Create a checklist of things to know about the other party to help the team prepare for negotiation (see Form 6-2). Listed below are a few suggested questions which you should discuss with your team members to ensure you understand as much as possible about your organization and the other side.

Form 6-2
Things to Know About the Other Party

Buyer and Seller

- ❐ What is the organization's overall business strategy?
- ❐ What is its reputation?
- ❐ What is its current company business environment?
- ❐ Who is the lead negotiator?
- ❐ Who are the primary decision makers?
- ❐ What are their key objectives?
- ❐ What are their overall contract objectives?
- ❐ What are their personal objectives?
- ❐ Who or what influences the decision makers?
- ❐ What internal organization barriers do they face?

Seller Only

- ❐ When does the buyer need our products or services?
- ❐ How much money does the buyer have to spend?
- ❐ Where does the buyer want our products and services delivered?
- ❐ What benefits will our products and services provide?
- ❐ What is our company's past experiences with this buyer?

Date Prepared:_____ Lead Negotiator:_____

3. *Know the big picture:* In the words of Stephen R. Covey, author of *The Seven Habits of Highly Effective People,* "begin with the end in mind." Keep focused on the primary objectives. Be aware that the ability of either party to be flexible on some issues may be limited because of internal policies, budgets, or organizational politics.

   One of the proven best practices to keep the negotiation focused is using interim summaries. The key is not to get caught up in small, unimportant details that take the negotiation off track.

4. *Identify objectives:* Know what both you and the other party want to accomplish. Successful negotiators know that nearly everything affects price (see Figure 6-3): changes in schedule, technology, services, terms and conditions, customer obligations, contract type, products, and other contracting elements.

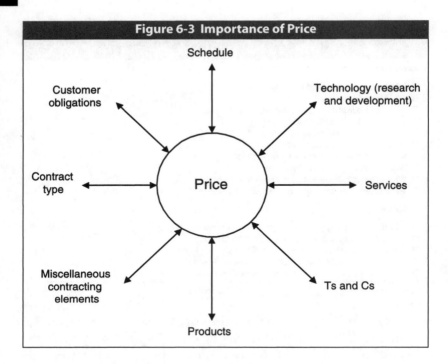

Figure 6-3 Importance of Price

You can easily identify a novice or apprentice negotiator because they always want to discuss price first. An experienced negotiator knows you should agree to all of the terms and conditions (Ts and Cs) first. Price is the last item a master negotiator will discuss and agree to with the other side. Master negotiators know what the big print giveth and the little print taketh away.

Form 6-3	
Objectives Identification	
Seller Objectives	**Buyer Objectives**
Personal 1	Personal 1
2	2
3	3
4	4
5	5
Professional 1	Professional 1
2	2
3	3
4	4
5	5
6	6
7	7

Date Prepared:_____   Lead Negotiator:_____

5. *Prioritize objectives:* Although all terms and conditions are important, some are clearly more important than others. Prioritize your objectives to help you remain focused during negotiation. Figure 6-4 shows that various terms and conditions affect cost, risk, and value.

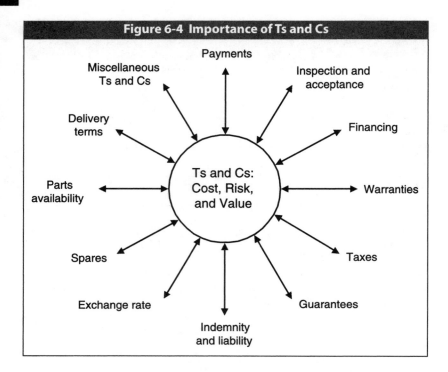

Figure 6-4 Importance of Ts and Cs

It is important for contract negotiators to truly understand and appreciate that all terms and conditions (Ts and Cs) contained in the deal have a cost, risk, and value associated with them and their specific wording. The exact wording of the deal is critical in contract negotiations.

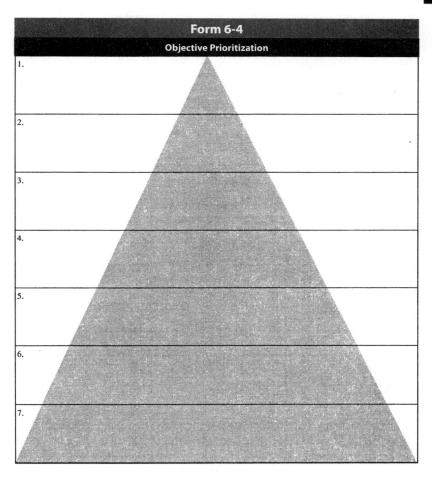

| Form 6-4 |
| Objective Prioritization |

1.

2.

3.

4.

5.

6.

7.

Date Prepared: _____   Lead Negotiator: _____

6. *Create options:* Creative problem solving is a critical skill of successful negotiators. Seek to expand options; do not assume that only one solution exists to every problem. Conducting team brainstorming sessions to develop a list of options to achieve negotiation objectives is a proven best practice of many world-class organizations (see Form 6-5).

Form 6-5		
Create Options for Achieving Negotiation Objectives		
Seller Objectives	**Possible Options**	**Buyer Objectives**

Date Prepared:_____ Lead Negotiator:_____

7. *Select fair standards:* Successful negotiators avoid a contest of wills by turning an argument into a joint search for a fair solution, using fair standards independent of either side's will. Use standards such as the—

■ Uniform Commercial Code
■ United Nations Convention on Contracts for the International Sale of Goods
■ American Arbitration Association standards
■ ISO 9000 quality standards
■ State, local, and federal laws
■ Market or industry standards

8. *Examine alternatives:* Prepare in advance your alternatives to the important negotiation issues or objectives. Successful negotiators know their best-case, most-likely, and worst-case (walk-away) alternatives for all major objectives (see Form 6-6).

Form 6-6		
Objectives and Alternatives-Worst Case, Most Likely, and Best Case		
Objective:		
Worst Case	Most Likely	Best Case

◆————————————————————————————◆

(Plot your most likely position)

Date Prepared:_____ Lead Negotiator:_____

9. *Select your strategy, tactics, and countertactics:* Negotiation strategies provide the overall framework that will guide how you conduct your negotiation. Negotiation strategies can be divided into two types: win-lose and win-win.

The win-lose negotiation strategy is about winning today, despite the potential long-term effect tomorrow and beyond. Common characteristics of the win-lose strategy include concealing one's own position and interests, discovering the other party's position and interests, weakening the other party's resolve, and causing the other party to modify its position or accept your position on all key issues. Although the win-lose negotiation strategy is not a politically correct approach, it is a commonly used negotiation strategy worldwide.

The win-win negotiation strategy is about creative joint problem solving, which develops long-term successful business relationships. The win-win negotiation strategy, however, may sometimes be difficult to accomplish. Among the obstacles to developing the win-win business environment are previous adverse buyer-seller relations, lack of training in joint problem solving and conflict resolution, and complex and highly regulated contracting procedures in some organizations, especially large companies and government agencies.

Winning or losing a contract negotiation is, indeed, a matter of perspective, which is based on your knowledge, experience, and judgment. The only way to know whether you have won or lost a negotiation is to compare the results to your negotiation plan. Did you get what you wanted? Is what you got closer to your best-case, most-likely, or worst-case alternative? Clearly, without a contract negotiation plan, you have no basis against which to evaluate the negotiation outcome.

To achieve your desired contract negotiation results, you need not only a strategy, but also tactics and countertactics, which are a means to a desired end.

10. *Develop a solid and approved team negotiation plan:* The conclusion of contract negotiation planning should be the summary and documentation of all planned actions. If necessary, have the negotiation plan reviewed and approved by higher management to ensure that all planned actions are in the best interests of the organization (see Form 6-7).

Form 6-7
Sample Negotiation Planning Summary

Negotiation Information

Location	Date	Time
1	1	1
2	2	2
3	3	3

Key Objectives (Plot your most likely position)

1. Price
Worst Case ———————————●——————— Best Case $10.5M $12.0M $12.5M

2. Payments
Worst Case ———————————●——————— Best Case After Delivery Progress payments Advance payments

3. Warranty period
Worst Case ———————————●——————— Best Case 36 months 18 months 12 months Industry average

4.
Worst Case ————————————————— Best Case

5.
Worst Case ————————————————— Best Case

Form 6-7 – Continued

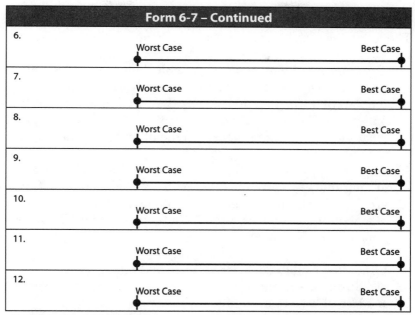

6.

Worst Case   Best Case

7.

Worst Case   Best Case

8.

Worst Case   Best Case

9.

Worst Case   Best Case

10.

Worst Case   Best Case

11.

Worst Case   Best Case

12.

Worst Case   Best Case

Possible Tactics and Countertactics

Objective	Planned Tactics — Buyer	Planned Countertactics — Seller

Contract Price

Range	
Best Case	
Most Likely	
Worst Case	

Date Prepared:_____ Lead Negotiator:_____
Approved by:_____ Date Approved:_____

Conduct the Negotiation

The following activities are necessary to conduct the negotiation:

11. *Determine who has authority:* If possible, before the negotiation, determine who has the authority to negotiate for each party. At the start of the negotiation, ensure that you know who has that authority, who the lead negotiator is for the other party, and what limits, if any, are placed on the other party's authority.

12. *Prepare the facility:* Most buyers want to conduct the negotiation at their offices to provide them with a sense of control. If you are the seller try to conduct the negotiation at your location or at a neutral site, such as a hotel, conference center, via conference call, or Net-meeting.

    Other key facility considerations include the—
    ■ Size of the room
    ■ Use of break-out rooms
    ■ Lighting
    ■ Tables (size, shape, and arrangement)
    ■ Seating arrangements
    ■ Use of audiovisual aids
    ■ Schedule (day and time)
    ■ Access to telephone, fax, e-mail/Internet access, restrooms, food, and drink

13. *Use an agenda:* A proven best practice of successful negotiators worldwide is creating and using an agenda for the negotiation. Provide the agenda to the other party before the negotiation begins (see Form 6-8). An effective agenda helps a negotiator to—
    ■ Set the right tone
    ■ Control the exchange of information
    ■ Keep the focus on the objectives
    ■ Manage time
    ■ Obtain the desired results

Form 6-8	
Negotiation Agenda	

Contract

Title	Date
Location	Time

Topics of Action	**Time**
❏ Introduce team members	_____
❏ Provide overview and discuss purpose of negotiation	_____
❏ Exchange information on key interests and issues	_____
❏ Quantity of products	_____
■ Quality of products and services	
■ Past performance	
■ Delivery schedule	
■ Maintenance	
■ Training	
❏ Have a break	_____
❏ Review agreement on all key interests and issues	_____
❏ Agree on detailed terms and conditions	_____
❏ Agree on price	_____
❏ Review and summarize meeting	_____

Date Prepared:_____ Lead Negotiator:_____

14. *Introduce the team*: Introduce your team members, or have team members make brief self-introductions. Try to establish a common bond with the other party as soon as possible.

15. *Set the right tone:* After introductions, make a brief statement to express your team strategy to the other party. Set the desired climate for contract negotiation from the start.

16. *Exchange information:* Conducting contract negotiation is all about communication. Be aware that information is exchanged both orally and through body language, visual aids (pictures, diagrams, photographs, or videotapes), and active listening.

17. *Focus on objectives:* Never lose sight of the big picture.

18. *Use strategy, tactics, and countertactics:* Do what you said you were going to do, but be flexible to achieve your objectives. Anticipate the other party's tactics, and plan your countertactics. Adjust them as necessary.

19. *Make counteroffers:* A vital part of conducting the negotiation is providing substitute offers, or counteroffers, when the other party does not accept what you are offering. Document all offers and counteroffers to ensure that both parties understand any changes in the terms and conditions.

When offers and counteroffers are done right, they are part art and science. A seller should know the approximate range (monetary amount) the buyer intends to spend. Plus, a well prepared seller should know approximately what their competitors are likely to offer and the approximate price. Likewise, well informed and prepared Buyer's know what approximate range (monetary amount) the seller's are likely to seek. When well prepared Buyers and Sellers enter into the exchange of offers and counteroffers there should exist a negotiation zone (see Table 6-3).

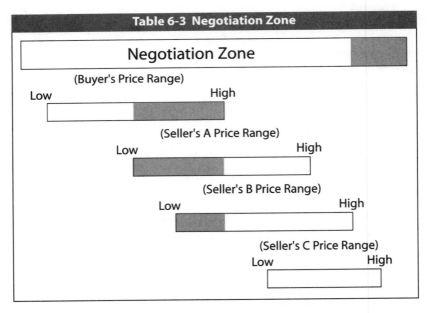

Table 6-3 Negotiation Zone

Given a competitive source business environment, sellers must ensure their initial offer is not so high that they will be eliminated from the competition. However, a seller must also ensure they maintain a healthy profit margin and still have room in their offer to give further price reductions if necessary to capture the business. Clearly, every seller must perform a balancing act between their desire to win business vs. their need to reduce/mitigate risks, while maximizing revenue and profit.

As illustrated in the Negotiation Zone (Table 6-3), every Buyer has a monetary range they expect to spend for their required products and/or services, which vary (low to high) based upon numerous variables typically contained within contract terms and conditions. Further, as depicted in Table 6-3, each Seller (A, B, or C) has a monetary range, typically described in their approved business case, within which they can make offers and counteroffers, based upon their costs, risks, desired profit margin, and preferred terms and conditions.

Once both parties have made their initial offer, then the fun really begins. How do you determine how much to move? Do you alter your terms and conditions in conjunction with changes in pricing? Do you offer a different type of pricing arrangement i.e. Fixed-Price to Time & Materials or Cost-Plus-Fixed Fee (see Table 6-4 Advantages, Disadvantages & Suitability of Various Contract types)? Should you refuse to move to force the other party to counteroffer? The answers to all of the above questions is – it depends! That is why, experienced highly skilled master contract negotiators are a valuable asset to every organization involved in detailed, complex, and expensive contract negotiations.

Table 6-4

Advantages, Disadvantages, and Suitability of Various Contract Types

Type	Essential Elements and Advantages	Disadvantages	Suitability
Firm Fixed Price (FFP)	Reasonably definite design or performance specifications available. Fair and reasonable price can be established at outset. Conditions for use include the following: Adequate competition Prior purchase experience of the same, or similar, supplies or services under competitive conditions. Valid cost or pricing data. Realistic estimates of proposed cost. Possible uncertainties in performance can be identified and priced. Sellers willing to accept contract at a level that causes them to take all financial risks Any other reasonable basis for pricing can be used to establish fair and reasonable price.	Price not subject to adjustment regardless of seller performance costs. Places 100% of financial risk on seller. Places least amount of administrative burden on contract manager. Preferred over all other contract types. Used with advertised or negotiated procurements.	Commercial products and commercial services for which reasonable prices can be established.
Fixed Price with Economic Price Adjustment (FP/EPA)	Unstable market or labor conditions during performance period and contingencies that would otherwise be included in contract price can be identified and made the subject of a separate price adjustment clause. Contingencies must be specifically defined in contract. Provides for upward adjustment (with ceiling) in contract price. May provide for downward adjustment of price if escalated element has potential of falling below contract limits. Three general types of EPAs, based on established prices, actual costs of labor or material, and cost indexes of labor or material.	Price can be adjusted on action of an industry-wide contingency that is beyond seller's control. Reduces seller's fixed-price risk. FP/EPA is preferred over any CR-type contract. If contingency manifests, contract administration burden increases. Used with negotiated procurements and, in limited applications, with formal advertising when determined to be feasible. CM must determine if FP/EPA is necessary either to protect seller and buyer against significant fluctuations in labor or material costs or to provide for contract price adjustment in case of changes in seller's established prices.	Commercial products and services for which reasonable prices can be established at time of award.

	Table 6-4 - continued		
Type	**Essential Elements and Advantages**	**Disadvantages**	**Suitability**
Fixed Price Incentive (FPI)	Cost uncertainties exist, but there is potential for cost reduction or performance improvement by giving seller a degree of cost responsibility and a positive profit incentive.	Requires adequate seller accounting system.	Development and production of high-volume, multiyear contracts.
	Profit is earned or lost based on relationship that contract's final negotiated cost bears to total target cost.	Buyer must determine that FPI is least costly and award of any other type would be impractical.	
	Contract must contain target cost, target profit, ceiling price, and profit-sharing formula.	Buyer and seller administrative effort is more extensive than under other fixed-price contract types.	
	Two forms of FPI: firm target (FPIF) and successive targets (FPIS).	Used only with competitive negotiated contracts.	
	FPIF: Firm target cost, target profit, and profit-sharing formula negotiated into basic contract; profit adjusted at contract completion.	Billing prices must be established for interim payment.	
	FPIS: Initial cost and profit targets negotiated into contract, but final cost target (firm) cannot be negotiated until performance.		
	Contains production point(s) at which either a firm target and final profit formula, or a FFP contract, can be negotiated.		
	Elements that can be incentives: costs, performance, delivery, quality.		
Cost-Reimbursement Contracts (Greatest Risk on Buyer)			
Cost	Appropriate for research and development work, particularly with nonprofit educational institutions or other nonprofit organizations, and for facilities contracts.	Application limited due to no fee and by the fact that the buyer is not willing to reimburse seller fully if there is a commercial benefit for the seller. Only nonprofit institutions and organizations are willing (usually) to perform research for which there is no fee (or other tangible benefits)	Research and development; facilities.
	Allowable costs of contract performance are reimbursed, but no fee is paid.		

Table 6-4 - continued

Type	Essential Elements and Advantages	Disadvantages	Suitability
Cost Sharing (CS)	Used when buyer and seller agree to share costs in a research or development project having potential mutual benefits. Because of commercial benefits accruing to the seller, no fee is paid. Seller agrees to absorb a portion of the costs of performance in expectation of compensating benefits to seller's firm or organization. Such benefits might include an enhancement of the seller's capability and expertise or an improvement of its competitive position in the commercial market.	Care must be taken in negotiating cost-share rate so that the cost ratio is proportional to the potential benefit (that is, the party receiving the greatest potential benefit bears the greatest share of the costs).	Research and development that has potential benefits to both the buyer and the seller.
Cost-Reimbursement Contracts (Greatest Risk on Buyer)			
Cost Plus Incentive Fee (CPIF)	Development has a highly probability that is feasible and positive profit incentives for seller management can be negotiated. Performance incentives must be clearly spelled out and objectively measurable. Fee range should be negotiated to give the seller an incentive over various ranges of cost performance. Fee is adjusted by a formula negotiated into the contract in accordance with the relationship that total cost bears to target cost. Contract must contain target cost, target fee, minimum and maximum fees, fee adjustment formula. Fee adjustment is made at completion of contract.	Difficult to negotiate range between the maximum and minimum fees so as to provide an incentive over entire range. Performance must be objectively measurable. Costly to administer; seller must have an adequate accounting system. Used only with negotiated contracts. Appropriate buyer surveillance needed during performance to ensure effective methods and efficient cost controls are used.	Major systems development and other development programs in which it is determined that CPIF is desirable and administratively practical.

	Table 6-4 - continued		
Type	**Essential Elements and Advantages**	**Disadvantages**	**Suitability**
Cost Plus Award Fee (CPAF)	Contract completion is feasible, incentives are desired, but performance is not susceptible to finite measurement. Provides for subjective evaluation of seller performance. Seller is evaluated at stated time(s) during performance period. Contract must contain clear and unambiguous evaluation criteria to determine award fee. Award fee is earned for excellence in performance, quality, timeliness, ingenuity, and cost-effectiveness and can be earned in whole or in part. Two separate fee pools can be established in contract: base fee and award fee. Award fee earned by seller is determined by the buyer and is often based on recommendations of an award fee evaluation board.	Buyer's determination of amount of award fee earned by the seller is not subject to disputes clause. CPAF cannot be used to avoid either CPIF or CPFF if either is feasible. Should not be used if the amount of money, period of performance, or expected benefits are insufficient to warrant additional administrative efforts. Very costly to administer. Seller must have an adequate accounting system. Used only with negotiated contracts.	Level-of-effort services that can only be subjectively measured, and contracts for which work would have been accomplished under another contract type if performance objectives could have been expressed as definite milestones, targets, and goals that could have been measured.
Cost Plus Fixed Fee (CPFF)	Level of effort is unknown, and seller's performance cannot be subjectively evaluated. Provides for payment of a fixed fee. Seller receives fixed fee regardless of the actual costs incurred during performance. Can be constructed in two ways: Completion form: Clearly defined task with a definite goal and specific end product. Buyer can order more work without an increase in fee if the contract's estimated costs are increased. Term form: Scope of work described in general terms. Seller obligated only for a specific level of effort for stated period of time. Completion form is preferred over term form. Fee is expressed as percentages of estimated cost at time contract is awarded	Seller has minimum incentive to control costs. Costly to administer. Seller must have an adequate accounting system. Seller assumes no financial risk.	Completion form: Advanced development or technical services contracts. Term form: Research and exploratory development. Used when the level of effort required is known and there is an inability to measure risk.

Table 6-4 - continued		
Type	**Essential Elements and Advantages**	**Disadvantages**	**Suitability**
Time and Materials			
Time and Material (T&M)	Not possible when placing contract to estimate extent or duration of the work, or anticipated cost, with any degree of confidence. Calls for provision of direct labor hours at specified hourly rate and materials at cost (or some other basis specified in contract). The fixed hourly rates include wages, overhead, general and administrative expenses, and profit. Material cost can include, if appropriate, material handling costs. Ceiling price established at time of award.	Used only after determination that no other type will serve purpose. Does not encourage effective cost control. Requires almost constant surveillance by buyer to ensure effective seller management. Ceiling price is required in contract.	Engineering and design services in conjunction with the production of suppliers, engineering design and manufacture, repair, maintenance, and overhaul work to be performed on an as-needed basis.

Form 6-9, provides a simple, yet, effective means of documenting offers and counteroffers exchanged during contract negotiations. Remember, the number of offers and counteroffers exchanged is not as important as the value of the concessions made.

Form 6-9	
Offers and Counteroffers Summary	
Seller	**Buyer**
Offer	Counteroffer
Offer	Counteroffer
Offer	Counteroffer
Offer	Counteroffer
Date Prepared:_____	Lead Negotiator:_____

20. *Document the agreement or know when to walk away:* Take time throughout the negotiation to take notes on what was agreed to between the parties. If possible, assign one team member to take minutes. To ensure proper documentation, periodically summarize agreements on all major issues throughout the negotiation. At the end of the negotiation, summarize your agreements both orally and in writing (see Form 6-10). If a settlement is not reached, document the areas of agreement and disagreement. If possible, plan a future meeting to resolve differences.

Remember: Do not agree to a bad deal—learn to say, "No thank you," and walk away.

Form 6-10	
Negotiation Results Summary	

Contract Title	Date of Contract
Parties Involved	Date(s) of Negotiation
Brief Product/Service Description	Location
Agreed to Price	
Key changes from Approved Proposal	

Date Prepared:_____ Lead Negotiator:_____

Document the Negotiations and Form the Contract

The following activities are conducted to document the negotiation and form the contract.

21. *Prepare the negotiation memorandum (minutes or notes):* Document what was discussed during the negotiation. After having the memorandum word processed, spell checked, and edited, have it reviewed by someone within your organization who attended the negotiation and someone who did not. Then determine whether they have a similar understanding.

22. *Send the memorandum to the other party:* As promptly as possible, provide a copy of your documented understanding of the contract negotiation to the other party. First, e-mail or fax it to the other party. Then send an original copy by either overnight or 2-day mail. Verify that the other party receives your negotiation memorandum by following up with an e-mail or telephone call, or send by registered mail, return receipt requested.

23. *Offer to write the contract:* As the seller, offer to draft the agreement so that you can put the issues in your own words. Today, most contracts are developed using electronic databases, which facilitate reviews, changes, and new submissions.

24. *Prepare the contract:* Writing a contract should be a team effort with an experienced contract management professional at the lead. Typically, automated standard organizational forms, modified as needed, are used with standard terms and condi-

tions that were tailored during negotiation. At other times, a contract must be written in full. Ensure that no elements of the contract are missing (see Form 6-11). After the initial contract draft, obtain all appropriate reviews and approvals, preferably through electronic data.

Form 6-11		
Essential Contract Elements Checklist		
Project Name	Prepared by (Print)	Date Prepared
Cus-tomer	Telephone/Fax	e-mail
❑ Deliverables and prices (provide a listing of deliverables and their prices)		
❑ Deliverable conformance specifications		
❑ Requirements in statement of work (determine SOW requirements not listed as deliverables)		
❑ Delivery requirements (list delivery requirements, deliverable packaging and shipping requirements, and service performance instructions)		
❑ Deliverable inspection and acceptance		
❑ Invoice and payment schedule and provisions (include in contract tracking summary)		
❑ Representations and certifications		
❑ Other terms and conditions		

25. *Prepare negotiation results summary:* Prepare an internal-use-only summary of key negotiation items that have changed since originally proposed. Many organizations have found such a summary to be a valuable tool for explaining changes to senior managers.

26. *Obtain required reviews and approvals:* Depending on your organizational procedures, products, services, and other variables, one or more people may be required to review and approve the proposed contract before signature. Typically, the following departments or staff review a contract: project management, financial, legal, procurement or contract management, and senior management. Increasingly, organizations are using automated systems to draft contracts and transmit them internally for the needed reviews and approvals.

27. *Send the contract to the other party for signature:* Send a copy of the contract to the other party via e-mail or fax, and then follow up with two mailed original copies. With all copies include an appropriate cover letter with a return mail address and time/date suspense for prompt return. Verify receipt of

the contract by phone or e-mail. Today, many organizations, as well as the laws of many nations, recognize an electronic signature to be valid.

28. *Provide copies of the contract to affected organizations:* The contract is awarded officially after it is executed, signed by both parties, and delivered to both parties. Ensure that all other affected organizations or parties receive a copy.

29. *Document lessons learned:* Take the time to document everything that went well during the contract negotiation process. Even more important, document what did not go well and why, and what should be done to avoid those problems in the future.

30. *Prepare the contract administration plan:* At the end of the contract negotiation process, follow a proven best practice by having the team that negotiated the contract help the team that is responsible for administering it develop a contract administration plan.

The following graphic (Table 6-5), provides a checklist of proven effective contract negotiation Best Practices. How many of the actions listed in Table 6-5 do you and your organization both know and do? Remember, knowing what to do is good, but, doing it is better!

Table 6-5
Checklist of Buyer - Contract Negotiation Best Practices

The Buyer Should:
- Know what you want-lowest price or best value
- State your requirements in performance terms and evaluate accordingly
- Conduct market research about potential sources before selection
- Evaluate potential sources promptly and dispassionately
- Follow the evaluation criteria stated in the solicitation: management, technical, and price
- Use absolute, minimum, or relative evaluation standards to measure performance as stated in your solicitation
- Develop organizational policies to guide and facilitate the source selection process
- Use a weighting system to determine which evaluation criteria are most important
- Use a screening system to prequalify sources
- Obtain independent estimates from consultants or outside experts to assist in source selection
- Use past performance as a key aspect of source selection, and verify data accuracy
- Conduct price realism analysis
- Create a competitive analysis report
- Use oral presentations or proposals by sellers to improve and expedite the source selection process

Table 6-5 (cont)
Checklist of Contract Negotiation Best Practices

The Buyer and Seller Should:
- Understand that contract negotiation is a process, usually involving a team effort
- Select and train highly skilled negotiators to lead the contract negotiation process
- Know market and industry practices
- Prepare yourself and your team
- Know the other party
- Know the big picture
- Identify and prioritize objectives
- Create options-be flexible in your planning
- Examine alternatives
- Select your negotiation strategy, tactics, and countertactics
- Develop a solid and approved team negotiation plan
- Determine who has the authority to negotiate
- Prepare the negotiation facility at your location or at a neutral site
- Use an agenda during contract negotiation
- Set the right tone at the start of the negotiation
- Maintain your focus on your objectives
- Use interim summaries to keep on track
- Do not be too predictable in your tactics
- Document your agreement throughout the process
- Know when to walk away
- Offer to write the contract
- Prepare a negotiation results summary
- Obtain required reviews and approvals
- Provide copies of the contract to all affected parties
- Document negotiation lessons learned and best practices
- Prepare a transition plan for contract administration
- Understand that everything affects price
- Understand the Ts and Cs have cost, risk, and value
- Tailor Ts and Cs to the deal, but understand the financial effects on price and profitability
- Know what is negotiable and what is not

Desired Outputs

- **Contract:** The output from negotiations and contract formation may be the contract, which is both a document and a relationship between parties.

    Or it may be best to—

- **Walk away:** Do not agree to a bad deal. No business is better than bad business.

Straight Talk: Suggestions for Significant Improvement

It is our belief most organizations do not maximize their contract negotiation talent, skills, and best practices. Rather, most organizations have one or a few top contract negotiators, which they leverage to conduct most or all of their big deals. Few organizations have really created a knowledge transfer/management program to ensure contract negotiation skills and best practices are effectively transferred throughout their organization. Few organizations have created contract negotiator mentor programs, to help develop future world-class contract negotiators. Very few organizations have developed internal contract negotiation workshops or even conduct mock negotiations to help business professionals properly prepare for major contract negotiations. Too much time is spent learning the latest software program and how to fill out the basic forms and charts to report status to management and not enough time is spent training and preparing contract managers to negotiate deals, tailor terms and conditions, form an appropriate contract, and administer large complex contracts with frequent contract changes.

Summary

Contract negotiation and contract formation is vital to the success of buyers and sellers worldwide. When skilled contract negotiators follow a proven process approach, successful business agreements are reached. Through effective contract formation practices, win-win contracts are developed and documented, yielding beneficial results for both parties.

Remember, in the words of Dr. Chester Karrass, author, consultant, and master contract negotiator, "You don't get what you deserve, you get what you have the ability to negotiate." A major goal of the reader should be mastering the contract negotiation process by using a logical, organized, documented, step-by-step approach to build successful business relationships. The highly effective contract negotiation process discussed in this chapter has been taught to more than 20,000 business professionals worldwide via the National Contract Management Association (NCMA), The George Washington University School of Business, The Keller Graduate School of DeVry University, Villanova University On-Line Masters Certificate Program in Contract Management, the University of California at Los Angeles, the U.S. Naval Postgraduate School, just to name a few, with outstanding results. I hope that you will consider using the contract negotiation process, forms, and best practices discussed in this chapter and throughout this book.

Questions to Consider

1. How would you describe your organization's typical contract negotiation preparation process?

2. How effectively does your organization share knowledge regarding the use of successful contract negotiation strategies, tactics, and countertactics?

3. How well do you plan, conduct, and document contract negotiations?

4. What areas of the contract negotiation process does your organization really need to improve?

CHAPTER 7

POST-BID/
PROPOSAL PHASE
CONTRACT
PERFORMANCE,
ADMINISTRATION,
& CLOSEOUT

INTRODUCTION

According to the International Association for Contract and Commercial Management (IACCM) "the average contract management group spends most of its time on pre-award contract development, bid support and negotiation." Now there is a surprise – not! Contract performance is simply each party doing what they said they were going to do in the solicitation, bid/proposal, and in the contract. Contract administration is the process of ensuring that each party's performance meets contractual requirements. On larger projects with multiple product and service providers, a key aspect of contract administration is managing the interfaces among the various providers. Because of the legal nature of the contractual relationship, the project team must be acutely aware of the legal implications of actions taken when administering the contract.

The principal objective of contract administration is the same for both parties–to ensure the fulfillment of the contractual obligations by all the parties to the contract. If the parties are individuals, this task is a matter of self-discipline. However, when organizations are involved, the problem is more complicated. Organizations must perform as systems, integrating the efforts of many people who compose the components of the organization. Thus, for organizations to function efficiently requires communication and control, which is the primary task of contract administration, see Figure 7-1, The Buying & Selling Life-Cycle.

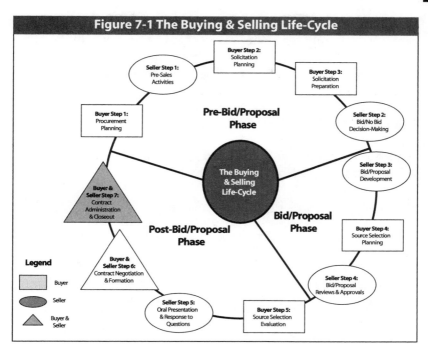

Figure 7-1 The Buying & Selling Life-Cycle

Effective contract administration is critical to effective project management, because an organization's failure to fulfill its contractual obligations could have legal consequences. Thus, someone must observe performance of contractual obligations. That person is the contract manager, who must always be aware of the legal consequences of an action or a failure to act and who must take steps to ensure that required actions are taken and prohibited actions are avoided. In a real sense, a contract manager is a project manager, and the principles of project management apply to his or her work. IACCM's survey on the Contract Management role, structure, and headcount was targeted at Sales Contracting (the sellers side) not the procurement groups (the buyers side). IACCM's survey revealed a virtual dead-heat in Contract Management reporting line, with 27% reporting to Finance, 27% reporting to Sales and 25% reporting to Legal. The next largest group 15% was business operations. No matter where contract management reports contract administration needs to be accomplished, but, clearly some functional areas care more about contract performance and administration than others.

Each party to the contract should appoint a contract manager, who monitors not only his or her own organization but also the other party to ensure that both parties are keeping their promises. The contract manager must maintain these two perspectives throughout contract performance. Contract performance and administration is largely commitment management, as illustrated by Figure 7-2, Contract Administration, & Closeout Process.

Figure 7-2 Buyer and Seller Step 7: Contract Performance, Administration, & Closeout Process

Input	Tools & Techniques	Output
• Contract • Work results • Change requests • Invoices and payments • Contract administration policies	• Contract analysis and planning • Preperformance conference • Performance measuring and reporting • Payment system • Change control system • Dispute management system • Contract closeout checklist	• Documentation • Contract changes • Payment • Completion of work • Contract closeout or • Contract termination

Adapted from: World Class Contracting, by Gregory A. Garrett, CCH, 2003

Contract administration includes applying the appropriate project management processes to the contractual relationships and integrating the output from these processes into the general management of the project.

Inputs

Inputs to contract administration consists of the following items:

■ *Contract:* The contract document is the primary guide for administering the contract.
■ *Work results:* The results of performing the requirement will affect the administration of the contract.
■ *Change requests:* Change requests are a common element of most contracts. An effective process for managing change must be in place to ensure that all requests are handled smoothly. Changes may be called amendments, modifications, add-ons, up-scopes,

or down-scopes. Changes are opportunities either to increase or decrease profitability for the seller. Changes are a necessary aspect of business for buyers, because of changes in their needs.

■ *Invoices and payments:* An efficient process must be developed for handling invoices and payments throughout contract administration. Few areas cause more concern to sellers than late payment. Buyers can realize savings by developing an efficient and timely payment process, because sellers are often willing to give discounts for early payment.

■ *Contract administration policies:* Although the specific policies that will apply to contract administration depend on the contracting parties, four policies are key: compliance with contract terms and conditions, effective internal and external communication and control, effective control of contract changes, and effective resolution of claims and disputes. These policies will be discussed further in this chapter in "Contract Administration Policies."

Tools and Techniques

The following tools and techniques are used for contract administration:

■ *Contract analysis and planning:* Before the award of a contract, each party should develop a contract administration plan and assign the responsibility of administering the contract to a contract manager. To whom should the job be assigned? A project manager could do double duty as contract manager. However in most large companies, contract administration is a specialized function, usually performed by someone in the contracting department, because doing the job will require special knowledge and training.

Contract administration is an element of both contract management and project management. If the project is under a contract, then project management and contract administration will overlap considerably, depending on how the company defines those terms. If the project is not under a contract but contracts to obtain goods and services essential to project implementation, contract administration will be a smaller element of project management.

Assume for the moment that a project is under a contract and that the project manager and contract manager are different people. What should their relationship be? Although organizations divide the responsibilities differently, in general, the project manager will have overall responsibility for executing the project, and the contract manager will oversee the contractual aspects of the project. The contract manager's special knowledge and training about contracts will be an asset to the project manager. Whether the contract manager reports to the project manager or to someone else will depend on whether the work is organized along project, functional, or matrix lines of authority.

In anticipation of contract award, the project manager and contract manager should analyze the terms and conditions of the prospective contract and develop a work breakdown structure that reflects both the technical and administrative aspects of contract performance. They should then determine which departments of the organization will be affected by those terms and conditions.

Many functional managers will be affected by contract terms and conditions. Consider, for example, the following clause from a services contract:

Fitness of Employees

Seller shall employ on or in connection with the Project only persons who are fit and skilled for the Project. Should any objectionable person be employed by Seller, Seller shall, upon request of ABC Company, cause such person to be removed from the Project.

Clauses of this type are not unusual in services contracts, particularly when the work will be performed at the buyer's facility. The clause is not unreasonable, and to many it would even seem innocuous. Not so, however, because this clause has potentially great significance to a company's human resources department and for labor relations in general. The human resources department may have specific procedures for removing an employee from an assignment. Therefore, the project manager and contract manager should contact that department to discuss the contract and the appropriate personnel procedures to be followed.

The project manager and contract manager must meet with the managers of all affected functional areas to inform them of the contract, the terms and conditions related to their operations, and contract administration policies and procedures. In some companies, the functional managers will already know about the contract and will have made preliminary preparations for performance. In others, they will not have been informed and may be completely unprepared for what they must do.

The project manager and contract manager should try to reach agreement on intermediate performance goals with each manager who has performance responsibility. Intermediate goals will enable the contract manager and the functional manager to measure progress, detect significant performance variances, take corrective action, and follow up. Of course, performance goals must reflect contract performance obligations.

The project manager, contract manager, and other business managers also must decide how and when to measure and report actual performance. The techniques, timing, and frequency of measurement and reporting should reflect the nature and criticality of the work. A reasonable balance must be struck between excessive reporting and no measurement or reporting of any kind. Functional managers may see these requirements as nuisances that are of little value to themselves.

The realities of contract administration, however, are often quite different from the ideal situation. First, most companies devote more effort to source selection and contract formation than to contract administration. Project commencement often depends on contract award, so more resources are devoted to startup than to oversight. Second, in performing these tasks, the project manager and contract manager will face all the challenges that confront all project managers, but their responsibility may not come with formal authority. In many companies, functional managers simply do not appreciate the importance of contracts and contract administration and will resent the imposition of what they see as additional performance burdens. Third, the project manager and contract manager may not have the luxury of working on only one project or contract at a time. Nevertheless, a reasonable effort must be made to ensure that all personnel recognize their responsibilities under the contract and attempt to ensure that those responsibilities are fulfilled.

■ *Preperformance conference:* Before performance begins, the buyer and the seller should meet to discuss their joint administration of the contract. The meeting should be formal; an agenda should be distributed in advance, and minutes should be taken and distributed. Each party should appoint a person who will be its organization's official voice during contract performance. At the meeting, the parties should review the contract terms and conditions and discuss who will do what. They also should establish protocols for written and oral communication and for progress measurement and reporting and discuss procedures for managing change and resolving differences. Buyer and seller department managers who will have performance responsibilities should attend the preperformance conference or, at the least, send a representative. Important subcontractors also should be represented. The meeting should be held at the performance site, if possible.

- *Performance measuring and reporting:* During contract administration, the project manager, contract manager, and responsible business managers must observe performance, collect information, and measure actual contract achievement. These activities are essential to effective control. The resources devoted to these tasks and the techniques used to perform them will depend on the nature of the contract work, the size and complexity of the contract, and the resources available. Performance measuring and reporting will be discussed further in this chapter in "Performance Measurement and Reporting."

- *Payment system:* Every contract must establish a clear invoicing and payment system or process. The buyer and seller must agree to whom invoices should be sent and what information is required. Sellers must submit proper invoices in a timely manner. Buyers should pay all invoices promptly. Sellers should insist that late payment penalty clauses be included in all contracts.

- *Change control system:* As a rule, any parties that can make a contract can agree to change it. Changes are usually inevitable in contracts for complex undertakings, such as system design and integration. No one has perfect foresight; requirements and circumstances change in unexpected ways, and contract terms and conditions must often be changed as a result (details are presented later in this chapter in "Change Management").

- *Dispute management system:* No one should be surprised when, from time to time, contracting parties find themselves in disagreement about the correct interpretation of contract terms and conditions. Most such disagreements are minor and are resolved without too much difficulty. Occasionally, however, the parties will find themselves entangled in a seemingly intractable controversy. Try as they might, they cannot resolve their differences. If the dispute goes unresolved for too long, one or both of the parties may threaten, or even initiate, litigation. Litigation is time consuming, costly, and risky. No one can ever be entirely sure of its result. It rarely results in a truly satisfactory resolution of a dispute, and it sours commercial relationships. For these reasons, it should be avoided. One goal of business managers and contract managers should be to resolve disputes without litigation whenever possible.

The keys to effective dispute resolution are as follows:

- Recognize that contract documents are not perfect
- Keep larger objectives in mind
- Focus on the facts
- Depersonalize the issues
- Be willing to make reasonable compromises

When disputes become intractable, seeking the opinion of an impartial third party can sometimes help. When this approach is formal, and the third party's decision is binding on the parties, it is called arbitration. Some companies include a clause in their contracts that makes arbitration the mandatory means of resolving disputes. Such a clause might read as follows:

Disputes

Should any dispute occur between the parties arising from or related to this Agreement, or their rights and responsibilities to each other, the matter shall be settled and determined by arbitration under the then current rules of the American Arbitration Association. The arbitration shall be conducted by a single arbitrator, the decision and award of the arbitrator shall be final and binding, and the award so rendered may be entered in any court having jurisdiction thereof. The language to be used in the arbitral proceeding shall be English.

In an international contract, the "Disputes" clause may be modified to provide for an international forum. The clause might read—

The arbitral tribunal shall be composed of three (3) arbitrators who shall be appointed by the Chairman of the Royal Arbitration Institute of the Stockholm Chamber of Commerce.

The arbitration process will be more formal than ordinary negotiation between the parties (which may be represented by attorneys), but it will be less formal than court proceedings.

Outputs

The following outputs result from contract administration:

- *Documentation:* Documentation is essential to provide proof of performance, management of changes, justification for claims, and evidence in the unlikely event of litigation.
  The most important documentation is the official copy of the contract, contract modifications, and conformed working copies of the contract. Other important forms of documentation include the following items:
  - *External and internal correspondence:* All contract correspondence should be electronically maintained by the contract manager in a central, chronological reading file, with separate data files for external and internal correspondence. Each piece of correspondence should be dated and assigned a file number. The project manager or contract manager should initial and date each piece of correspondence to acknowledge that it was read. Ideally, only one person should be authorized to correspond regarding contractual aspects with the other party to the contract. However, if more than one person on the project team is authorized to correspond with the other contract party, copies of all correspondence must be sent to the contract manager for filing. All mail, email, or faxes requiring an answer must be addressed promptly, preferably in writing; this is a fundamental rule of effective contract administration.
  - *Meeting minutes:* Minutes should be recorded for all meetings between the seller and the buyer. The minutes should state the date, time, and location of the meeting and identify all attendees by name, company or organization, and title. They should describe all issues discussed, decisions made, questions unresolved, and action items assigned. Copies of the minutes should be provided to each attendee and

to others interested in the meeting but unable to attend. Minutes of internal meetings must be kept only for purposes of project management, not for contract management.

- *Progress reports:* Progress reports should be electronically filed chronologically, by subject. The project manager and contract manager should initial and date each progress report to acknowledge that they have read it and are aware of its contents.
- *Project diaries:* On large projects, the project manager and contract manager should keep a daily diary, in which they record significant events of the day. They should update their diaries at the end of each workday. The entries should describe events in terms of who, what, when, where, and how. Preferably, the diary should be kept in a perfect-bound book with prenumbered pages or electronically in a shared-data file.

  A diary supplements memory and aids in recalling events. A diary is also useful as an informal project history when a new project manager or contract manager must take over. It can be of great assistance in preparing, negotiating, and settling claims or in the event of litigation. However, a diary may become evidence in court proceedings, so a diarist should be careful to record only facts, leaving out conclusions, speculations about motives, and personal opinions about people or organizations.
- *Telephone logs:* Another useful aid to memory is a telephone log, which is a record of all incoming and outgoing calls. It identifies the date and time of each call, whether it was incoming or outgoing, and if outgoing, the number called. It lists all parties to the call and includes a brief notation about the discussion.
- *Photographs and videotapes:* When physical evidence of conditions at the site of performance is important, a photographic or videotape record can be helpful. This record will greatly facilitate communication and will provide an excellent description of the exact nature of the site conditions. Whenever a contract involves physical labor, the project manager, contract manager, or other on-site representative should have a camera and film available for use.

The purpose of documentation is to record facts and reduce reliance on human memory. Efforts to maintain documentation must be thorough and consistent.

- *Contract changes:* As a result of changes in the buyers' needs, changes in technologies, and other changes in the marketplace, buyers need flexibility in their contracts. Thus changes are inevitable. Sellers must realize that changes are not bad, that they are in fact good, because changes are often an opportunity to sell more products or services.
- *Payment:* Cash is important—sellers want their money as quickly as possible. Buyers should seek product or service discounts for early payments. Likewise, sellers should improve their accounts receivable management and enforce late payment penalties.
- *Completion of work:* This last step is the actual accomplishment by the seller of the buyer's requirement for products, services, systems, or solutions.

Performance Measurement and Reporting

Observing, collecting information, and measuring progress will provide a basis for comparing actual achievement to planned achievement. Generally, observing and collecting information cover three categories of concerns: cost control, schedule control, and compliance with specifications and statements of work. Cost control and schedule control are usually integrated; the latter category is often addressed in quality assurance and control. However, a fourth category—compliance with paperwork requirements, that is, the administrative aspects of performance—is recommended. Observation in this area may be direct or indirect.

Direct Observation

Direct observation means personal, physical observation. The project manager, contract manager, or a representative is physically present at the site of the work during its performance to see how it is progressing. This approach is practical when the work is physical in nature and performed at a limited number of sites. Construction projects, for example, are good candidates for direct observation.

Direct observation by the project manager or contract manager is of limited use, however, if the work is largely intellectual in nature or if it is too complex for physical inspection alone to provide enough information to measure progress. In such cases, direct observation must be supplemented with or replaced by indirect observation.

Indirect Observation

Indirect observation includes testing, progress reports from many observers, and technical reviews and audits. Indirect observation is appropriate whenever direct observation would provide insufficient or ambiguous information. For example, determining by personal observation whether, at a given point in time, actual project costs are greater than, equal to, or less than budgeted costs would be difficult. Likewise, for projects involving an intellectual effort, such as system design, personal observations at the offices where the work is performed are unlikely to reveal whether the work is on, ahead of, or behind schedule.

In these circumstances, the project manager and contract manager must devise an indirect way to collect information. For some small, noncritical contracts, a telephone call may be all that is necessary to find out whether everything is proceeding according to plan. For large, complex contracts, however, the project manager or contract manager may require extensive reports, regular progress meetings, formal testing, and technical reviews and audits.

Sometimes a contract will specify such requirements, as in the following excerpt from a clause in a consultant agreement:

Reports

> Consultant shall provide ABC Company with monthly progress reports during the term of this Agreement, describing the status of the work, and shall participate in monthly status review meetings with ABC Company, at such times and locations reasonably specified by ABC Company. Additional meetings will be held if reasonably requested by either party.

Note that the clause does not describe specific information that must be included in the monthly report to describe the status of the work, so the seller may determine the information to be provided and its format. If the project manager or contract manager has specific information requirements, they should be described in the contract.

Reports

Generally, indirect observations are presented in reports that may be written or oral and may include raw data, informational summaries, analyses, conclusions, or a combination thereof. In the "Reports" clause, the monthly report is likely to be a collection of statements describing the seller's conclusions about the work's status. The conclusions may or may not be supported by raw data and an account of the seller's analysis. Often, this kind of report is adequate; other times, it is not.

Progress meetings are simply oral reports of progress. They have some advantages and some disadvantages. Listeners are able to ask questions about the information, analyses, and conclusions reported and have discussions with the reporter. However the listeners may not have time during the meeting to ponder the information provided and make their own analyses before the meeting ends.

Reports rarely provide real-time data. They do not describe how things are now; rather they provide a picture of some past point in time. How old the data are will depend on the nature and frequency of the report and on the reporter's capabilities. A cost and schedule performance report that is submitted on July 1 and depends on accounting data may actually describe cost and schedule status as of May 30, depending on the capabilities of the seller's accounting system.

Reported conclusions about project status are valid only if the information on which they are based is accurate and the analyst is competent, realistic, and honest. Sellers are renowned for their optimism during the period before a crisis emerges. Facts can be presented in ways that permit almost any conclusion to be drawn from them.

In deciding to rely wholly or in part on reports (including meetings), the project manager or contract manager also must decide what information each report must contain. Following are some issues that should be addressed:

- What aspects of performance should the report address?
- What information should the report include—conclusions about performance, analyses, raw information, or some combination thereof?

SEVEN

- How frequently must the report be submitted and at what points in time?
- What is the cut-off point ("as of" date) for information to be included in the report?
- In what format should the report be submitted?
- To whom should the report be submitted, and to whom should copies be sent?

Identification and Analysis of Performance Variances

Observed and collected information about project performance must be analyzed to determine whether the project is proceeding as planned. The analyst compares actual performance to performance goals to determine whether any variances exist. An analyst who discovers a variance between actual and expected performance must determine several things: Is it significant? What was its cause? Was it a one-time failure, or is it a continuing problem? What type of corrective action would be most effective?

Variance analysis must be timely, particularly when the information is obtained through reports. That information is already old by the time it is received. Delays in analyzing its significance may allow poor performance to deteriorate further, perhaps beyond hope of effective corrective action. Acting promptly is particularly important during the early phases of contract performance, when corrective action is likely to have the greatest effect.

It is not uncommon for project managers and contract managers to collect reams of information that sit in their in-baskets and file cabinets, never put to use. When a project has gone badly, a review of information in the project files frequently shows that there were warning signs—reports, meeting minutes, letters, memos—but that they were unnoticed or ignored. Often, several people, perhaps a variety of business managers, share the responsibility for monitoring performance. In these instances, the project manager and contract manager must take steps to ensure that those people promptly analyze the information, report their findings, and take corrective action.

Corrective Action

When the project manager and contract manager discover a significant variance between actual and expected performance, they must take corrective action if possible. They must identify the cause of the problem and determine a solution that will not only eliminate it as a source of future difficulty, but also correct the effect it has already had, if possible. If the effect cannot be corrected, the parties may need to negotiate a change to the contract, with compensation to the injured party, if appropriate.

Follow-Up

After corrective action has been taken or is under way, the project manager and contract manager must determine whether it has had or is having the desired effect. If not, further action may be needed. Throughout this corrective action and follow-up process, the parties must keep each other informed about what is going on. Effective communication between the parties is essential to avoid misunderstandings and disputes when things are not going according to plan. The party taking corrective action must make every effort to let the other party know that it is aware of the problem and is addressing it seriously. Sometimes this step is more important than the corrective action itself.

Change Management

With change comes the risk that the parties will disagree on the nature of their obligations to one another. This situation is particularly likely to occur in contracts between organizations in which many people on both sides are in frequent contact with one another. These people may make informal, undocumented arrangements that depart from the contract terms and conditions. Thus, performance may be at variance with expectations, which can lead to misunderstandings and disputes.

Even when the parties formally agree to make changes, they may disagree about who should bear the burden of the effect on cost and schedule. Changes can affect budgets and schedules in unexpected ways, leading to serious disputes. A risk also exists that a proposal for a formal change may provide one party with an opportunity to renegotiate the entire contract based on issues not connected with the change.

Best Practices: Seven Actions to Improve Change Management

These considerations demand careful management of change. Best practices in change control include the following:

- Ensure that only authorized people negotiate or agree to contract changes
- Make an estimate of the effect of a change on cost and schedule, and gain approval for any additional expense and time before proceeding with any change
- Notify project team members that they must promptly report (to the project manager or contract manager) any action or inaction by the other party to the contract that does not conform to the contract terms and conditions
- Notify the other party in writing of any action or inaction by that party that is inconsistent with the established contract terms and conditions
- Instruct team members to document and report in writing all actions taken to comply with authorized changes and the cost and time required to comply
- Promptly seek compensation for increases in cost or time required to perform, and negotiate claims for such compensation from the other party in good faith
- Document all changes in writing, and ensure that both parties have signed the contract; such written documentation should be completed before work under the change begins, if practical (see Form 18).

Managing change means ensuring that changes are authorized, their effect is estimated and provided for, they are promptly identified, the other party is properly notified, compliance and impact are reported, compensation is provided, and the entire transaction is properly documented.

Contract Change Clauses

Contracts frequently include a clause that authorizes the buyer to order the seller to conform with certain changes made at the buyer's discretion. Such clauses are called *change clauses*. The following clause is an example:

Changes

ABC Company reserves the right at any time to make changes in the specifications, drawings, samples, or other descriptions to which the products are to conform, in the methods of shipment and packaging, or in the time or place of delivery. In such event, any claim for an adjustment shall be mutually satisfactory to ABC Company and Seller, but any claim by Seller for an adjustment shall be deemed waived unless notice of a claim is made in writing within thirty (30) days following Seller's receipt of such changes. Price increases or extensions of time shall not be binding upon ABC Company unless evidenced by a purchase order change issued by ABC Company. No substitutions of materials or accessories may be made without ABC Company's written consent. No charges for extras will be allowed unless such extras have been ordered in writing by ABC Company and the price agreed upon.

This clause does not expressly tie the amount of the seller's claim to the effect of the change on its cost or time requirements. Moreover, there is no express mention of reductions in price or time. However, the clause does say that any claim must be "mutually satisfactory" to both parties. It is unclear what, if any, legal significance there is in these subtle differences in language.

The clause requires that "notice of a claim" by the seller be made in writing within 30 days of the seller's receipt of the change order.

Documentation of Change

Whenever the parties make a change in the contract, it is important that they maintain the integrity of that document as trustworthy evidence of the terms and conditions of their agreement. Logically, a change will add terms and conditions, delete terms and conditions, or replace some terms and conditions with others. Thus, when modifying the contract, the parties should decide what words, numerals, symbols, or drawings must be added, deleted, or replaced in the contract document.

Parties to a contract will often discuss the change they want to make but fail to describe the change in the context of their contract document. After a few such changes, the document will no longer accurately describe the current status of their agreement, and the parties may dispute what the current terms really are. Such an occurrence should surprise no one, human communication and memory being what they are.

The best way to avoid this problem is to draft the language of the change carefully in the context of the contract document, ensuring that the new language describes the intent of the parties. This action should be taken before making any attempt to estimate the cost and schedule effect of any change or to perform the work. People sometimes argue that expediency demands that the work proceed before reaching agreement on the precise language of the change. However, this practice is likely to create confusion over just what changed and how. If the parties cannot reach agreement on the language of the change in a reasonable time, they probably are not in agreement about the nature of the change and should not proceed.

Modification of the Contract Document

One party will have the original copy of the contract. The other party will usually have a duplicate original. These originals should remain with the contract manager, or in the contracts department or legal office.

When parties agree to change the contract, they should never alter the original documents. Instead, they should prepare modification documents that describe the contract changes. These changes can generally be described in two ways: First, the modification document can include substitute pages in which deleted original language is stricken out and new or replacement language is inserted in italics. Second, minor changes can be described in "pen and ink" instructions that strike out certain words and add others.

Copies of each modification should be distributed promptly to all project team members who have a copy of the original document. The project manager, contract manager, and other key team members should maintain a personal conformed working copy of the contract. This copy should be kept in a loose-leaf binder or electronic database so that pages can be replaced easily. The conformed working copy should be altered as necessary to reflect the current status of the agreement between the parties. Changes should be incorporated promptly. Each team member should always keep the conformed working copy readily available and bring it to meetings. The contract manager should periodically check to ensure that each team member's conformed working copy is up-to-date.

Effect of the Change on Price and Schedule

After the parties are in precise agreement as to how the contract was modified, they should try to estimate the cost and schedule impact of the change. They can do this independently, but the most effective approach is to develop the estimate together, as a team, working out the details and their differences in the process. If the parties are open and honest with one another, this approach can save time and give them greater insight into the real effect of the change on cost and schedule. A well-developed work breakdown structure and project schedule graphic can be of enormous value to this process. Work may proceed based either on an estimate of the cost and schedule impact, with a limit on the parties' obligations, or on a firm-fixed adjustment.

If the parties work out their estimates independently (the traditional approach), an agreement will entail a certain amount of bargaining. This approach can lead to time-consuming haggling and even to deadlock, and such delays can be costly when a change is needed during performance.

Another approach is for the parties to agree that the seller can proceed with the work as changed and submit a claim later. This method can spell trouble for both parties, however, particularly if the adjustments are unexpectedly high. For the buyer, it can mean unpleasant surprises about the effect on prices and schedules for changed work. For the seller, it can mean a dismayed buyer and delays in settling claims. For both, it can mean a damaged relationship. Working out the cost and schedule impact before committing to the change is better for both parties.

If the seller must proceed with the work before the change can be fully negotiated, the parties should agree to limits on their mutual obligations in relation to the change. It is common practice for parties to agree on cost and schedule ceilings when work must begin before agreement is complete. Obviously, such limits should be documented in writing.

Authorization of Performance Under the Change

After the parties have agreed to the change and to either an estimate of the impact on cost and schedule or a final price adjustment, the buyer should provide the seller with written authorization to proceed with the work as changed. The easiest way to accomplish this objective is to prepare, sign, and distribute a modification document. If this approach will take too long, a letter or other form of written documentation will suffice. The authorization should include a description of the change, its effective date, and a description of any limits on the obligations of the parties.

Submission, Negotiation, and Resolution of Claims

If price and schedule adjustments are not negotiated before authorizing performance under the change, the parties must negotiate such matters after performance. As a rule, the buyer should try to limit any price adjustments to the cost increases caused by the change, plus reasonable allowances for overhead and profit, and any additional time required to perform the work as changed. However, if the change reduces the cost or time of performance, the buyer should seek a reduction in price or schedule.

The project manager and contract manager should keep detailed records of all costs incurred in complying with changes. They must document the effect of changes on the time required to perform. The party submitting the claim should be able to make a reasonable demonstration of a cause-and-effect relationship between the change and the increased or decreased cost and time requirements. Ideally, the parties will have reached an advance agreement about the nature and extent of claim documentation. The objective of negotiation should be to seek a reasonable settlement that will fairly compensate the seller for performing additional work or fairly reduce the buyer's price when work is deleted.

Contract Administration Policies

Four contract administration policies are key to every contract. They are: compliance with contract terms and conditions, effective communication and control, effective control of contract changes, and effective resolution of claims and disputes.

Compliance with Contract Terms and Conditions

The policy of compliance with contract terms and conditions is the policy of keeping one's promises. Contracting parties should know and understand the contract terms and keep their promises to comply in good faith. Such a policy is essential to effective risk management for both parties. No one should enter into a contract intending not to comply with its terms and conditions, because doing so would risk legal and commercial consequences.

However, these principles can become problematic, particularly when contracting parties are organizations. Often the people who plan, select the seller, and negotiate and sign the contract are different from those who must perform the contract work, and each group may have different goals and objectives. The negotiators may agree to terms and conditions that conflict with the objectives, policies, practices, and customs of the functional departments that do the work.

In such circumstances, because of failures of internal communication and control, department managers may inadvertently or even willfully violate contract terms. Common explanations include: "I thought the contract was wrong, so we did it the right way;" "I didn't interpret it that way;" "I wasn't sure what it meant, so I did it the way we always do it;" "I never saw the contract, we just handled it in a routine manner;" and "What contract?" Thus, one of the greatest problems in contract administration is communicating contract obligations to all affected people and maintaining control over their contract performance.

Effective Communication and Control

The policy of compliance with contract terms and conditions requires that organizations maintain effective communication about, and control over, contract performance. Each party to the contract must establish both communication procedures to ensure that people within its organization know what they must do and the necessary controls to ensure that they do it. Good intentions about contract performance will not be enough to avoid legal consequences in the absence of effective communication and control. Contracts must specify who is the designated point of contact and who has the authority to modify the contract.

Ensuring that the parties to the contract communicate with each other is equally important. A contract is a relationship. Because virtually every contract entails some degree of interaction between the contracting parties, each party must keep the other informed of its progress, problems, and proposed solutions, so that the other can respond appropriately.

Like all human relationships, contracts are dynamic. As performance proceeds and events unfold, the parties will find that they must modify their original expectations and plans to adjust to real events. As they do so, they must modify the contract terms and conditions to reflect the current status of their agreement. Changes are an inevitable part of contracting, because no one can predict the future with perfect accuracy. However, the parties should make changes consciously and openly, so that they remain in agreement about what they should be doing. Lack of communication can result in dispute over what their obligations really are.

Effective Control of Contract Changes

Part of communication and control is the effective management of changes, which are inevitable. Effectively controlling changes includes establishing formal procedures for changing the contract and limiting the number of people entitled to make changes. It also entails establishing recognition and notification procedures in response to unauthorized changes. Finally, it requires establishing procedures for identifying, estimating, and measuring the potential and actual effect of changes on all aspects of contract performance.

It is natural for the functional managers of one party to work directly with their counterparts in the other party's organization—people who will speak their language and understand their policies and customs. These colleagues will often bypass formal channels of communication. Such relationships frequently lead to informal, undocumented agreements that depart from contract terms and conditions. These informal agreements can lead to trouble. Policy must be backed by procedures to ensure that the changes brought about through these relationships are controlled.

Effective Resolution of Claims and Disputes

The inherent shortcomings of language as a medium of communication, the organizational nature of the contracting process, and the dynamic nature of contract relationships all contribute to the potential for disagreements between the parties. In fact, like changes, disagreements are virtually inevitable. They should be expected as a normal part of contract management. The larger and more complex the project, the greater the potential for misunderstanding and disagreement.

However, the parties must not allow disagreements and disputes to prevent the execution of the contract. They must commit themselves to resolving disputes that will arise between them in an amicable way. Although claims and disputes cannot be avoided, they can be resolved effectively, fairly, and without rancor and litigation. Experienced parties to a contract will anticipate claims and disputes and recognize that they do not necessarily indicate incompetence or ill will but, rather, reflect the fact that human foresight, planning, and performance are imperfect.

Professional contract managers understand that contract disputes must be resolved dispassionately. They also recognize that personalities may affect disputes. But they know that the objective is final disposition in an inexpensive, expeditious, and less formal manner, before disputes fester and infect the contractual relationship.

Each party to the contract has the power to litigate if it believes it has been wronged. Ultimately a losing proposition for all involved, litigation is costly and time consuming, and its results are uncertain. Negotiation and arbitration are preferable to litigation, and the parties to the contract should strive to use those techniques to the fullest extent practical.

Contract Closeout and Termination

A contract can end in one of three ways: successful performance, mutual agreement, or breach. Most contracts end by successful performance. However, under some circumstances, the parties may agree to end their contract even though the original objectives were not met. They may reach this agreement through negotiation or arbitration. In a breach of contract, one or both of the parties fail to keep their promises. This could result in arbitration or litigation. Contract closure by mutual agreement or breach of contract is called *contract termination.*

Contract closeout refers to verifying that all administrative matters are concluded on a contract that is otherwise physically complete. In other words, the seller has delivered the required supplies or performed the required services, and the buyer has inspected and accepted the supplies or services.

Many sellers have a policy that their contract manager sign a contract completion statement confirming that all administrative actions were performed. Standard times for closing out a contract vary depending on many factors.

Occasionally, contracts take on lives of their own. For instance, "administrative convenience," "extensions of time" or "additional goods and services" are often added to an existing agreement that may have been completely executed by the seller. Closing out the completed contract and opening a new one may be more appropriate in such cases, especially when new or different terms and conditions might lead to confusion.

Contract closeout includes the following actions:

- *Completion of work:* A contract is physically complete when one of two events has occurred:

  - All required supplies or services are delivered or performed, inspected, and accepted, and all existing options were exercised or have expired
  - A contract completion notice was issued by one party to the other

- *Contract documentation:* The purpose of closeout is to ensure that no further administrative action is necessary on the contract. Part of this task is to check that all paperwork was submitted. The following forms, reports, and payments may be outstanding after a contract is physically complete:

  - For the buyer—
    - Closeout report
    - Certificate of completion or conformance
    - Seller's release of claims

  - For the seller—
    - Closeout report
    - Proof of buyer's final payment
    - Release of performance bonds and letter of credit

- *Termination notice (for termination only):* A written or oral notification to cancel the contract due to cause or default of contract, or for convenience, is issued in the event of contract termination.

- *Compliance verification:* Administrative tasks, incidental to contract performance, may have to be accomplished before closing out the file. Final payment cannot be authorized until the seller has accomplished all administrative tasks, such as:

  - Return, or other disposition, of buyer-furnished property
  - Proper disposition of intellectual property
  - Settlement of subcontracts
  - Fulfillment of procedural requirements of termination proceedings (for termination only)

- *Contract documentation:* Several types of documentation must be dealt with at this time:
  - *Outstanding claims or disputes:* Some issues related to basic contract performance may not be resolved, and the buyer may not have raised some issues. All outstanding issues must be addressed at this time. To avoid reopening a closed file, some sellers make a standard practice of requesting a signed statement from the buyer that all contract terms and conditions were met. Some unscrupulous buyers have attempted to coerce sellers into abandoning outstanding claims in return for getting paid amounts that are not in dispute. Such actions are bad faith on the part of the buyer.
  - *Payments:* Final payments or outstanding underpayment should be collected by the seller. The buyer's payment office should make payment based on the seller's invoice and its receipt of a receiving report. On more complex requirements, contract managers generally have a more active role in these tasks. Underpayment can be the result of many factors, including liquidated damages, adjustments after an audit, and retroactive price reductions.
  - *Files:* The project manager or contract manager must keep a log of closed-out files containing information, such as the date the file was closed out, date the file was transferred physically to a storage center, location of the storage center, and filing location provided by the storage facility. Some information in contract files must be kept for a certain number of years. Such information should be specified in the contract.
  - *Contract completion statement:* The contract manager should prepare a contract completion statement.

- *Contract closeout checklist:* A checklist can be a useful tool during contract closeout.

- *Termination (for termination only):* Termination is the administrative process exercising a party's contractual right to discontinue performance completely or partially under a contract. The three types of terminations are termination for cause or default, termination by mutual agreement (for convenience), and no-cost settlement. (See "Termination Types" later in this chapter for further discussion.)

- *Documented lessons learned:* At the completion of each contract, the project manager, contract manager, and project team should jointly develop a lessons-learned summary, which should describe the major positive and negative aspects of the contract. The lessons-learned summary focuses on sharing best practices with other company project teams, warning others of potential problems, and suggesting methods to mitigate the risks effectively to ensure success.

Termination Types

Termination with respect to a contract refers to an ending before the closure of the anticipated term of the contract. The termination may be by mutual agreement or may be by one party's exercising its remedies due to the other party's omission or failure to perform a contractual or contract law duty (default).

Termination by Mutual Agreement

Both parties may agree at any time that they do not wish to be bound by the contract and terminate their respective rights and obligations stemming from the contract.

Termination for Cause or Default

The right to terminate a contract may originate from either the general principles of contract law or the express terms of the contract. Contracts may be terminated for default for the following reasons:

- *Failure to tender conforming supplies or services:* If the seller fails, or is unable, to cure a nonconforming tender, the seller is in default and the contract can be terminated or other remedial action can be taken.

- *Failure to complete performance substantially within the time specified in the contract:* Usually, the buyer does not consider or have the legal right of termination for default actions when only minor corrective work remains on the contract.
- *Repudiation of the contract by the seller:* A repudiation, or anticipatory breach, occurs when a seller or buyer clearly indicates to the other party that it cannot or will not perform on the contract. Examples indicating that an anticipatory repudiation may exist include a letter stating an intention of nonperformance or job abandonment.
- *Failure to perform any other terms of the contract:* A failure to comply with bonding requirements, progress-schedule submission requirements, or fraud statutes would constitute a failure to perform other contract terms.

Although authority to terminate may be expressly provided to both parties, contract managers must exercise this authority in good faith based on conditions of the termination clause or a material breach of contract terms. The decision is highly discretionary, based on the business judgment of the contract manager and business advisors.

Factors to be considered before terminating a contract for default include—

- Contract terms and conditions and applicable laws and regulations
- Specific failure of the buyer or seller and the excuses made by the breaching party for such failure
- Availability from other sources
- Urgency of the need and time that would be required by other sources as compared with the time in which completion could be obtained from the current contract
- Degree of essentially of the seller, such as unique seller capabilities
- Buyer's availability of funds to finance repurchase costs that may prove to be uncollectible from the defaulted seller, and the availability of funds to finance termination costs if the default is determined to be excusable
- Any other pertinent facts and circumstances

Termination for Convenience

It is the right of the parties, usually the buyer, to terminate a contract unilaterally when completing the contract is no longer in the buyer's best interest. This has long been recognized in U.S. government contracts, and the consequences are defined by law. This type of termination of government contracts has been the subject of many U.S. court and legal decisions. In U.S. government contracts, the buyer has the right to terminate without cause and limit the seller's recovery to the—

- Price of work delivered and accepted
- Costs incurred on work done but not delivered
- Profit on work done but not delivered if the contract incurred no loss
- Costs of preparing the termination settlement proposal

In commercial contracts, the concept of buyer's best interest is not used. Termination occurs only as a result of default due to breach of contract or due to mutual agreement. Recovery of anticipated profit is generally precluded.

No-Cost Settlement

Used without normal termination procedures, no-cost settlement can be considered when—

- The seller has indicated it will accept it
- No buyer property was furnished under the contract
- No outstanding payments or debts are due the seller, and no other obligations are outstanding
- The product or service can be readily obtained elsewhere

Note that termination for convenience is not a commercial contracting concept. Thus, if a contract contains a statement allowing parties to terminate the contract unilaterally, the parties should exercise extreme caution in defining specific remedies and consequences of such action.

Best Practices: 30 Actions to Improve Results

Buyer and Seller

- Read and analyze the contract
- Develop a contract administration plan
- Appoint a contract manager to ensure that your organization does what it proposed to do
- Develop and implement contract administration policies or guidelines for your organization
- Comply with contract terms and conditions
- Maintain effective communication and control
- Control contract changes with a proactive change management process
- Resolve claims and disputes promptly and dispassionately
- Use negotiation or arbitration, not litigation, to resolve disputes
- Develop a work breakdown structure to assist in planning and assigning work
- Conduct preperformance conferences
- Measure, monitor, and track performance
- Manage the invoice and payment process
- Report on progress internally and externally
- Identify variances between planned versus actual performance
- Be sure to follow up on all corrective actions
- Appoint authorized people to negotiate contract changes and document the authorized representatives in the contract
- Enforce contract terms and conditions
- Provide copies of the contract to all affected organizations
- Maintain conformed copies of the contract
- Understand the effects of change on cost, schedule, and quality
- Document all communication—use telephone and correspondence logs
- Prepare internal and external meeting minutes
- Prepare contract closeout checklists
- Ensure completion of work
- Document lessons learned and share them throughout your organization
- Communicate, communicate, communicate!
- Clarify team member roles and responsibilities
- Provide leadership support to the team throughout the contract management process
- Ensure that leadership understands the contract management process and how it can improve business relationships from beginning to end.

Straight Talk: Suggestions for Significant Improvement

The primary focus of nearly every contract management organization is get deals signed. The majority of contract management resources and talent, from both the buyers and sellers, are dedicated to preparing solicitations, bids or proposals, reviewing bids or proposals, and negotiating and awarding contracts. Unfortunately, in both the public and private business sectors too little time and resources are allocated to properly manage contracts after they have been awarded. As a result, contract administration is often either poorly performed by individuals not properly trained, not performed at all, or only performed by exception, i.e. when a problem arises someone must be assigned to fix the problem. Those organizations which do have full-time contract administrators often have them heavily overbooked, managing far too many contracts for them to provide sufficient proactive contract management. Most organizations do not really appreciate the value-added of professional contract administration, via timely contract interpretation, effective contract change management, timely contract invoicing and payment, effective dispute resolution, and efficient contract closeout.

Summary

The post-bid/proposal phase: contract administration and closeout step is simply a matter of both parties doing what they promised to do. The on-going challenge is maintaining open and effective communication, timely delivery of quality products and services, responsive corrective actions to problems, and compliance with all other agreed-on terms and conditions. After the project has been successfully completed, proper procedures are put into place to close out the contract officially. In those instances where the contract is terminated due to cause of default, action is taken to legally cancel the contract.

Remember the power of precedent. Your organization is always evaluated based on your past performance and the precedents it sets. Your contract management actions taken years ago affect your organization's reputation today. Likewise, the contract management actions that you take today form your organization's reputation for tomorrow.

QUESTIONS TO CONSIDER

1. How well does your organization staff the right quality and quantity of resources to perform contract administration?

2. Who has the lead role for contract administration and closeout in your organization?

3. How well does your organization manage contract changes?

4. How well does your organization manage contract closeouts?

CHAPTER 8

U.S. FEDERAL GOVERNMENT MARKETPLACE ACQUISITION PLANNING, SOLICITATIONS, & SOURCE SELECTION BEST PRACTICES

INTRODUCTION

The U.S. Federal Government marketplace is huge, complex, and highly regulated. For sellers, the U.S. Federal Government marketplace is difficult to initially penetrate and the typical profitability is far lower than in commercial business transactions. For buyers, the U.S. Federal Government marketplace is highly constrained by the funding rules and actions or inactions of the U.S. Congress. The Federal Acquisition Regulation (FAR) System has been somewhat streamlined during the past 20+ years, but is still far too restrictive and forces lengthy acquisition cycle-time for most large procurements.

Acquisition planning, as it is called by the U.S. Federal Government, begins as soon as the agency identifies a need, and should start well in advance of the fiscal year in which the contract will be solicited and awarded. Planning can be an informal process of identifying needs and the means to fulfill those needs. Not all acquisitions will require the full extent of acquisition planning. Generally, as supplies and services become more complex, so does the extent and nature of the planning process and the acquisition plan.

Formal planning, especially complex or high-dollar value requirements, will be accomplished by a team of experts that usually includes financial, technical, legal, and contracting personnel. The Federal Acquisition Regulation (FAR) 7.103 specifies the responsibilities of the agency head in setting forth procedures for acquisition planning. Where urgency is a factor, the agency head or designee can waive requirements for detail and formality as necessary in planning for and executing the acquisition.

In this chapter, we will discuss the following:

- Acquisition Planning Best Practices
- Solicitation Planning Best Practices
  - Conduct Market Research
  - Use Performance Work Statements (PWS) or Statements of Objectives (SOO)
  - Develop Work Breakdown Structure (WBS)
  - Structure Contract Line Item Numbers (CLINs)
  - Improve Proposal Preparation Guidelines
- Source Selection Best Practices
- Best Value Contracting Best Practices

THE U.S. GOVERNMENT'S ACQUISITION PLAN & TEAM

The U.S. Government's acquisition plan addresses all technical, business, management and other considerations that will control the acquisition. The specific content will vary depending on the nature of the supplies and services, the circumstances surrounding the acquisition, and even the stage of the acquisition. The acquisition plan usually consists of two parts: Part A, a discussion of the requirement and the mission need, and Part B, the plan of action for contracting to satisfy the requirement. The U.S. Government's acquisition team will typically include a wide range of functional specialists depending upon then nature, complexity, and urgency of the agency's needs. Table 8-1 provides a list of the typical functional specialists who participate in acquisition planning, which leads to the creation of the solicitation.

Table 8-1
U.S. Federal Government Functional Specialists Participating in the Acquisition Planning Process

• Contract Specialist/Manager	• Contracting Officer (CO)
• Budget Analyst	• Contracting Officer's Technical Representative (COTR)
• Business Manager	• Procurement Attorney/Lawyer
• Configuration Manager	• Program/Project Manager (PM)
• Financial Analyst	• Quality Assurance Representative (QAR)
• Logistics Manager	• Small Business Advocate

Acquisition Background and Objectives

Statement of Need – The acquisition plan begins with a brief, but concise, discussion of the statement of need. Then a technical and contractual history of the requirement is provided, as well as the acquisition alternatives for satisfying the needs.

Applicable Conditions – Certain conditions, such as system compatibility, will affect the acquisition of an end item. These conditions can affect the method of contracting to be selected, as well as the type of contract to be used. This section identifies such conditions and discusses strategies which would take them into account. This includes any cost, schedule, and performance constraints. Cost and schedule constraints can range from insufficient funds to early operational requirements.

Cost – This section of the acquisition plan identifies the cost goals and the cost concept that will be employed:

Life-Cycle Cost – If life-cycle cost will be used to track and control cost goals, the acquisition plan must discuss how it will be applied and which cost model will be employed to develop life-cycle cost estimates.

Design-to-Cost – Design-to-cost is a technique requiring the contractor to design the item or system to a specific cost goal. When design-to-cost is employed, the acquisition plan must determine the assumptions for its use, including the rationale for quantities, learning curves, and appropriate economic adjustment factors. In addition, the plan should identify how objectives will be applied, tracked, and enforced. Finally, the acquisition plan should determine the specific solicitation and contractual provisions that will be used as requirements for design-to-cost performance.

Should-Cost – This technique is usually reserved for production programs, which is used to determine what a system would cost if all the contractor's inefficiencies were eliminated or reduced. If the acquisition plan supports a production program, then it should provide the assumptions and applications of should-cost techniques.

Capability or Performance – While the acquisition plan contains an earlier discussion of the agency's need, this section should identify the desired performance characteristics of a product or capabilities of a service. While the general description of the need was provided earlier, this section sets forth performance characteristics, specifically the actions required to satisfy the need.

Delivery or performance period requirements – For non-complex items or services, the performance period may be relatively short. However, for complex items like a major system, the performance period and delivery requirements will span several years. If urgency is a major factor, this section should identify the reasons and the effect such urgency will have on deliveries and the performance period.

Trade-offs – This section provides the expected consequences of trade-offs among schedule, cost, capability or performance goals. For a complex, major system, trade-offs between performance and schedule or performance and cost often become necessary. Obtaining the required performance is usually more important than meeting the schedule and, therefore, represents the required trade-off.

Acquisition Streamlining — Best Practices

A major thrust in the U.S. Federal Government today is to streamline the acquisition process by reducing paperwork, reducing the size of solicitation documents, and reducing reliance on government standards and specifications. Streamlining should be a primary consideration throughout the development of the acquisition plan. In general, streamlining involves thoroughly reviewing the technical package to ensure that only performance-based requirements are stated and counter-productive, nice-to-have or highly detailed specifications are eliminated. Unnecessary requirements include:

- How-to-manage (externally imposed management systems)
- Premature (design solutions before development begins)
- Untailored (overspecification, unneeded provisions, etc.)
- Accidentally referenced (referenced by implication.)

Contract streamlining means using more off-the-shelf, commercial products or services and relying less on unique government equipment. It seeks to avoid such problems as overly voluminous specifications for common items. Acquisition streamlining is a mandatory requirement for new DOD system acquisition programs.

Table 8-2 provides a listing of some of the many proven effective acquisition streamlining best practices currently used in the U.S. Federal Government marketplace.

Table 8-2
U.S. Federal Government Marketplace Acquisition Streamlining — Best Practices
• Understand and focus on performance-based mission requirements
• Streamline acquisition strategy plan in view of time, technical risk, and cost
• Conduct market research and industry focused-meetings
• Use a Statement of Objectives (SOO) to obtain contractors proposed solutions, performance standards, metrics, and quality plan
• Encourage contractors to develop creative solutions
• Use strategic sourcing
• Specify system level broad mission performance requirements at onset of development
• Challenge every detailed requirement
• Specify what results are required, not how-to-manage (all phases) or how to do it
• Use oral presentations
• Pursue economically producible, operationally suitable and field supportable designs (all phases)
• Select the best value partner

U.S. Federal Government Marketplace: The Solicitation Document

In contracts, as in computers, the rule is "garbage in – garbage out." Contractors provide only what is required under the contract, and if the government does not clearly define its requirements in the solicitation, the performance will probably be inadequate. Developing the requirements for a contract is the same as defining work requirements for an in-house operation. Developing the requirements is a management exercise and success depends on the ability to employ the basic principles of management.

■ The work to be done and the performance standards expected (quality, quantity, and timeliness) must be clearly defined.
■ A formal performance measurement system must be in place to assess actual performance.
■ Specific actions must be taken if work does not meet the standards specified.

Use of Integrated Project Team (IPT) to Develop Objectives, Requirements, & Oversee the Acquisition Process

The creation of a true Integrated Project Team (IPT) is essential for a buyer to gather all of their organizations and end user objectives, requirements, and guide the acquisition process. The IPT is typically composed of a multi-functional team including senior representatives from:

■ End-Customers
■ Project/Program Management (PM)
■ Technical Operations
■ Supply Chain Management
■ Financial Management/CFO
■ Information Management/CIO
■ Contract Management/Purchasing
■ Legal

Use a Performance Work Statement (PWS) or Statement of Objectives (SOO) — A Solicitation Planning Best Practice

The WBS is the management framework of the requirement, but it is not the description of the government's requirement. The WBS does not contain any of the technical, engineering or other specific requirements. Often the buyer will choose to create a Statement of Objectives (SOO) and ask prospective sellers to assess the SOO and propose how they would do the work via a performance work statement with appropriate standards, measures, metrics, and performance incentives. The performance requirements are contained in the performance work statement (PWS), which is a form of a statement of work (SOW).

Contract managers frequently encounter problems with incomplete SOWs. A well planned PWS can clearly communicate all of the performance-based requirements to the contractor. However, these requirements must also be clearly stated. As the complexity and dollar value of the contract requirement increases, so does the need for a structured approach.

The Work Breakdown Structure (WBS) — A Solicitation Planning Best Practice

A Work Breakdown Structure (WBS) is a tool for organizing, defining, and graphically displaying the product or service to be provided, as well as the work to be accomplished to achieve the specified results. In preparing an RFP, an important step is to examine what are the government agency's needs. A WBS can be the first step in establishing a management framework, which the government's requirements can be clearly identified. The WBS acts as the foundation for a management control system for both government and contractor project personnel. It organizes the project and provides a consistent and visible framework that:

- Provides an effective management and technical baseline for planning and assigning responsibilities within the government and contractor organizations.
- Structures the reporting process for progress and status reports.
- Organizes the project as a whole and ensures consideration of total life cycle effects when making system development and acquisition decisions.

Contractors can use the WBS as a framework in preparing their offers, as well as managing the project or program. Specifically, the contractor's management control systems use the WBS as a guide in deciding policies, procedures, and methods to accomplish the following:

- Define all authorized work and related resources to meet the requirement of the contract.

- Integrate the contractor's planning, scheduling, and budgeting with each other and with the contract work breakdown structure (CWBS).
- Integrate the CWBS with the contractor's organizational structure to permit cost and schedule performance measurement, via an Earned Value Management System (EVMS).
- Assign each direct cost from cost accounts into a single branch of the WBS.
- Report data elements and variances (budgeted costs scheduled and performed, indirect costs, and cost variances) to the level specified in the contract.
- Reconcile original budgets with current measurement budgets.

Work breakdown structures are required for major system acquisitions. When a specific acquisition is identified, the project manager may prepare a project summary WBS by selecting applicable elements from a list of summary WBSs contained in MIL-STD-881B. The MIL-STD lists three upper levels of summary WBSs for the following categories:

- Aircraft systems
- Electronics systems
- Missile systems
- Ordinance systems
- Ship systems
- Space systems
- Surface vehicle systems

Contract Work Breakdown Structure (CWBS) – Only one preliminary CWBS will be used in each request for proposal and ensuing contract. The preliminary CWBS is structured by selecting those elements of the approved project summary WBS that apply to a contract. The solicitation may identify the preliminary CWBS to prospective contractors. Contract line items numbers, configuration items, work statement tasks, and specifications are all expressed in terms of the preliminary CWBS. During negotiations contractors may propose changes to the preliminary CWBS based on the objectives of the particular acquisition.

Structuring Contract Line Item Numbers (CLINS) — A Solicitation Planning Best Practice

In the RFP, Section B of the Uniform Contract Format describes the supplies or services to be delivered under the contract. These items are referred to as contract line item numbers (CLINs). The structure and description of these items can have significant impact on both the government and the contractor. CLINs should be based on the work breakdown structure. The only effective way to determine exactly what the government requires is to analyze the work breakdown structure and then design the CLINs to match this structure.

Proposal Preparation Guidelines — A Solicitation Planning Best Practice

The portion of a solicitation upon which most contractors initially focus is the proposal preparation instructions located in Section L of the Uniform Contract Format. This section depicts the proposal format and content that the government desires.

Formatting Best Practices

The government can provide very specific or very general instructions on how it would like to see the contractor's proposal. For ease of evaluation and selection of the best contractor, however, the government must ensure that the proposals it receives contain the critical information in an appropriate format. Solicitations should provide guidance to offerors regarding proposal page limitations, number of copies required, and the division of proposals into separate volumes on technical, management cost, and other criteria.

Proposal Content Best Practices

Along with the proposal format requirements, the content of the proposal should be clearly specified, including whether the proposals can be submitted in several volumes, and separated according to agency needs. Distinct volumes allow for separate evaluation of technical and cost or pricing data. The instructions may specify further differentiation of proposal parts, including such volumes as administrative and management. Section L of the solicitation spells out what specific information the government would like to see in the various parts of the proposal. In this section the government can also request any plans that would aid the evaluators and decision makers. It would also specify what type of contract will be used, what technical information will be available, and when the proposals are due. In general, section L of the solicitation should contain any and all information that would allow the contractor to submit the best possible proposal while at the same time providing the selection team the right data to make their decision.

Form 8-1
U.S. Federal Government Marketplace: Solicitation Best Practices Checklist

❏ *Draft RFP* — Providing industry with the most complete draft package possible and then allowing sufficient time to analyze industry's response and incorporate good ideas into the actual RFP helps create a clearer, more effective solicitation. Contractors should be encouraged to challenge cost drivers, restrictive specifications and excessive data requirements. Draft RFPs are especially effective in sole source procurements; however, they can also be useful in competitive situations.

❏ *Electronic Submission of Solicitation Notices, Frequently Asked Questions & Answers, and Industry Pre-Solicitation Meetings* — Can be used to identify interested sources and to explain complicated requirements to interested sources. They can reduce undue expenditures of time, effort, and money.

❏ *Amendments to Solicitations* — If changes need to be made or ambiguities need to be corrected in a solicitation, a formal amendment can be issued to all prospective offerors. Additional response time should be given to allow offerors the opportunity to address the changes.

❏ *RFP Tracking* — An RFP is made up of many separate components — line items, statement of work, data requirements, proposal preparation instructions, evaluation criteria — that have been prepared by a variety of personnel. Therefore, it is extremely important to ensure that the parts constituting the whole communicate a consistent message to prospective offerors. Cross references should be provided throughout the RFP, within each separate component where appropriate and any conflicting information must be eliminated.

❏ *Solicitation Review Board* — Sometimes referred to as a "Murder Board," a solicitation review board is comprised of functional experts from outside the RFP process. The board asks questions and makes recommendations about the RFP's adequacy and clarity. This process provides an objective analysis and evaluation of the solicitation.

❏ *Executive Summary* — A concise introductory letter that conveys the salient features of the solicitation. It normally will include a brief description of the program.

❏ *Oral Presentation(s)* — The use of oral presentations by contractors can facilitate better and more effective decision-making by the U.S. Government.

❏ *Elimination or Limited Use of the Bid Protest Process* — See details provided in Chapter 5.

U.S. Federal Government Marketplace: Source Selection Best Practices

The process for selecting a contractor is called source selection and is described in FAR Part 15.3. The Department of Defense (DOD) and many civil agencies also have their own policies governing this very formal process. The primary objective of a source selection effort is to select the source whose proposal has the highest degree of creditability and whose performance can be expected to best meet the needs of the government at a reasonable cost.

Therefore, the following best practices must be followed: (1) the process must be fair, impartial, and equitable, and must reflect a comprehensive evaluation of the competitor's proposals, (2) the selection of evaluation criteria should balance technical, functional, and economic considerations with the acquisition objectives, and (3) specific criteria communicate to the contractor the basis for selection; however, the government must also specify the standards it will use to determine whether the criteria were met. The areas of consideration will vary according to the product being sought, but will generally include technical, management, past performance, and cost. Development of the selection criteria is a crucial step in the source selection process - well defined criteria will allow the source selection to proceed smoothly and in a timely manner.

The specific number and types of evaluation factors will depend on the nature of the procurement. FAR 15.304 gives some guidance, stating that:

> "Price or cost to the Government shall be evaluated in every source selection."

> "The quality of the product or service shall be addressed in every source selection through consideration of one or more factors such as past performance, compliance with solicitation requirements, technical excellence, management capability, personnel qualifications, prior experience, and any other relevant factors."

The use of too few evaluation factors will result in insufficient guidance for preparation and evaluation of proposals, whereas, too many factors may cause confusion. Most often, the agencies arrange evaluation factors into major categories and varying levels of subcategories. The major categories often include Technical, Management, and Cost factors.

Technical evaluation factors must be independent of each other to avoid redundancy, which may skew scores. Planners must attempt to include all appropriate factors; however, all factors should be determinate – they must be useful in the source selection decision. If a factor will not vary from offer to offer, it need not be counted highly as an evaluation criterion.

Management criteria that are most often included as evaluation factors includes such items as:

- Company experience on a similar project
- Available company resources and facilities
- Management and program plans

The cost criteria that are included as evaluation factors will differ among fixed price, incentive, and cost reimbursement contracts. When a fixed price contract is involved, the offeror's proposed price is the factor that will be considered in the evaluation; however, the agency should use its own cost estimate as an indicator of cost realism and the offeror's understanding of the requirements. Incentive contracts are structured and evaluated as a package of cost factors including target cost, share ratio, ceiling price, or maximum/minimum fee. On the other hand, in cost reimbursement contracts, the agency's estimate of realistic cost (plus the proposed fee) must be used as the measure of cost realism.

Supplies or services purchased by the government, on either fixed price or cost reimbursement contracts, may result in additional costs to the government as a result of ownership. These costs, such as transportation, storage, or life cycle costs, can also be considered in the evaluation. As with any evaluation factor, these criteria must be identified in the solicitation if they are to be evaluated (see Figure 8-1).

Figure 8-1 Source Selection—Best Practice: The Common Framework

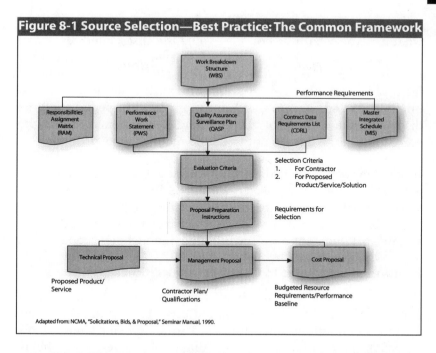

Adapted from: NCMA, "Solicitations, Bids, & Proposal," Seminar Manual, 1990.

U.S. Federal Government Marketplace: Conducting Best Value Source Selection and Contract Negotiations — Best Practices

The term "best value" can have several meanings, depending on one's particular perspective. FAR Subpart 2.101 defines best value as the expected outcome of an acquisition that in the Governments estimation provides the greatest overall benefit in response to the requirement. Best value is usually associated with the source selection process, per FAR 15.101. However, the concept can also be applied to other situations.

In all source selection situations, best value is a tool for the buyer and seller to establish a proper balance between factors such as price, quality, technical and performance. Best value applies to products and services already developed, as opposed to value engineering (also referred to as value analysis), which examines tradeoffs during the design process.

Perhaps it would be more helpful to define best value in terms of what it is and what it is not. Best value is a disciplined, balanced approach, an assessment of tradeoffs between price and performance, a team effort, an evaluation of qualitative and quantitative factors, and an integrated risk assessment. It is not price cutting, uncompensated overtime, accounting gimmicks, special one-time discounts, the shifting of all price and performance risk to the contractor, or an excuse not to define requirements properly.

Best value source selection is a determination of which offer presents the best tradeoff between price and performance, where quality is considered an integral performance factor, see FAR 15.101-1. The best value source selection decision can and should be made using a variety of qualitative and quantitative management tools.

Relation of Best Value to Contract Negotiation

Best value source selection is intrinsically tied to the process of contract negotiations for several reasons. First of all, to be successful, negotiations must focus on some specific quantifiable objective. Best value offers a meaningful objective to each negotiation party. In addition, contract negotiation typically requires tradeoffs among a variety of interrelated factors. Using best value techniques helps contract management professionals assess the impact of these tradeoffs to ensure a successful negotiation session. These techniques also help determine the range of values, e.g., cost, production, quality requirements, life-cycle cost, etc., where tradeoffs can be made and still obtain the optimal balance between price, performance, and quality. Lastly, realistic negotiation objectives are established up front. For example, best value contracting techniques can discourage the use of unrealistic initial negotiation positions by contractors seeking to win a contract with practices such as uncompensated overtime or unrealistically low initial prices.

To be successful, best value contracting must be an integral part of the acquisition strategy planning process, which means early planning must occur. Best value contracting also requires a team effort among various disciplines such as engineering, accounting, legal, manufacturing, and contracts, to clearly identify all acquisition requirements and determine the optimum tradeoffs among various factors.

Tradeoffs in Best Value Contract Negotiations

Tradeoffs in making a best value decision should always consider the objectives of both the buyer and seller, which were discussed previously. Tradeoffs may have to be revisited as negotiations progress, since the needs of the buyer and seller will be revealed (usually incrementally) during the course of negotiations. The level of analysis in best value tradeoff decision depends on the complexity of the particular procurement. Low-technology procurements usually require a simple, straight-forward tradeoff approach, since price is normally the primary factor. However, high-technology procurements normally require more sophisticated tradeoff analysis tools, because price is usually a secondary factor to technical and/or quality concerns.

Due to the many types of contracting situations, there is not a single best way to determine best value. Rather, it requires a combination of techniques that should be used, preferably integrating quantitative and qualitative factors. The use of a team approach helps with rationally making the necessary tradeoffs (see Figure 8-2).

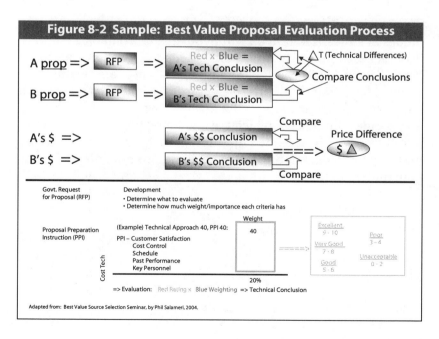

Figure 8-2 Sample: Best Value Proposal Evaluation Process

Adapted from: Best Value Source Selection Seminar, by Phil Salameri, 2004.

The Evolution of Best Value Contracting

The practice of best value contracting has continued to grow in importance over the past decade. One reason is due to the fact that the federal regulatory environment has continually evolved, gradually allowing for increased best value contracting techniques. Government contractors have responded to these changes by offering best value pricing as a part of an overall value-based cost and technical approach. This has helped make the government's contractors more efficient and competitive. In addition, the technical nature and complexity of the items and services to be purchased has continued to increase, e.g., sophisticated consulting, advanced hardware, software, and professional services. This often results in quality and past performance factors becoming more important than price-related factors. In addition, the emphasis on making best value purchasing decisions will increase as the government attempts to obtain more value for its money. Finally, the continual improvement in increasing the professional qualifications and credentials, of both government and industry acquisition workforce personnel, has fostered the use of best value on both sides.

The commercial sector has long used best value contracting techniques as a means to remain competitive and profitable. The U.S. Federal Government has not been able to use the same degree of flexibility enjoyed by private companies when employing best value. This is due to the need to comply with various laws that have no material bearing on the business aspects of the contract, e.g., socioeconomic, but which are mandated by law as a matter of public policy to be included in all federal acquisitions. As a result, best value implementation has not achieved its full potential in the government contracting arena (see Forms 8-2 and 8-3).

EIGHT

Form 8-2
Checklist Best Value Negotiation "Dos"

Do:

☐ Develop or obtain proven best value contracting tools.

☐ Select best value measurement tools that are easy to understand and use.

☐ Ensure quality factors do not become secondary to cost issues, except for noncomplex acquisitions.

☐ Consider using automation tools for best value decision support during source selection.

☐ Tailor best value measurement tools to specific procurement situations, realizing that complexity increases with the size and scope of the acquisition.

☐ Use a contract type that fairly allocates risks.

☐ Provide contract incentives for superior (quality) performance.

☐ Implement guidance throughout the agency or company.

☐ Continue to improve techniques.

☐ Make each best value decision a team effort between contracts, engineering, production, quality assurance, and other related offices.

☐ Ensure a best value approach supports the overall negotiation strategy.

☐ Realize the best value approach works only if you know what you're buying. This means all relevant price and performance-related issues need to be researched.

☐ Document the rationale for best value decisions.

☐ Allow flexibility for tradeoffs

From: Negotiating a Quality Contract, NCMA, 1992.

Form 8-3
Checklist Best Value Negotiation "Don'ts"

Don'ts:

☐ Don't use: 1) the low bid or 2) the lowest cost, technically acceptable offer or as a substitute for best value, when best value is applicable.

☐ Don't expect to make a good best value decision without clearly defining your approach up front.

☐ Don't attempt to implement best value contracting without properly training acquisition personnel.

☐ Don't forget to research all relevant issues, especially technical factors.

☐ Don't' make best value decision tools unnecessarily complex.

☐ Don't allow for such practices as a "buy-in" or uncompensated overtime.

☐ Don't use auctioning, technical leveling, or technical transfusion techniques as a substitute for best value contracting.

☐ Don't forget to formalize the elements of the best value agreement as soon as possible after contract negotiations.

☐ Don't allow an offeror's low initial price to overshadow life-cycle cost considerations.

☐ Don't expect to obtain the maximum level of economy when buying noncommercial off-the-shelf items.

From: Negotiating a Quality Contract, NCMA, 1992.

Summary

In this chapter we have provided a summary of numerous proven best practices when developing acquisition plans, preparing solicitations, evaluating proposals, and negotiating contracts within the U.S. Federal Government Marketplace. The next chapter will provide similar best practices for the U.S. Commercial Marketplace.

Questions to Consider

1. How well does your organization conduct acquisition planning?

2. Does your organization implement all of the solicitation planning best practices contained within this chapter?

3. How effectively has your organization streamlined your buying/acquisition process?

4. Does your organization implement all of the solicitation best practices discussed in this chapter?

CHAPTER  9

U.S. COMMERCIAL MARKETPLACE SOLICITATIONS, BIDS, PROPOSALS, & CONTRACTS

Introduction

Many top U.S. corporations understand the importance to have a strong link between contract management processes and policies and their brand image. Approaches to contract management have a significant impact on how a company is perceived in the marketplace. In the highly competitive U.S. commercial marketplace, most companies must try to hold down the cost of getting products and services to market while still ensuring product and service quality, ease of doing business, on-time delivery, and customer satisfaction. World-class companies continually benchmark, internally and externally, to discover innovative and proven practices that can offer better results. Prominent among these practices are effective means of bid/proposal/capture management and contract management.

Purchasing Annual Survey Results (2005)

Purchasing Magazine has an annual survey of U.S. Commercial businesses, which in 2005 yielded some insightful, but not surprising results. Based upon the results of this survey, a direct correlation could be determined between how buyers view their sellers/suppliers and how pricing is handled. For instance, buyers who typically award contracts or place orders based on lowest price are less likely to give their selected sellers good performance ratings. In contrast, buyers who conduct competitive negotiations based upon best value, including total cost of ownership, often view their selected sellers/suppliers as providing good to excellent performance.

Furthermore, according to the Purchasing Survey of 2005, what buyers want from sellers/distributors most are: quality, price, availability, total cost of ownership, and service, in that order (se Table 9-1).

Table 9-1		
What Buyers Want from Sellers/Distributors Most		
The following get top priority (on a scale of 1 - 10, with 10 the highest):		
	2006	**2005**
Quality	7.8	7.2
Price	6.9	5.8
Availability	6.5	4.6
Total cost	5.9	5.7
Service	5.2	5.7
Ease of doing business	3.3	NA
Brands carried	3.0	NA
Inventory assistance	2.1	3.6
E-commerce capability	2.1	NA
Technical assistance	1.9	3.7
Emergency assistance	1.3	NA
Source: *Purchasing Survey (2005)*		

The results of the Purchasing Survey of 2005 also clearly stated what buyers like about sellers/distributors and what the "buyer's biggest problems with sellers/distributors" (see Tables 9-2 and 9-3).

Table 9-2
What Buyers Like About Sellers/Distributors
(Order of responses)
Customer service
Geographic range of service
e-commerce capability
Range of products}
Handling of delivery and lead time issues
Source: *Purchasing Survey (2005)*

Table 9-3
Buyers' Biggest Problems With Sellers/Distributors
(Order of responses)
Product and technical knowledge
Cost
Availability
Relationships with manufacturer suppliers
Quality
Source: *Purchasing Survey (2005)*

These results clearly demonstrate that it really comes down to how a Buyer measures performance. A company that embraces strategic sourcing, best value, and supply chain management measures performance of its purchasing operations on how well costs are managed. Generally, a purchasing operation's primary tactic is to evaluate buyers in an effort to get the lowest price possible from their sellers/distributors. More knowledgeable buyers understand the value of the total cost of ownership and are rewarding the sellers that provide a lower life-cycle cost.

Today, U.S. federal, state, and local governments are seeking ways to provide more to their constituents with less. In conjunction, the U.S. federal government is re-examining their own, often highly regulated, processes for buying and selling. Seeking to free those processes from unnecessary constraints, they are looking to the private sector or commercial marketplace for streamlined contract management models in an effort to do business better, faster, and cheaper.

To help organizations pursue these goals, this chapter provides a summary of some of the most important commercial best practices for solicitations, bids, proposals, and contracts.

Using U.S. Commercial Best Practices to Improve Solicitations, Bids, Proposals & Contracts

■ *Use a contract management methodology:* Every company should have a logical, organized, yet flexible, process by which it buys and sells goods and services. An effective contract management methodology thoroughly addresses the entire buying and selling process. It sets forth all steps required and clearly defines the roles and responsibilities of everyone involved. Some companies have a process in place detailing the roles and responsibilities of employees, in all stages of an acquisition. This includes from sales through negotiation, contract formation through project management and contract administration. Such a process sets forth all the steps required and clearly defines the roles and responsibilities of everyone involved.

- *Commit to a contract management professional development program:* As business transactions become increasingly customized and complex, more organizations are recognizing that successful contract management, including contract negotiation, requires trained, experienced, professional personnel. Simply hiring clerks will not suffice. Villanova University, Regis University, The George Washington University, and others have established a professional development program composed of continuing education training, which leads to a master's certificate in commercial contract management.

- *Establish a list of pre-qualified suppliers:* Many private-sector companies are taking this proactive approach, which is widely practiced among government agencies. Potential suppliers are screened in advance to determine which ones are qualified for subsequent contract negotiation opportunities. The buying lead time is thus reduced.

- *Take advantage of electronic contract management software applications:* Many private-sector entities, like many agencies in the U.S. Federal government, use electronic means of issuing solicitations, submitting bids and proposals, forming contracts, awarding contracts, exchanging contract correspondence, submitting invoices, and receiving payments. In fact, many large manufacturers and retailers are requiring that suppliers institute an electronic data reduces cycle time, cuts costs, increases productivity, and improves customer service.

- *Use corporate credit cards:* More companies are using credit cards to simplify relatively small-scale or routine purchases. Most establish clear controls, including dollar thresholds, limited access, and specific purchasing guidelines. Through this practice, cycle times, internal documentation, and overhead costs are all being lowered, as the need to spend time negotiating deals for small purchases of commercially available off-the-shelf items is eliminated.

- *Adopt value-based pricing when sensible:* Value-based pricing, sometimes called customer-based pricing, is top down rather than cost based. Instead of pricing products and services by estimating the cost to manufacture or provide them, and then adding a desired margin, value-based pricing focuses on the customer's needs and the benefits the customer expects to reap. In other words, it offers a sound business rationale for charging more for the same products and service, thereby increasing profitability. One's success in the practice of value-based pricing is often closely linked to the individual's contract negotiation skills.

■ *Use universal sales agreements:* Such agreements – in the form of distributor agreements, supply agreements, master agreements, framework agreements, basic ordering agreements, and more – are widely used in commercial contracting. They greatly reduce administrative time, effort, and paperwork by establishing a mutually agreed-on set of terms and conditions that apply to all business transactions made pursuant to the agreement. Universal sales agreements allow contract negotiators to get deals set-up faster and then allow the contract negotiators to focus on tailoring the Ts and Cs to the specific purchase order as needed.

■ *Conduct risk versus opportunity assessment:* Nothing is more profitable than a good bid/no-bid decision. The ability to make informed bid/no-bid decisions, intelligently weighing risk against opportunity, is critical in today's highly competitive marketplace. Many companies have developed sophisticated tools that help their managers identify and quantify both risk and opportunity. Remember, risk must either be bound by the Ts and Cs or priced into the contract.

■ *Simplify standard contract terms and conditions:* Too many companies use standard terms and conditions that are needlessly wordy, overly legalistic, and difficult to understand. More companies are realizing that such terms and conditions are viewed negatively by the other party and constitute obstacles to successful business deals. Some are attacking the problem head-on by rewriting their standard terms and conditions in language that is clear, concise, and easy for all parties involved to understand. Master contract negotiators understand the power, value, and risk associated with Ts and Cs.

■ *Permit oral presentation of proposals:* This time-saving practice is used increasingly by purchasing organizations worldwide. Most establish a few presentation guidelines and state them expressly in their solicitations to ensure that all competing sellers use the same rules. Master contract negotiators understand the value of oral presentations and when to use them.

- *Employ highly skilled contract negotiators:* For many years, companies have realized the value of developing and maintaining a team or group of master contract negotiators to negotiate the mega-deals for their organizations.

- *Conduct mock contract negotiations:* Many headaches can be avoided and a lot of money saved through conducting mock contract negotiations, internally, before the actual negotiations. The primary purpose of conducting mock contract negotiations is to ensure that the parties are fully aware and prepared for the actual contract negotiations with the other party. Mock contract negotiations may be face-to-face meetings or they may be videoconferences, teleconferences, net-meetings, or a combination.

- *Adopt a uniform solicitation, proposal, and contract format:* This logical, organized approach – issuing all solicitations in a common format, requiring that proposals follow the same format, and awarding contracts that use the format – has been used by the U.S. Federal government for many years. Although only a few private-sector entities use this practice, it greatly simplifies the source selection and proposal evaluation process, as well as facilitating contract management for both parties.

- *Create a Paperless Contracting Process:* Many major corporations, including IBM, are going paperless. Effective June 2006 IBM is making it possible for their contract management organization and their vendor partners to manage any type of contract required for product sales and services through a Web application called Contracts Online.

- *Use of Key Performance Indicators (KPIs):* Establishing and reporting on Key Performance Indicators (KPIs) is critical to the success of any contract. The most popular U.S. Commercial Procurement KPIs include:
  - Total Indirect and Direct Spend
  - % of Spend managed thru Procure-to-Pay system
  - % of Invoices paid late
  - % of Purchase Orders (PO's) generated after receipt of Invoice
  - Number of Active Suppliers and % Decrease
  - Discounts taken
  - PO's and Invoices per employee

Charles E. Rumbaugh, Esq. offers the following additional commercial contracting best practices.

■ Use of Changes Clauses in Commercial Contracts

In a commercial context, most buyers do not sufficiently focus-in on the critical nature of changes, which may be required subsequent to the award of a contract. Changes are common, especially for supply/production contracts calling for the delivery of sophisticated systems and/or contracts having a long performance period. In addition, some sellers do not look at the associated high-level discriminator concept in this area for (potential) incorporation into winning proposal(s).

For instance, the "normal" changes clause provides for those that may be negotiated, but it requires bilateral agreement prior to implementation. By requiring mutual agreement, these types of clauses could frustrate the ultimate evolving needs of the end-user. This is especially true as the number of purchases in the form of commercial contracts increase within the Federal Government, which is critical given the bilateral nature of the applicable Federal Acquisition Regulation commercial changes clause.

Perhaps an example is necessary to set the stage. A few years ago, a major government agency bought some sophisticated, *albeit* expensive, commercial systems that required several years of production prior to delivery. Several months post-contract award, certain enhancements to those systems were coming into the marketplace, either through the purchase of new systems incorporating same or as a modification to existing systems under contract. With a mutual consent changes clause under the existing contract, those negotiations became very prolonged and exhausting given the absence of a contractual vehicle, e.g., a pricing mechanism that may be deemed fair to both parties. Some could argue that the buyer had neglected to perform the requisite market research, which would have revealed that this commercial industry was dynamic and robust with increasing number of enhancements, product options, etc. that had been arising post-award.

One answer to this predicament from a buyer's perspective, and for those sellers that would be so accommodating (or desiring to provide a discriminator in their proposal), is having a fair and reasonable methodology for the pricing of changes. One evolving business technique used where the relationship of the parties is of utmost importance is derived through the use of Alternative Dispute Resolution (ADR) techniques and assists in the formation of contracts, especially where that relationship is central to the deal. The use of ADR in this scenario can be briefly described as follows:

> The specific parameters or areas within which changes could be made would be specified and negotiated into the clause with an agreed upon formula to determine the final/fair price for same. Absent a formula, ADR could assist in the process to determine that final/fair price – a process that can be best described as an adaptation of "Baseball Arbitration" may be utilized. Basically, "Baseball Arbitration" is an ADR technique that creates requisite environment that is conducive for the parties to negotiate the pricing of open items, yet if the parties are unable to agree on same, provides that mechanism (or alternative) for the resolution of same whereby an arbitrator may be called upon, after a mini-hearing, to decide which of the final price offers from each party shall be the price of the contract modification. Another approach is where the arbitrator could decide final price, but only within a range that the parties specified. In any event, the objective is to negotiate the price while providing an alternative in case the negotiations prove unsuccessful. Suffice to state here that the overwhelming number of times where the parties have agreed to use "Baseball Arbitration," they have mutually agreed to a price without resort to arbitration! While the details behind how "Baseball Arbitration" is used as a negotiating tool in business, as well as in the game of baseball, are beyond the scope of this writing, readers are directed to my two part series on the topic published in the October and November 2002 issues of the National Contract Management Association (NCMA), *Contract Management* magazine under the title, *Having Trouble Getting to the Negotiation Table? Try Baseball Arbitration.*

■ Ensure Letter Contracts and Letter Subcontracts Have a Provision/Process to Determine the Definitive Price in the Event the Parties Fail to Agree

As an adjunct to the discussion above on commercial "changes clauses," and of equal import is the absence of a process that will establish a fair and reasonable price for work under a letter contract or subcontract - in commercial or government contracting.

What is the alternative in the absence of the parties' agreement that operate under a letter agreement? Is it the buyer that has all the flexibility in finalizing a price? Why would sellers allow buyers this unilateral, unbridled authority? However, most sellers allow buyers to have that option without a thorough analysis as to the risk associated with the passage of time on those negotiations. What is the incentive for a buyer to negotiate a definitive price under a letter contract or subcontract? Again, agreeing upon an ADR process, as noted above for "changes" in regards to these types of transactions.

Usually having a special provision requiring the parties to negotiate in good faith, and if non-agreement exists at the end of a reasonable period of time, the price of the letter agreement is deemed finalized at the last price from the seller to the buyer. If the buyer is of the opinion that the price is "unfair/unreasonable," then the special provision would call for the use of "Baseball Arbitration." In most cases the parties do negotiate an agreement on price without resort to this "default" mechanism, but the parties know their alternatives!

Again, refer to the October and November 2002 NCMA *Contract Management* magazine articles on "Baseball Arbitration."

- Place Greater Emphasis on Acceptance/Warranties in Performance Based Acquisitions (PBAs)

    Another facet is the acknowledged controversial topic of the seemingly over-abundance or heightened emphasis of PBAs having "detailed" quality provisions. It is submitted that if buyers want to further streamline their processes toward those in a commercial setting, then they should reconsider the calculus and, where appropriate, tailor those "old" quality percepts to align with the new reality in commercial contracts.

    Specifically, the issue may not necessarily be whether quality specifications in PBAs "do the job," but rather on whether the deliverables "do the job!" Will "elaborate" measurement matrices on quality related issues satisfy the users' needs? In particular, it may be more appropriate for buyers, and for sellers looking for that all important discriminator in their proposals, to consider a more cost-effective approach with potentially less oversight, i.e. having the necessary post-delivery product with the "right" (lower) life-cycle costs and the "right" acceptance criteria and/or warranty. These important provisions will drive the quality equation. By having greater weight placed on acceptance and/or warranty provisions the end user may get the item they want and need and at the right cost/price.

The acceptance and warranty obligations could be used to a greater degree in determining, or driving, the quality specification in PBAs – but completed by the seller in order to ensure the acceptance/warranty obligations are achieved – and with greater adherence to this fundamental philosophy of PBAs! The case study on how Hyundai, an automobile company, reinvented itself with a great warranty and with outstanding market (buyer) acceptance should be reviewed by all.

- Develop and maintain a contract management best-practices and lessons-learned database

  Corporations are increasingly realizing the value of maintaining a database containing comprehensive information – both current and historical – about customers, suppliers, contract negotiation plans, business results, and actual contracts. The database, ideally in electronic form, must be user friendly and accessible to all appropriate personnel. Few companies pursue this practice and even fewer pursue it well. This is primarily due to the initial and continuing investment in cost, time, and effort. Yet that investment can pale in comparison with the benefits of significant cost avoidance, increased customer satisfaction, and more successful, long-term business relationships.

Summary

The learning process is a two-way street. As illustrated by several items in the discussion of best practices, those responsible for contract management in the commercial realm are benefiting by adopting practices long used by government. Ironically, government contract managers are benefiting just as much from adopting commercial best practices.

What matters most is that senior leadership of an organization realizes the value of contract management as a critical aspect of integrated business management. For sellers, it is not enough to have good sales managers, proposal managers, and quality products and services – an organization must have professional contract managers to successfully manage the entire buying and selling life-cycle. For buyers, it is not enough to know what they need to purchase – organizations must have a process to ensure that they effectively communicate their needs, select the right source, negotiate a successful contract, and obtain quality products and services. Teamwork is the essential element of business success. In today's highly complex commercial world of integrated products (hardware and software), services, and business solutions, it takes a highly talented, focused, and multi-functional teams to deliver results, with buyers and sellers working together as business partners.

Questions to Consider

1. How many of the best practices discussed in this chapter does your organization routinely practice?

2. What other commercial best practices does your organization practice?

3. How well educated and trained are your organization's contract managers, sales managers, and/or purchasing managers in commercial contracting best practices?

CHAPTER 10

MULTINATIONAL/ GLOBAL BUYING & SELLING BEST PRACTICES

INTRODUCTION

According to the International Association for Contract and Commercial Management (IACCM) "the approach to contract management and the way that risk is managed must become much more collaborative and much more open to cross-cultural influences. Thus, the contract management processes, both buyer-side and seller-side must become more sensitive to local practices and expectations. Products and services must be offered with terms and conditions that make sense for different cultural and socio-economic segments." Clearly, buying and selling products, services, and solutions outside the borders of the U.S. has numerous unique aspects associated with it, including: political, cultural, socio-economic, and technological just to mention a few. This chapter is focused on the following key points of discussion:

- Globalization – What is It?
- Global Thinking
- Global Sources of Demand
- Global Sources of Supply
- Global Sales, Manufacturing, & Execution
- Multinational Trade Organizations and Agreement
- Challenges of the International Contracting Environment

GLOBALIZATION — WHAT IS IT?

Globalization can be defined in several ways depending on the level you choose to focus on. People speak of globalization in reference to the entire world, a single country, a specific industry, a specific company or function within a company and even a particular line of business. At the worldwide level, globalization refers to the growing economic interdependence between countries as reflected by the continuous increase of cross-border flows of goods, services, capital and know-how. At the level of a specific country, globalization refers to the extent of the interlinkages between a country's economy and the rest of the world. At the level of a specific industry, globalization refers to the degree of a company's competitive position within that specific industry of one country in relation to its interdependency within that same industry of another country (Financial Times, London, 1998).

Clearly, since the terrible terrorist attacks on the United States on September 11, 2001, the entire world has been forced to reevaluate how the complex process of globalization will continue to evolve. In fact, most organizations and companies are continually evaluating the changing characteristics that shape the global business environment.

GLOBAL THINKING

In order to make globalization work you must practice global thinking. There are three critical dimensions to global thinking.

- Understand Global Sources of Demand
- Understand Global Sources of Supply and The Global Supply Chain
- Understand Global Marketing, Sales, and Execution

Global Sources of Demand – IBM, Toys R Us, and *NCR* are three very different companies with very different products and services, yet all three have successfully mastered global thinking and the art of globalization. All three understand the multinational demands for their respective products and services, especially in developed countries with higher per capita income.

Toys R Us for example has learned the opportunities and challenges one must face in the $6 Billion Japanese toy market. Likewise, *NCR* has worked hard and made considerable international investments in Europe, Japan, and South America to penetrate the multi-billion dollar Automated Teller Machine (ATMs), optical scanner, and computer cash register markets. *IBM* likewise realizes the tremendous global demand of businesses both large and small to outsource computer support services.

GLOBAL SOURCES OF SUPPLY

The Limited is regarded as one of the world's most successful retailers of apparel. While all of The Limited's retail outlets are located inside the United States, the company has successfully established global sourcing practices. The entire process, beginning with product design through the final stage of shipping garments to the individual stores, takes less than 60 days. This is a dramatically reduced cycle-time compared to its competitors. In addition, due to superior global supply-chain management, *The Limited* is able to have their garments designed by numerous companies throughout Europe and produced in Asia and other countries by local manufacturers. These garments are then shipped via a global logistics networks to Columbus, Ohio, where they are distributed to thousands of retail outlets including: *The Limited Express, Victoria's Secret, Abercrombie and Fitch, Lerner,* and *Henri Bendel.*

In the article, *The Essence of Global Sourcing,* by Dr. George L. Harris, Contract Management Magazine, NCMA, March 2006, Dr. Harris states:

The Global Supply Chain

In domestic markets, an order is usually placed through a sales organization, and the order is then either produced or shipped from inventory. Payment is made directly to the supplier once the product is deemed acceptable to the buyer. Product shipments are normally accomplished through one transport organization, which then invoices its services to either the buyer or seller. In international markets, the chain can potentially become very difficult to control. Figure 10-1 illustrates the typical international order.

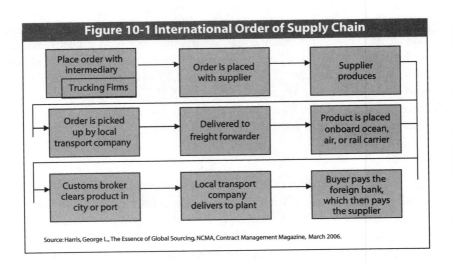

Figure 10-1 International Order of Supply Chain

Source: Harris, George L., The Essence of Global Sourcing, NCMA, Contract Management Magazine, March 2006.

In a domestic case, one transport supplier "touches" the product. In an international case, four different transport companies touch the goods. A freight forwarder handles all the local in-country paperwork and logistics, and the customs broker ensures the product sufficiently clears customs and all appropriate tariffs are charged.

The payment process is usually different in foreign countries as well. With most international purchases, payment is made through a letter of credit. A letter of credit is established between the buyer and a foreign bank, which is typically a branch of the buyer's primary bank. The bank and the buyer agree on the terms of payment, and the supplier submits each invoice to the bank for payment subject to those terms. The buyer deposits enough money to cover each invoice, which is usually related to the product shipments. Once payment is made, the amount of the letter of credit is drawn down accordingly.

Another element of this international supply chain that may be different, is the use of a third party to receive the order. A buyer may need to contract with a local partner, often a trading company, in the supplier's country to help identify potential suppliers or assist in securing the contract with the selected supplier. These trading companies are value-added resources, especially when language barriers exist. Typically, they receive a commission or a percentage of the value of products shipped. These companies can assist in performing quality system audits, expediting parts, and resolving problems. Most organizations do wean themselves away from these trading companies once they have become more experienced. Another option is for the buyer to create a locally based international procurement organization (IPO). As an example, Lucent Technologies started an IPO in Hong Kong for a minicomputer maker, hired local staff, and began regional purchasing of products from Hong Kong, Korea, and Taiwan. The evolution of these relationships can be reflected as shown in Figure 10-2.

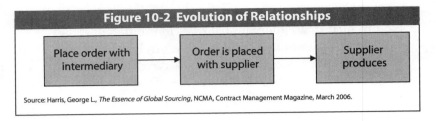

Figure 10-2 Evolution of Relationships

Place order with intermediary → Order is placed with supplier → Supplier produces

Source: Harris, George L., *The Essence of Global Sourcing*, NCMA, Contract Management Magazine, March 2006.

Of course, the creation and maintainability of these relationships is dependent on dollar expenditures, future plans, and risk management.

Global Sourcing

Creating relationships and setting up the appropriate infrastructure for global sourcing is critical to success. An analysis of the skill set and knowledge inherent in the current supply management organization is also necessary to be successful.

It is shortsighted of companies to ask supply management staff to perform domestic and international procurement. Based on the earlier comparison that was made, the differences in making these two types of purchases are striking,. Language, cultural influences, time differences, and the need for more specific and managed communications also contribute to the philosophy that separate and distinct responsibility should be considered. Small organizations may have problems justifying the headcount, but they can structure sourcing activities to ensure proper segregation of duties.

The global purchaser must:

- Have explicit product knowledge
- Have excellent written and verbal communication skills
- Be patient and organized
- Know a foreign language (when appropriate)
- Be process-oriented
- Possess quality systems knowledge
- Understand supplier business assessment
- Comprehend blueprint reading
- Understand value analysis
- Have logistics knowledge.

Some of these skills and aptitudes can be provided by other supply chain staff, but the most successful foreign purchasers have the entire package of skills, particularly technical and market knowledge. Also, because corporations generally buy from more than one foreign country or region, the purchaser must be able to shift approaches when appropriate. Figure 10-3 shows how cultural perspectives in certain countries influence how problems are addressed and how relationships are formed. People refer to this difference in terms of cultural context.

Figure 10-3 Cultural Perspectives

Focus on Personal Relationships		Focus on Problem	
		Low	High
High		Japan Brazil Mexico	Canada Singapore
Low			Germany United Kingdom United States

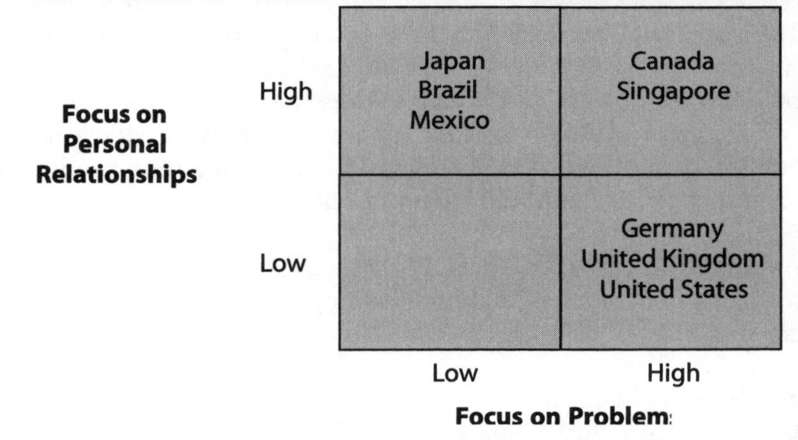

Source: Harris, George L., *The Essence of Global Sourcing*, NCMA, Contract Management Magazine, March 2006.

These reflections are generalizations and should not be used to pigeonhole specific cultures; rather they provide a framework for discussion. As an example, they can be used to establish an approach to be taken in negotiations, relationship building, and problem resolution. They can also be used to provide an initial focus to the sourcing strategy. A global purchasing strategy should be composed of the following components:

- Organization
- Goals
- Focused Regions/Countries

- Supply Management Process
- Relationships
- Time Frame/Schedule
- Budget

Case Study: Royal Philips Electronics

Royal Philips Electronics is one of the world's largest global electronics companies, with a multinational workforce of 160,900 employees in more than 60 countries. Headquartered in Amsterdam, Netherlands, the firm has products and services related to healthcare (including medical systems), technology (including semiconductors), and lifestyle (including lighting, domestics appliances, and consumer electronics).

The purchasing organization has a global spend of 23 billion euros, supporting 30.3 billion euros in total sales. There are global and regional commodity teams that address particular materials. The entire global sourcing process (deployed for nearly 10 years) is very process-driven. There are survey tools, self-audits, roadmaps for improvement, and third-party audits.[1]

As might be expected, there is also a formalized process for in-sourcing/outsourcing decisions and implementation. The process consists of five basic stages:

- Business Planning
- Reorganize and Prepare
- Formal Approval
- Execute and Implement
- Post-Evaluation.

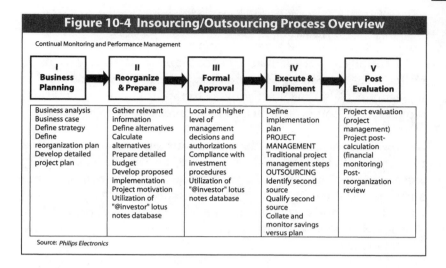

Figure 10-4 Insourcing/Outsourcing Process Overview

Continual Monitoring and Performance Management

I Business Planning	II Reorganize & Prepare	III Formal Approval	IV Execute & Implement	V Post Evaluation
Business analysis Business case Define strategy Define reorganization plan Develop detailed project plan	Gather relevant information Define alternatives Calculate alternatives Prepare detailed budget Develop proposed implementation Project motivation Utilization of "@investor" lotus notes database	Local and higher level of management decisions and authorizations Compliance with investment procedures Utilization of "@investor" lotus notes database	Define implementation plan PROJECT MANAGEMENT Traditional project management steps OUTSOURCING Identify second source Qualify second source Collate and monitor savings versus plan	Project evaluation (project management) Project post- calculation (financial monitoring) Post- reorganization review

Source: *Philips Electronics*

GLOBAL SALES, MANUFACTURING AND EXECUTION

ABB has successfully learned that as companies become global in scope, managers face increased responsibility for marketing and sales to foreign countries, as well as managing adaptation to significant cultural differences. *ABB* helps key managers develop their cultural awareness and foreign language skills, and provides them the opportunity to manage multi-national programs while fully utilizing the support of local subcontractors and local country hires for much of the execution of the actual work.

Global thinking is critical to the success of many companies. Globalization is not limited to just large corporations like *General Motors (GM), IBM, Sony, Phillips, Ikea, Honda, McDonalds,* etc. Surprisingly, small firms tend to be more flexible, which due to their size, allows them to quickly and effectively adapt to local markets far better than large firms. In fact, over 80 percent of the more than 100,000 companies in the U.S. that export are small businesses.

Both large and small businesses throughout the United States and worldwide are forming partnerships or alliances to leverage their strengths, which will help each of the partners sell more products and services. In November 2002, *Sun Microsystems and Lucent Technologies* announced their global partnership to target sales of their products and related services for wireline, wireless, and enterprise customers worldwide.

Case Study: Mattel, Inc.

Mattel, Inc. is one of the world's premiere toy enterprises that designs, manufactures, and markets such brands as Barbie, Matchbox, Fisher Price, American Girl, and Sesame Street. Headquartered in El Segundo, California, the company has approximately 25,000 employees in 42 countries with 2004 revenues totaling $5.1 billion.

Mattel, Inc. has worldwide operations encompassing global procurement, global logistics, finance, and worldwide quality assurance. Within the quality assurance area, the company has a global sustainability group whose mission is to "promote and protect our brands by balancing people, planet, and profit." The global sustainability group oversees three tiers that manufacture Mattel products:

- Facilities fully owned and operated by Mattel around the world
- Supplier locations in various regions of the world
- Licensee facilities: 600 licensees operating 3,000 factories in 30 countries

All three tiers require efficient management and expertise. Keep in mind that the second and third tiers specifically relate to outsourcing, as the facilities are not owned or operated by Mattel. One aspect of outsourcing that Mattel exemplifies is the need for brand protection, even across the outsourcing relationships. Consumers who recognize and trust a brand name do not make the distinction between the original company and any portion of its supply chain. Anything having to do with a Mattel brand is going to reflect on Mattel, even if the work is performed by an outsourcer.[2]

To ensure that Mattel's reputation and values are embodied within its outsource partners and those manufacturing locations owned by Mattel, the firm created Global Manufacturing Principles (GMP) in 1997. The idea came after a national news program did an expose about workers in an underdeveloped region where Barbie clothes were manufactured. The news story became the cornerstone for how Mattel treats people around the world and GMP was rolled out to all the entities that manufacture its branded products.

The GMP program checklist consists of 12 parts covering the following categories: management systems, wages and working hours, age requirements, forced labor, discrimination, freedom of association, living conditions (dorms and canteens), workplace safety, health, emergency planning, environmental protection, and customs. While each checklist is based on a standard template, there are country-specific variations.[3]

MULTINATIONAL TRADE ORGANIZATIONS AND AGREEMENTS

After World War II, the first real attempt to form a world trade organization failed because the U.S. Congress refused to ratify the proposed agreement. Later in 1947, 23 nations signed the General Agreement on Tariffs and Trade (GATT). Almost 40 years later, the Secretariat of the GATT effectively evolved into the World Trade Organization (WTO).

General Agreement on Tariffs and Trade (GATT)

GATT essentially served as an international forum focused on increasing international trade. GATT accomplished its mission by bringing member nations together in meetings, called Rounds, to negotiate reductions in their respective import duties. GATT also served as an important forum for discussion and settlement of trade disputes. The coverage of GATT expanded to more than 100 nations.

The Uruguay Round

The Uruguay Round of GATT lasted for several years, resulting in numerous agreements, which were signed by 113 countries on May 3, 1994, in Morocco. The governments signed the GATT 1994, plus agreements in the following areas of international trade.

- Agriculture
- Pre-shipment Inspections
- Import Licensing Procedures
- Rules of Origin
- Trade in Services
- Trade-Related Aspects of Intellectual Property Rights
- Rules and Procedures Governing Settlement of Disputes
- Trade in Civil Aircraft
- Government Procurement
- Dairy Products
- Others

World Trade Organization (WTO)

The World Trade Organization (WTO) was established on April 15, 1995, in Morocco. The mission of the WTO is to provide a common framework for the conduct of international trade among member nations. The WTO holds a meeting of its trade ministers every two years. WTO meetings were held in 1996, 1998, 2000, and 2002 at various cities worldwide including Singapore (1996) and Seattle (2000). Despite some protests at each of the meetings, the WTO has grown in both members and influence since its inception. Today 141 nations are members of the WTO, including China, which joined on January 1, 2002.

The WTO has numerous councils that meet more frequently than the general biyearly meetings. These include the General Council (that acts as a forum to settle trade disputes), a Council for Trade in Goods, a Council for Trade-Related Aspects of Intellectual Property Rights, and others. In addition, the WTO has established numerous committees including: Trade and Development Committee, Budget Committee, Finance and Administration Committee, and others. The former Secretariat of the GATT became the Secretariat of the WTO. Simply said, the WTO is a legal entity which serves as the champion of fair trade worldwide.

North American Free Trade Agreement (NAFTA)

The North American Free Trade Agreement (NAFTA) was signed on December 1992 and was ratified by the United States, Canada, and Mexico on January 1, 1994. NAFTA, to a large extent, was an expansion of the U.S. – Canada Free Trade Agreement, which was ratified fives years earlier. The mission of NAFTA is to increase trilateral trade and investment through the elimination of both tariff and non-tariff barriers over time.

NAFTA requires a special Certificate of Origin form which must be used for all shipments for which NAFTA duty rates are requested. NAFTA also covers trade in services, investment, protection of intellectual property rights, and settlement of disputes. NAFTA has been successful in increasing both trade and investments between all three countries. For more information see the official NAFTA web site *www.nafta-sec-alen.org*.

European Union(EU) and European Free Trade Association (EFTA)

The European Union (EU) has grown to 15 nations and may continue to grow. The EU cooperates closely with the European Free Trade Association (EFTA), which consists of seven additional countries, not currently in the EU. Clearly, the EU and EFTA have placed the U.S. and Canadian exports to Europe at a disadvantage, because they face entry barriers that are not faced by any of the member nations of the EU and EFTA. Mexico faces far fewer barriers to its exports to Europe, because it receives special consideration under the EU's Generalized System of Preferences. For more information about the EU, see the web site, *www.s700.uminho.pt/ec.html.*

United Nations — Contracts for the International Sale of Goods (UNCISG)

The United Nations Convention on Contracts for the International Sale of Goods (CISG) sets forth rules intended to govern sales and purchases between companies from different nations; however, its scope of influence is limited. First, not all nations have agreed to the CISG. As of January 15, 2006, only 67 nations are signatories. Second, although the nation in which a company is incorporated has signed the CISG, that company need not select the CISG as the source of law that will govern its contracts. The CISG represents a compromise between the UCC and other sources that have arisen out of English common law and the different civil laws prevailing in many other countries. The CISG may be excluded in favor of another source of law, as long as both parties agree and expressly so state in the contract.

One troublesome issue in the international sale of goods is the absence of a "Statute of Frauds" under the CISG. Accordingly, the absence of a writing or an electronic record may result in a finding that a contract was formed by the uninitiated! Good international business practices strongly favor executing an agreement from the get-go that ensures phone calls, emails, correspondence, etc. are not misconstrued as forming a contract for the sale of goods. This type of pre-agreement then allows business development and others to con-tact an international company without fearing such correspondence might be deemed as the formation of a contract to sell goods.

The published "Guide for Managers and Counsel" for applying the CISG generally recommends the best way to ensure the parties do not "unknowingly" enter into an international contract for the sale goods is by having a threshold protocol/agreement that provides in part the following:

> "There shall be no contract until each of us has accepted and signed a writing stating that it contains all of the terms or incorporates by reference to another writing all of the terms of a binding contract between us."

The CISG Guide is available at http://www.cisg.law.pace.edu/cisg/contracts.html.

International Contracting Terms (INCOTERMS)

The International Contracting Terms (INCOTERMS) are standard "terms" for allocating the costs and risks of shipping goods in international trade. Domestic U.S. terms used such as "FOB origin" and "FOB destination" are entirely inadequate for international transactions and would result in considerably different allocation of costs and risks than under current UCC in the United States. Every purchaser and seller should have a set of terms to consult when establishing international T&C. INCOTERMS are available from the International Chamber of Commerce in New York at a nominal cost. For more information, visit *www.iccwbo.org*. Some large commercial banks may also provide copies to their customers.

CHALLENGES OF THE INTERNATIONAL CONTRACTING ENVIRONMENT

In the article, *Challenges of the International Contracting Environment,* by Ernest Gabbard, Esq., CPCM, C.P.M., Contract Management Magazine, March 2006, Gabbard states:

> "While there are many domestic laws that will not apply to our transaction, there are many that *do apply* and with which we should be familiar. A partial list of the more substantive ones follows.
>
> 1. *Anti-Boycotts Legislation.* This one is erroneously presumed to apply only to transactions occurring in the Middle East (Arab-Israeli boycott). However, it also applies to "boycotts" in other areas such as India versus Pakistan and People's Republic of China (mainland) versus Republic of China (Tai-

wan). The issues are often subtle and frequently occur in such innocuous-looking documents as the letters of credit for the global transaction. This law is particularly problematic for the unwary contracts professionals, because it not only prohibits participation in a boycott, but it also requires *reporting of any request* for participation in a boycott. It is therefore prudent to carefully review all documents to identify any request and report such a request to the U.S. Office of Export Compliance (*www.bis. doc.gov/AntiboycottCompliance/*).

2. *Foreign Corrupt Practices Act (FCPA).* Although this impacts the seller more frequently than the buyer, it should not be overlooked in any significant transaction. This law prohibits payments by U.S. companies or citizens to influence a foreign official. The law is extremely complex and includes both anti-bribery provisions, as well as accounting requirements. The contracting and procurement professional should be aware of any actions of its foreign intermediaries, such as brokers or consultants, because the U.S. company could be held liable if those agents violate FCPA when acting on behalf of the company. You should include a prohibition of such actions in contracts with all foreign intermediaries. While such a clause will not completely insulate the U.S. firm from liability, it is an important step toward mitigating such risk. It would be valuable to review the FCPA with your legal counsel to help you recognize the issues that trigger its provisions.

3. *Customs Laws and Regulations.* This body of law and regulation governs the importation of goods into the United States. Virtually all goods can be affected by these laws. An initial or threshold decision can be made on applicability of customs requirements for groups of commodities by some preliminary research and then coordinating with an authority in customs law and regulation. The classification of the product for customs purposes can have significant economic and other ramifica-

tions. Not only can the customs duty vary significantly based upon the proper customs classification, but the ability to import the product at all could also be impaired by that classification. The prudent purchaser/importer will therefore likely employ a customs broker or other import specialist to assure the appropriate classification and to obtain assistance with the importation process.

4. *Export Administration Act (EAA).* Most sellers are aware of this law, which protects U.S. technology by restricting its export. However, this law is frequently overlooked by procurement professionals, because they do not perceive themselves as "exporting." In reality, whenever a specification, drawing, prototype, etc., is provided to a foreign person or entity, an "export" of technology occurs. Therefore, the purchaser may be exporting technology when providing such items to the seller or potential seller."

International T&C Checklist	
Payment Issues	❑ What currency will be used? ❑ What exchange rate will apply? ❑ How will payment be secured? E.g., letter of credit?
Taxation	❑ Are there any export taxes, import duties, etc.? ❑ If so, how should they be allocated in the contract?
Governing Law	❑ What body of law will apply to the contract? ❑ What country will have jurisdiction in the event of litigation?
Risk of Loss	❑ Who bears the risk of loss? ❑ How will that risk be allocated? ❑ Where will title transfer? ❑ Should we use INCOTERMS from ICC?
Contract Interpretation	❑ In what language(s) will the contract be created? ❑ Which language will take precedence if there is an error in translation?
Dispute Resolution	❑ How will contract disputes be resolved? International litigation can be problematic, so consider international arbitration? ❑ Where will disputes be resolved? Agree on the location, whether by arbitration or by litigation. ❑ Would liquidated damages be appropriate for this transaction in the event of contract default?
Counter Trade	❑ Are there any issues regarding barter, offset, counterpurchase, etc.?
❑ Always consider the cultural perspective of the other contracting party!	
International Terms & Conditions Checklist: Minimum Considerations to Supplement Domestic U.S. T&C Issues	

Challenges of International Contracting Environment, Ernest Gabbard, Esq, Contract Management Magazine, NCMA, March 2006

Multinational/Global - Buying & Selling Web Resources
CIA World Factbook — *www.odci.gov/gia/publications/factbook*
Country culture and business practices — *www.worldculture.com*
Dun and Bradstreet — *www.dnb.com*
Global Procurement Group — *www.globalpg.com/resources.htm*
Global Sourcing Solutions & Commerce — *www.globalssc.com*
Institute for Supply Management — Global Group — *www.ismoglobal.org*
Travel Advisory — *www.travel.state.gov/travelwarnings.html*
U.S. Chamber of Commerce — *www.uschamber.org*
U.S. Commercial Service — *www.ustrade.gov*
U.S. Department of Commerce — *www.doc.gov*
U.S. Department of State Bureau of Diplomatic Security — *www.ds.state.gov/terrorism*

Summary

So in retrospect, in this chapter we discussed some of the many unique aspects associated with buying and selling on a multinational or global basis. Understanding globalization, global sources of demand and supply, global sales, and global manufacturing and execution is critical to successful business. Likewise, understanding the multinational trade organizations and agreements, and the numerous complexities of international contracting, can help an organization be better prepared for both the challenges and opportunities to achieve success.

Questions to Consider

1. How well does your organization think globally but act locally?

2. What key challenges does your organization need to overcome to achieve success when buying and/or selling products, services, or solutions beyond its borders?

3. Does your organization fully understand the impact of numerous multinational trade organizations and agreements on your contracts?

4. Does your organization effectively manage risk on your organizational contracts?

Endnotes

[1] Duffy, Roberta J., Critical Issues Report, CAPS, Scottsdale, AZ, October 2005.

[2] Duffy, Roberta J., Critical Issues Report, CAPS, Scottsdale, AZ, October 2005. *Id.*

[3] Duffy, Roberta J., Critical Issues Report, CAPS, Scottsdale, AZ, October 2005. *Id.*

APPENDIX

ACQUISITION BID/NO BID ASSESSMENT TOOL (ABAT)

EXECUTIVE SUMMARY

The Acquisition Bid/No Bid Assessment Tool is designed to support the supplier's assessment of a potential opportunity viability before committing the resources required to develop a Project Plan and customer bid or proposal. It is to be completed by the sales team closest to the customer project under evaluation, with support from the Project Management Organization (PMO). The tool provides a high-level, evaluation of the risks associated with a project. It will support the Sales Team and senior management in determining which opportunities to concentrate on and the risks that must be managed to ensure project success. It is meant to provide assistance in making a "bid/no bid" decision.

HOW TO USE ABAT

The process for performing the project opportunity and risk assessment using the Acquisition Bid/No Bid Assessment Tool (ABAT) involves three basic steps:

- *Assessing the opportunity.* A series of ten questions on Opportunity Analysis are to be answered, with a score for each to be calculated. The questions have been weighted on a scale of 1 (low weight) to 5 (high weight) in terms of their relative importance to each other. This score is calculated by multiplying the raw score (Opportunity Factor (O)) by a pre-established weight value (W). After each question has been scored, it should be documented on the ABAT scoring sheet.
- *Assessing the risk.* A series of eleven questions on Risk Analysis are to be answered, with a score for each to be calculated. The score is calculated by multiplying the raw score (Risk Factor (R)) by the pre-established weight value (W). After each question has been scored, it should be documented on the ABAT scoring sheet.
- *Plotting the opportunity and risk scores on the Matrix.* The total scores for opportunity and risk, calculated on the ABAT scoring sheet are plotted on the matrix provided within the model. The location of this score on the matrix helps determine the quality of an opportunity and serves as an indicator of the level of risk that will need to be managed in order to assure project success.

WHEN TO USE ABAT

The questions provided in this tool can be applied to a project at any time during the sales cycle prior to issuing a proposal to the customer. However, the complete process is intended to be used primarily when the project requirements are defined with such detail that the customer could issue or has issued a Request for Proposal (RFP), Request for Quotation (RFQ), or similar solicitation document. The model has been designed so that it should be completed by a Core Team in a hour or less.

ASSESSING THE ABAT RESULTS

Once the scores have been plotted on the model's matrix, the Sales Team including the Bid/Capture Manager, and the Project Manager can determine the next appropriate step. Normally, a meeting with management is held to review the opportunity. This meeting should include representation from each of the organizations that would be responsible for performing detailed assessment, developing a Project Plan, and providing input to the customer proposal. These same organizations will ultimately be responsible for project execution if the bid is won.

If the project assessment is unfavorable, the Sales Team, in conjunction with the Project Manager may search for ways to improve the opportunity and/or reduce the risk before presenting the opportunity to management. Alternatively, the Sales Team, with concurrence from the Capture Manager, Project Manager and senior management as appropriate may conclude the opportunity should not be pursued.

OPPORTUNITY ANALYSIS

The Supplier's Perspective

	Weight Factor (W)	x	Oppt. Factor (O)	=	Total Score (W x O)

1. Promotes Supplier's Strategic Direction

Any project, if properly executed, will promote the reputation and image of the Supplier. However, the more valuable opportunities are those that are consistent with the Supplier's core business and strategic direction.

These projects:

_ Support our strategic market direction
_ Support our focus on key accounts
_ Utilize our knowledge of specific industries
_ Represent an excellent example of the type of business Supplier seeks and will serve as as a reference for future sales efforts with other accounts

The more of these attributes a project has, the better the opportunity. If properly executed, a project has all of the above attributes promotes Supplier as a industry leader.

Opportunity Factor (O)

$$\underline{\quad 5 \quad} \quad x \quad \boxed{\begin{array}{cccc} 1 & 2 & 3 & 4 \end{array}} \quad = \quad \underline{\qquad}$$

How many of the Supplier's major strategies as outlined above are matched by this project?

1. One
2. Two
3. Three
4. Four

OPPORTUNITY ANALYSIS

The Supplier's Perspective

Weight Factor (W)	x	Oppt. Factor (O)	=	Total Score (W x O)	

2. Revenue Plan

At this point in the project assessment, exact pricing has not yet been performed. However, an estimate of the amount of revenue expected as a result of the project should be developed. The estimate should include only revenue that will be generated within the scope of the project as defined by the contract. The revenues should include all hardware, software, and service revenues (do not include future revenue potential beyond the scope of this project).

Opportunity Factor (O)

$$\underline{\quad 4 \quad} \quad x \quad \boxed{\begin{array}{cccc} 1 & 2 & 3 & 4 \\ & & & \end{array}} \quad = \quad \underline{\qquad}$$

What is the estimated value of the project in U.S. dollars, including all hardware, software, and services?

1. $500,000 or less
2. Greater than $500,000, but less than $2,500,000
3. At least $2,500,000, but less than $5,000,000
4. $5,000,000 or greater

Notes
[Local currency could be substituted if necessary].

OPPORTUNITY ANALYSIS

The Supplier's Perspective

	Weight Factor (W)	x	Oppt. Factor (O)	=	Total Score (W x O)

3. Margin Plan

Estimate the percentage gross margin that is likely to be realized on the revenue generated by this project. This gross margin (GM) should be the aggregate for the project combining hardware, software, and service margins. Ideally, the margin should be consistent with the margin plan for the organization bidding on the project. However, competitive pressures and the need to win may cause Supplier to consider break-even or a loss on the project. Such might be the case when the project will lead to a high volume of profitable business in the future (when generating the profit estimate, do not include the margins generated by future revenues beyond the scope of this project).

Opportunity Factor (O)

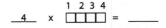

$$\underline{4} \quad x \quad \boxed{\begin{array}{c}1\ 2\ 3\ 4\\ \end{array}} \quad = \quad \underline{}$$

How does the project gross margin in this project compare to the percentage margin goals stated in the annual plan for the organization bidding on the project?

1. Negative margins, or break-even
2. Margins up to 50% of annual plan
3. Margins greater than 50%, but less than 100% of annual plan
4. Margins equal to or in excess of annual plan

Example
An organization's annual plan states a 50% GM goal for a given year. For a project that is projected to generate up to 30% margin, you should select the second answer.

OPPORTUNITY ANALYSIS

The Supplier's Perspective

Weight Factor (W)	x	Oppt. Factor (O)	=	Total Score (W x O)

4. Future Sales

A project may represent a good opportunity because of the future business potential. The project may provide the means to enter a new account, or may be required to protect an existing account. Participation in the project (either in whole or in part) may be required for the Supplier to be considered for future business. Consider the need to do this project relative to its effect on the relationship between Supplier and this Customer, and the potential for future Supplier hardware, software, and services opportunities within this Customer.

Opportunity Factor (O)

1 2 3 4

__3__ x ☐☐☐☐ = _____

What impact will successful conclusion of the project have on future Supplier opportunities with this Customer?

1. The project has little or no bearing on future business.
2. Future business is possible as a result of this project.
3. Future business is likely as a result of this project.
4. Future business is assured as a result of this project, or project participation is mandatory to remain a viable supplier.

Notes

OPPORTUNITY ANALYSIS

The Supplier's Perspective

Weight Factor (W)	x	Oppt. Factor (O)	=	Total Score (W x O)

5. Provides Value Added Experience and/or New Skills

Occasionally, a project is desirable for the education and/or experience to be gained by the Supplier. While learning and experience occur on any project, those that will significantly improve the skills of the Supplier Project Team, and/or develop previously nonexistent critical skills, are the more favored projects. Skills such as managing the project, delivering new products and technologies, and supporting the Customer are just a few examples.

Opportunity Factor (O)

1 2 3 4

___3___ x ▢▢▢▢ = _____

What is the value of the experience and skills to be gained from the project?

1. Little improvement in existing skills is expected because the Project Team is very experienced.
2. Significant improvement in existing skills will be gained by the Project Team members.
3. Little improvement in existing skills is expected, but some new skills and expertise will be developed.
4. Significant improvement in existing skills is expected, and new skills and expertise also will be developed by the Project Team members.

Notes

OPPORTUNITY ANALYSIS

The Supplier's Perspective

	Weight Factor (W)	x	Oppt. Factor (O)	=	Total Score (W x O)

6. Resource Utilization

A project may be highly desirable if it makes good use of the Supplier's resources and assets that are either currently or projected to be underutilized. Even a project that might otherwise be declined may be desirable for its positive impact on the Supplier's resource and asset utilization. The impact on the sales, project management, and support personnel and the use of technical facilities and equipment should be considered. Evaluate current resource utilization and the number and type of projects currently underway. Consider how senior management would react to requests for additional resources.

Opportunity Factor (O)

1 2 3 4

___2___ x ☐☐☐☐ = _____

What impact will this project have on the Supplier's resource and asset utilization?

1. The project will drain significant resources allocated to other projects.
2. The project will drain some resources allocated to other projects.
3. The project will have a normal impact on resources.
4. The project will make use of currently underutilized resources.

Notes

OPPORTUNITY ANALYSIS

The Supplier's Perspective

Weight Factor (W)	x	Oppt. Factor (O)	=	Total Score (W x O)

7. Customer Favors the Supplier

A project involving Customer who favors
the Supplier before the project has been
proposed (for reasons other than price) is
highly desirable. Customer's may prefer the
Supplier for any number of reasons, including
our technology, reputation, past experience,
industry commitment, and so on. Of course,
they may favor the competition for the same
reasons. Consider the number of competitors
vying for the project, as well as the Customer's
past experience with the Supplier and/or the
competition.

Opportunity Factor (O)

$$\underline{\quad 3 \quad} \quad x \quad \begin{array}{c} 1\ 2\ 3\ 4 \\ \boxed{\ \ \ \ } \end{array} = \underline{\qquad}$$

How does the Customer consider the Supplier in
comparison to the competition for this project?

1. The Customer favors the competition and
   is negative towards the Supplier for this
   project.
2. The Customer favors the competition and is
   neutral towards the Supplier for this project.
3. The Customer is neutral towards all potential
   suppliers for this project.
4. The Customer prefers the Supplier for this
   project.

Notes

OPPORTUNITY ANALYSIS

The Supplier's Perspective

	Weight Factor (W)	x	Oppt. Factor (O)	=	Total Score (W x O)

8. Supplier's Revenue and Direct Control of Products and Services

Most projects will require some outsourcing of products and/or services by other vendors or supply-chain partners. The more products and services are outsourced by various vendors, generally the greater the risk and lower the direct revenues.

Opportunity Factor (O)

$\underline{\quad 2 \quad}$ x $\begin{array}{cccc} 1 & 2 & 3 & 4 \\ \hline \quad|\quad|\quad|\quad| \end{array}$ = $\underline{\quad\quad}$

What percentage of the revenue will be generated by the Supplier's products and services?

1. Less than 50% of the project revenue will come from the Supplier's products and services.
2. 50% to 70% of the project revenue will come from the Supplier's products and services.
3. Between 70% and 90% of the project revenue will come from the Supplier's products and services.
4. 90% or more of the project revenue will come from the Supplier's products and services.

Notes

OPPORTUNITY ANALYSIS

The Supplier's Perspective

	Weight Factor (W)	x	Oppt. Factor (O)	=	Total Score (W x O)

9. Proposal or Bid Expense

Every project has presale expense associated with it. The amount of presale expense varies greatly from bid to bid. Some projects are largely a replication of an existing project with this account or another account. In other projects, a significant amount of planning and even a demonstration of the system (including a benchmark) are required before the bid is considered by the account. Projects with little presale expense are more desirable. Examples of items that increase the level of presale expense include:

_ Additional local resources beyond those normally assigned to this account

_ A benchmark system to be constructed

_ Non-Seller's product(s) to be acquired for evaluation before the proposal is generated

_ Resources from other organizations, such as country or group home office

_ Professional services from outside the Supplier's sources

Opportunity Factor (O)

$$\underline{\quad 1 \quad} \quad x \quad \boxed{\begin{array}{|c|c|c|c|} 1 & 2 & 3 & 4 \\ \hline & & & \\ \hline \end{array}} \quad = \quad \underline{\qquad}$$

What is the estimated level of presale expense for this Project?

(Use the items listed above as a guide).

1. High (all of the above apply).
2. Moderate (three or four of the above apply).
3. Low (one or two of the above apply).
4. Minimal presale expense is expected (none of the above).

Notes

OPPORTUNITY ANALYSIS

The Supplier's Perspective

Weight Factor (W)	x	Oppt. Factor (O)	=	Total Score (W x O)

10. Sales Executive Assessment of Opportunity

The Sales Executive, with the support from the Project Leader, should provide an overall assessment of the need to win the opportunity. This is the point at which the Sales Executive and Project Leader can express an opinion on the need to win based on the more tangible aspects of the opportunity. Perhaps they are aware of other opportunity factors not yet considered.

Opportunity Factor (O)

1 2 3 4

$\underline{\quad 3 \quad}$ x $\boxed{\ \ \ \ }$ = $\underline{\qquad}$

On a scale of 1 (low need) to 10 (high need), which is the Sales Executive's overall assessment of the need to win this project business (briefly describe those reasons in the space provided below)?

1. 5 or less
2. 6 or 7
3. 8 or 9
4. 10

Reasons for overall assessment:

_____

_____

_____

_____

_____

_____

_____

RISK ANALYSIS

The Supplier's Perspective

	Weight Factor (W)	x	Risk Factor (R)	=	Total Score (W x R)

1. Customer's Commitment

Customer commitment is a vital factor in the success of a project. A committed Customer will place a high degree of importance on the project and will make it part of its business plan. A committed Customer will apply resources, such as a Project Manager, as well as a budget to implement the project. A committed Customer is less likely to change or cancel the project, and therefore represents a lower risk.

Risk Factor (R)

1 2 3 4

__5__ x ☐☐☐☐ = _____

How committed is the Customer to the project?

1. The Customer has assigned personnel and a budget.
2. The Customer has assigned a budget, but no personnel.
3. The Customer has assigned personnel, but no budget.
4. The Customer has not assigned personnel or a budget.

Notes

RISK ANALYSIS

The Supplier's Perspective

	Weight Factor (W)	x	Risk Factor (R)	=	Total Score (W x R)

2. Project Delivery Schedule

All projects have a set start and completion date. The Customer will normally require that the project be completed within a specific time. Typically, this is driven by the Customer's business cycle, and end-customer demands. The ability to meet the project schedule requirements is highly dependent on the magnitude of the project and the availability and coordination of the right talent at the right time. A project schedule that is reasonable and can be established by the Supplier, with no penalty clauses, represents the least risk.

Risk Factor (R)

$$\underline{\quad 4 \quad} \quad \text{x} \quad \boxed{\begin{array}{c|c|c|c} 1 & 2 & 3 & 4 \\ & & & \end{array}} \quad = \quad \underline{\qquad}$$

How has the project delivery schedule been established?

1. Project start and end dates are flexible and will be established by the Supplier.
2. Project start and end dates will be mutually established by the Customer and the Supplier.
3. Project start and end dates have been set by the Customer. There is no penalty clauses, but changing the schedule and milestones is difficult and must be negotiated with the Customer.
4. Project start and end dates have been set by the Customer and are not changeable. Penalty clauses may exist for not meeting milestones.

Notes

RISK ANALYSIS

The Supplier's Perspective

Weight Factor (W)	x	Risk Factor (R)	=	Total Score (W x R)

3. Project Performance Period

The performance period of the project has a bearing on the level of risk associated with the project. The longer the project, the greater the chance of significant changes. Personnel, customer environment, and the business climate are a few examples of areas subject to significant change as time passes. These changes can pose substantial risk to the project.

Risk Factor (R)

1 2 3 4

$\underline{\quad 3 \quad}$ x ☐☐☐☐ = $\underline{\qquad}$

What is the estimated performance period of the project from the time a contract is awarded to the time it is expected to be completed?

1. Three months to six months
2. Between six months and one year
3. One year
4. More than one year

Notes

RISK ANALYSIS

The Supplier's Perspective

Weight Factor (W)	x	Risk Factor (R)	=	Total Score (W x R)

4. Supplier's Experience

Experience with a previous project that was similar to this one can reduce risk. Determine how many of the project requirements can be met using products, technologies, and/or skills that have been used by the Supplier on other projects. Consider:

_ The skills available at the local level to manage and carry out this project

_ How much of the system solution needs to be developed as opposed to having been done before somewhere within the Supplier

_ The Supplier's experience with the non-Supplier's products needed for the solution

_ The Supplier's experience with their supply-chain partners and other customer selected 3rd parties

Risk Factor (R)

1 2 3 4

__4__ x ☐☐☐☐ = _____

What is the Supplier's experience with similar solutions?

1. The project is a replication of a previous project managed locally.
2. A majority (50% or greater) of the project requirements replicate a previous project done by the Supplier.
3. A minority (less than 50%) of the project requirements replicate a previous project done by the Supplier.
4. None of the project requirements can be satisfied using previous experience, either local or worldwide.

Notes

RISK ANALYSIS

The Supplier's Perspective

Weight Factor (W)	x	Risk Factor (R)	=	Total Score (W x R)

5. The Supplier's Participation in Project Definition

Many Customers develop project requirements without the participation of those who will bid on the projects. In this type of situation, those who bid will have had little or no input regarding schedules, technology, product selection, and so on. The less the Supplier is involved in the development of the requirements, the higher the risk presented by the project.

Risk Factor (R)

    1 2 3 4
__3__ x ☐☐☐☐ = _____

Did the Supplier have any involvement in the development of the requirements?

1. The Supplier developed requirements for the Customer.
2. The Supplier guided the Customer in developing requirements.
3. The Supplier was asked for comments after requirements were developed.
4. The Supplier had no involvement in developing the requirements.

Notes

RISK ANALYSIS

The Supplier's Perspective

	Weight Factor (W)	x	Risk Factor (R)	=	Total Score (W x R)

6. Level/Extent of Outsourcing

Most projects that provide a customized solution outsource the resources of one or more vendors or subcontractors. External organizations can also include non-Supplier hardware and software manufacturers and/or distributors, application software developers, professional Service Providers, and consultants. The number of external organizations involved with a project directly relates to the amount of risk in the project; the more external resource coordination needed, the higher the risk.

Risk Factor (R)

1 2 3 4

__3__ x ☐☐☐☐ = _____

Not including the Customer, how many suppliers and/or subcontractors will need to be coordinated for this Project?

1. None
2. One or two
3. Three to five
4. Six or more

Notes

RISK ANALYSIS

The Supplier's Perspective

Weight Factor (W)	x	Risk Factor (R)	=	Total Score (W x R)

7. Bid/Proposal Turnaround Time

Bid requests usually specify a date when a response must be returned to the requester. This time requirement presents an element of risk. A request requiring a quick response may not give the Supplier the necessary time to do a thorough evaluation of the request. A complex project requiring a bid response (proposal) in 30 days or less could be considered aggressive. Conversely, a simple project allowing more than 30 days for a response could be considered conservative. The shorter the time allowed to develop a response, the higher the risk.

Risk Factor (R)

1 2 3 4

___3___ x ☐☐☐☐ = _____

Which of the following best describes the time frame allotted for assessing Customer requirements and generating a proposal?

1. Not a significant factor
2. Moderate
3. Aggressive
4. Very Aggressive

Notes

RISK ANALYSIS

The Supplier's Perspective

	Weight Factor (W)	x	Risk Factor (R)	=	Total Score (W x R)

8. Technology and Product Maturity

Consider the maturity of the technologies and products to be used in this solution. Many products available today are so widely used that they have been accepted as industry standards. Products that have a substantial field population and have been in use for a year or more are considered mature. These types of products are typically very reliable and pose little risk. However, prereleased and newly released products, or products using leading-edge technology, pose greater risks.

Risk Factor (R)

1 2 3 4

___2___ x ☐☐☐☐ = _____

What percentage of the products needed to satisfy the requirements are mature?

1. All requirements can be satisfied with mature, released products.
2. Less than 30% of the products will be prereleased or new products, or products using leading-edge technology.
3. Between 30% to 70% of the products will be prereleased or new products, or products using leading-edge technology.
4. 70% or more of the products will be prereleased or new products, or products using leading-edge technology.

Notes

RISK ANALYSIS

The Supplier's Perspective

Weight Factor (W)	x	Risk Factor (R)	=	Total Score (W x R)

9. Geographic Distribution

The geographic distribution of the project adds complexity and risk. The greater the geographic distribution, the greater the risk due to factors such as distance, time zone differential, and language barriers.

Risk Factor (R)

1 2 3 4

__2__   x   ☐☐☐☐   =   _____

What is the geographic distribution of the project as it relates to the Supplier's locations?

1. Confined to one location
2. Confined to one region, with multiple locations
3. Confined to one country
4. Distributed across multiple countries

Notes

RISK ANALYSIS

The Supplier's Perspective

	Weight Factor (W)	x	Risk Factor (R)	=	Total Score (W x R)

10. Project Leader Assessment of Project

The Project Leader should provide an overall assessment of the doability of the project. This is the point at which the Project Leader can express an opinion on the likelihood that the Organization could effectively manage the risk and satisfy the customer project requirements to deliver within the scope and terms of the contract. The Project Leader may be aware of other risk factors (such as economic or political instability) not yet considered.

Risk Factor (R)

1 2 3 4

__3__ x ☐☐☐☐ = _____

On a scale of 1 (low risk) to 10 (high risk), what is the Project Leader's overall risk assessment of the Supplier's ability to successfully manage this project (briefly describe those reasons in the space provided below)?

1. 5 or less — Manageable risk
2. 6 or 7 — Risk mitigation likely
3. 8 or 9 — Very high risk
4. 10 — Extremely high risk

Reasons for overall assessment:

_____

_____

_____

_____

_____

_____

ABAT Scoring Sheet

OPPORTUNITY ANALYSIS   RISK ANALYSIS

Weight Factor (W)	x	Oppt. Factor (O)	=	Total Score (W x O)

Weight Factor (W)	x	Risk Factor (R)	=	Total Score (W x R)

1.	__5__	x	____	=	____
2.	__4__	x	____	=	____
3.	__4__	x	____	=	____
4.	__3__	x	____	=	____
5.	__3__	x	____	=	____
6.	__2__	x	____	=	____
7.	__3__	x	____	=	____
8.	__2__	x	____	=	____
9.	__1__	x	____	=	____
10.	__3__	x	____	=	____

1.	__5__	x	____	=	____
2.	__4__	x	____	=	____
3.	__3__	x	____	=	____
4.	__4__	x	____	=	____
5.	__3__	x	____	=	____
6.	__3__	x	____	=	____
7.	__3__	x	____	=	____
8.	__2__	x	____	=	____
9.	__2__	x	____	=	____
10.	__3__	x	____	=	____

Total Opportunity Score = _____   **Total Risk Score** = _____

Acquisition Bid/No Bid Matrix

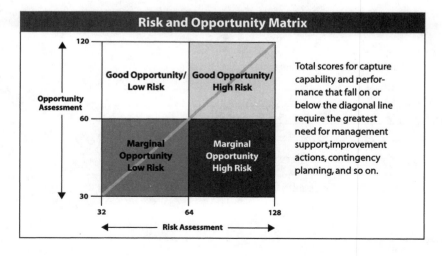

Risk and Opportunity Matrix

120

Opportunity Assessment

| Good Opportunity/ Low Risk | Good Opportunity/ High Risk |

60

| Marginal Opportunity Low Risk | Marginal Opportunity High Risk |

30

32   64   128

Risk Assessment

Total scores for capture capability and performance that fall on or below the diagonal line require the greatest need for management support, improvement actions, contingency planning, and so on.

GLOSSARY

acceptance
(1) The taking and receiving of anything in good part, and as if it were a tacit agreement to a preceding act, which might have been defeated or avoided if such acceptance had not been made. (2) Agreement to the terms offered in a contract. An acceptance must be communicated, and (in common law) it must be the mirror image of the offer.

acquisition cost
The money invested up front to bring in new customers.

acquisition plan
A plan for an acquisition that serves as the basis for initiating the individual contracting actions necessary to acquire a system or support a program.

acquisition strategy
The conceptual framework for conducting systems acquisition. It encompasses the broad concepts and objectives that direct and control the overall development, production, and deployment of a system.

act of God
An inevitable, accidental, or extraordinary event that cannot be foreseen and guarded against, such as lightning, tornadoes, or earthquakes.

actual authority
The power that the principal intentionally confers on the agent or allows the agent to believe he or she possesses.

actual damages
See *compensatory damages*.

affidavit
A written and signed statement sworn to under oath.

agency
A relationship that exists when there is a delegation of authority to perform all acts connected within a particular trade, business, or company. It gives authority to the agent to act in all matters relating to the business of the principal.

agent
An employee (usually a contract manager) empowered to bind his or her organization legally in contract negotiations.

allowable cost
A cost that is reasonable, allocable, and within accepted standards, or otherwise conforms to generally accepted accounting principles, specific limitations or exclusions, or agreed-on terms between contractual parties.

alternative dispute resolution
Any procedure that is used, in lieu of litigation, to resolve issues in controversy, including but not limited to, settlement negotiations, conciliation, facilitation, mediation, fact finding, mini-trials and arbitration.

amortization
Process of spreading the cost of an intangible asset over the expected useful life of the asset.

apparent authority
The power that the principal permits the perceived agent to exercise, although not actually granted.

as is

A contract phrase referring to the condition of property to be sold or leased; generally pertains to a disclaimer of liability; property sold in as-is condition is generally not guaranteed.

assign

To convey or transfer to another, as to assign property, rights, or interests to another.

assignment

The transfer of property by an assignor to an assignee.

audits

The systematic examination of records and documents and/ or the securing of other evidence by confirmation, physical inspection, or otherwise, for one or more of the following purposes: determining the propriety or legality of proposed or completed transactions; ascertaining whether all transactions have been recorded and are reflected accurately in accounts; determining the existence of recorded assets and inclusiveness of recorded liabilities; determining the accuracy of financial or statistical statements or reports and the fairness of the facts they represent; determining the degree of compliance with established policies and procedures in terms of financial transactions and business management; and appraising an account system and making recommendations concerning it.

base profit

The money a company is paid by a customer, which exceeds the company's cost.

best value

The best trade-off between competing factors for a particular purchase requirement. The key to successful best-value contracting is consideration of life-cycle costs, including the use of quantitative as well as qualitative techniques to measure price and technical performance trade-offs between various proposals. The best-value concept applies to acquisitions in which price or price-related factors are *not* the primary determinant of who receives the contract award.

bid

An offer in response to an invitation for bids (IFB).

bid development

All of the work activities required to design and price the product and service solution and accurately articulate this in a proposal for a customer.

bid phase

The period of time a seller of goods and/or services uses to develop a bid/proposal, conduct internal bid reviews, and obtain stakeholder approval to submit a bid/proposal.

bilateral contract

A contract formed if an offer states that acceptance requires only for the accepting party to promise to perform. In contrast, a *unilateral contract* is formed if an offer requires actual performance for acceptance.

bond

A written instrument executed by a seller and a second party (the surety or sureties) to ensure fulfillment of the principal's obligations to a third party (the obligee or buyer), identified in the bond. If the principal's obligations are not met, the bond ensures payment, to the extent stipulated, of any loss sustained by the obligee.

breach of contract

(1) The failure, without legal excuse, to perform any promise that forms the whole or part of a contract. (2) The ending of a contract that occurs when one or both of the parties fail to keep their promises; this could lead to arbitration or litigation.

buyer

The party contracting for goods and/or services with one or more sellers.

cancellation

The withdrawal of the requirement to purchase goods and/or services by the buyer.

capture management
The art and science of winning more business.

capture management life cycle
The art and science of winning more business throughout the entire business cycle.

capture project plan
A document or game plan of who needs to do what, when, where, how often and how much to win business.

change in scope
An amendment to approved program requirements or specifications after negotiation of a basic contract. It may result in an increase or decrease.

change order/purchase order amendment
A written order directing the seller to make changes according to the provisions of the contract documents.

claim
A demand by one party to contract for something from another party, usually but not necessarily for more money or more time. Claims are usually based on an argument that the party making the demand is entitled to an adjustment by virtue of the contract terms or some violation of those terms by the other party. The word does not imply any disagreement between the parties, although claims often lead to disagreements. This book uses the term *dispute* to refer to disagreements that have become intractable.

clause
A statement of one of the rights and/or obligations of the parties to a contract. A contract consists of a series of clauses.

collaboration software
Automated tools that allow for the real-time exchange of visual information using personal computers.

collateral benefit

The degree to which pursuit of an opportunity will improve the existing skill level or develop new skills which will positively affect other or future business opportunities.

compensable delay

A delay for which the buyer is contractually responsible that excuses the seller's failure to perform and is compensable.

compensatory damages

Damages that will compensate the injured party for the loss sustained and nothing more. They are awarded by the court as the measure of actual loss, and not as punishment for outrageous conduct or to deter future transgressions. Compensatory damages are often referred to as "actual damages." See also *incidental* and *punitive damages*.

competitive intelligence

Information on competitors or competitive teams which is specific to an opportunity.

competitive negotiation

A method of contracting involving a request for proposals that states the buyer's requirements and criteria for evaluation; submission of timely proposals by a maximum number of offerors; discussions with those offerors found to be within the competitive range; and award of a contract to the one offeror whose offer, price, and other consideration factors are most advantageous to the buyer.

condition precedent

A condition that activates a term in a contract.

condition subsequent

A condition that suspends a term in a contract.

conflict of interest
Term used in connection with public officials and fiduciaries and their relationships to matters of private interest or gain to them. Ethical problems connected therewith are covered by statutes in most jurisdictions and by federal statutes on the federal level. A conflict of interest arises when an employee's personal or financial interest conflicts or appears to conflict with his or her official responsibility.

consideration
(1) The thing of value (amount of money or acts to be done or not done) that must change hands between the parties to a contract. (2) The inducement to a contract – the cause, motive, price, or impelling influence that induces a contracting party to enter into a contract.

contract negotiation
Is the process of unifying different positions into a unanimous joint decision, regarding the buying and selling of products and/or services.

contract negotiation process
A three phased approach composed of planning, negotiating, and documenting a contractual agreement between two or more parties to buy or sell products and/or services.

constructive change
An oral or written act or omission by an authorized or unauthorized agent that is of such a nature that it is construed to have the same effect as a written change order.

contingency
The quality of being contingent or casual; an event that may but does not have to occur; a possibility.

contingent contract
A contract that provides for the possibility of its termination when a specified occurrence takes place or does not take place.

contra proferentem

A legal phrase used in connection with the construction of written documents to the effect that an ambiguous provision is construed most strongly against the person who selected the language.

contract

(1) A relationship between two parties, such as a buyer and seller, that is defined by an agreement about their respective rights and responsibilities. (2) A document that describes such an agreement.

contract administration

The process of ensuring compliance with contractual terms and conditions during contract performance up to contract closeout or termination.

contract closeout

The process of verifying that all administrative matters are concluded on a contract that is otherwise physically complete – in other words, the seller has delivered the required supplies or performed the required services, and the buyer has inspected and accepted the supplies or services.

contract fulfillment

The joint Buyer/Seller actions taken to successfully perform and administer a contractual agreement and met or exceed all contract obligations, including effective changes management and timely contract closeout.

contract interpretation

The entire process of determining what the parties agreed to in their bargain. The basic objective of contract interpretation is to determine the intent of the parties. Rules calling for interpretation of the documents against the drafter, and imposing a duty to seek clarification on the drafter, allocate risks of contractual ambiguities by resolving disputes in favor of the party least responsible for the ambiguity.

contract management

The art and science of managing a contractual agreement(s) throughout the contracting process.

contract type
A specific pricing arrangement used for the performance of work under the contract.

contractor
The seller or provider of goods and/or services.

controversy
A litigated question. A civil action or suit may not be instigated unless it is based on a "justifiable" dispute. This term is important in that judicial power of the courts extends only to cases and "controversies."

copyright
A royalty-free, nonexclusive, and irrevocable license to reproduce, translate, publish, use, and dispose of written or recorded material, and to authorize others to do so.

cost
The amount of money expended in acquiring a product or obtaining a service, or the total of acquisition costs plus all expenses related to operating and maintaining an item once acquired.

cost of good sold (COGS)
Direct costs of producing finished goods for sale.

cost accounting standards
Federal standards designed to provide consistency and coherency in defense and other government contract accounting.

cost-plus-award fee (CPAF) contract
A type of cost-reimbursement contract with special incentive fee provisions used to motivate excellent contract performance in such areas as quality, timeliness, ingenuity, and cost-effectiveness.

cost-plus-fixed fee (CPFF) contract
A type of cost-reimbursement contract that provides for the payment of a fixed fee to the contractor. It does not vary with actual costs, but may be adjusted if there are any changes in the work or services to be performed under the contract.

cost-plus-incentive fee (CPIF) contract

A type of cost-reimbursement contract with provision for a fee that is adjusted by a formula in accordance with the relationship between total allowable costs and target costs.

cost-plus-a-percentage-of-cost (CPPC) contract

A type of cost-reimbursement contract that provides for a reimbursement of the allowable cost of services performed plus an agreed-on percentage of the estimated cost as profit.

cost-reimbursement (CR) contract

A type of contract that usually includes an estimate of project cost, a provision for reimbursing the seller's expenses, and a provision for paying a fee as profit. CR contracts are often used when there is high uncertainty about costs. They normally also include a limitation on the buyer's cost liability.

cost-sharing contract

A cost-reimbursement contract in which the seller receives no fee and is reimbursed only for an agreed-on portion of its allowable costs.

cost contract

The simplest type of cost-reimbursement contract. Governments commonly use this type when contracting with universities and nonprofit organizations for research projects. The contract provides for reimbursing contractually allowable costs, with no allowance given for profit.

cost proposal

The instrument required of an offeror for the submission or identification of cost or pricing data by which an offeror submits to the buyer a summary of estimated (or incurred) costs, suitable for detailed review and analysis.

counteroffer

An offer made in response to an original offer that changes the terms of the original.

customer revenue growth

The increased revenues achieved by keeping a customer for an extended period of time.

customer support costs

Costs expended by a company to provide information and advice concerning purchases.

default termination

The termination of a contract, under the standard default clause, because of a buyer's or seller's failure to perform any of the terms of the contract.

defect

The absence of something necessary for completeness or perfection. A deficiency in something essential to the proper use of a thing. Some structural weakness in a part or component that is responsible for damage.

defect, latent

A defect that existed at the time of acceptance but would not have been discovered by a reasonable inspection.

defect, patent

A defect that can be discovered without undue effort. If the defect was actually known to the buyer at the time of acceptance, it is patent, even though it otherwise might not have been discoverable by a reasonable inspection.

definite-quantity contract

A contractual instrument that provides for a definite quantity of supplies or services to be delivered at some later, unspecified date.

delay, excusable

A contractual provision designed to protect the seller from sanctions for late performance. To the extent that it has been excusably delayed, the seller is protected from default termination or liquidated damages. Examples of excusable delay are acts of God, acts of the government, fire, flood, quarantines, strikes, epidemics, unusually severe weather, and embargoes. See also *forbearance* and *force majeure clause*.

depreciation

Amount of expense charged against earnings by a company to write off the cost of a plant or machine over its useful live, giving consideration to wear and tear, obsolescence, and salvage value.

design specification

(1) A document (including drawings) setting forth the required characteristics of a particular component, part, subsystem, system, or construction item. (2) A purchase description that establishes precise measurements, tolerances, materials, in-process and finished product tests, quality control, inspection requirements, and other specific details of the deliverable.

direct cost

The costs specifically identifiable with a contract requirement, including but not restricted to costs of material and/or labor directly incorporated into an end item.

direct labor

All work that is obviously related and specifically and conveniently traceable to specific products.

direct material

Items, including raw material, purchased parts, and subcontracted items, directly incorporated into an end item, which are identifiable to a contract requirement.

discount rate

Interest rate used in calculating present value.

discounted cash flow (DCF)

Combined present value of cash flow and tangible assets minus present value of liabilities.

discounts, allowances and returns

Price discounts, returned merchandise.

dispute

A disagreement not settled by mutual consent that could be decided by litigation or arbitration. Also see *claim*.

e-business

Technology-enabled business that focuses on seamless integration between each business, the company, and its supply partners.

EBITDA

Earnings Before Interest, Taxes, Depreciation and Amortization, but after all product/service, sales and overhead (SG&A) costs are accounted for. Sometimes referred to as Operating Profit.

EBITDARM

Acronym for Earnings Before Interest, Taxes, Depreciation, Amortization. Rent and Management fees.

e-commerce

A subset of e-business, Internet-based electronic transactions.

electronic data interchange (EDI)

Private networks used for simple data transactions, which are typically batch-processed.

elements of a contract

The items that must be present in a contract if the contract is to be binding, including an offer, acceptance (agreement), consideration, execution by competent parties, and legality of purpose.

enterprise resource planning (ERP)

An electronic framework for integrating all organizational functions, evolved from Manufacturing Resource Planning (MRP).

entire contract

A contract that is considered entire on both sides and cannot be made severable.

e-procurement

Technology-enabled buying and selling of goods and services.

estimate at completion (EAC)

The actual direct costs, plus indirect costs allocable to the contract, plus the estimate of costs (direct or indirect) for authorized work remaining.

estoppel

A rule of law that bars, prevents, and precludes a party from alleging or denying certain facts because of a previous allegation or denial or because of its previous conduct or admission.

ethics

Of or relating to moral action, conduct, motive, or character (such as ethical emotion). Also, treating of moral feelings, duties, or conduct; containing precepts of morality; moral. Professionally right or befitting; conforming to professional standards of conduct.

e-tool

An electronic device, program, system, or software application used to facilitate business.

exculpatory clause

The contract language designed to shift responsibility to the other party. A "no damages for delay" clause would be an example of one used by buyers.

excusable delay

See *delay, excusable.*

executed contract

A contract that is formed and performed at the same time. If performed in part, it is partially executed and partially executory.

executed contract (document)

A written document, signed by both parties and mailed or otherwise furnished to each party, that expresses the requirements, terms, and conditions to be met by both parties in the performance of the contract.

executory contract

A contract that has not yet been fully performed.

express

Something put in writing, for example, "express authority."

fair and reasonable

A subjective evaluation of what each party deems as equitable consideration in areas such as terms and conditions, cost or price, assured quality, timeliness of contract performance, and/or any other areas subject to negotiation.

Federal Acquisition Regulation (FAR)

The government-wide procurement regulation mandated by Congress and issued by the Department of Defense, the General Services Administration, and the National Aeronautics and Space Administration. Effective April 1, 1984, the FAR supersedes both the Defense Acquisition Regulation (DAR) and the Federal Procurement Regulation (FPR). All federal agencies are authorized to issue regulations implementing the FAR.

fee

An agreed-to amount of reimbursement beyond the initial estimate of costs. The term "fee" is used when discussing cost-reimbursement contracts, whereas the term "profit" is used in relation to fixed-price contracts.

firm-fixed-price (FFP) contract

The simplest and most common business pricing arrangement. The seller agrees to supply a quantity of goods or to provide a service for a specified price.

fixed cost

Operating expenses that are incurred to provide facilities and organization that are kept in readiness to do business without regard to actual volumes of production and sales. Examples of fixed costs consist of rent, property tax, and interest expense.

fixed price

A form of pricing that includes a ceiling beyond which the buyer bears no responsibility for payment.

fixed-price incentive (FPI) contract

A type of contract that provides for adjusting profit and establishing the final contract price using a formula based on the relationship of total final negotiated cost to total target cost. The final price is subject to a price ceiling, negotiated at the outset.

fixed-price redeterminable (FPR) contract

A type of fixed-price contract that contains provisions for subsequently negotiated adjustment, in whole or in part, of the initially negotiated base price.

fixed-price with economic price adjustment

A fixed-price contract that permits an element of cost to fluctuate to reflect current market prices.

forbearance

An intentional failure of a party to enforce a contract requirement, usually done for an act of immediate or future consideration from the other party. Sometimes forbearance is referred to as a nonwaiver or as a onetime waiver, but not as a relinquishment of rights.

force majeure clause

Major or irresistible force. Such a contract clause protects the parties in the event that a part of the contract cannot be performed due to causes outside the control of the parties and could not be avoided by exercise of due care. Excusable conditions for nonperformance, such as strikes and acts of God (e.g., typhoons) are contained in this clause.

fraud

An intentional perversion of truth to induce another in reliance upon it to part with something of value belonging to him or her or to surrender a legal right. A false representation of a matter of fact, whether by words or conduct, by false or misleading allegations, or by concealment of that which should have been disclosed, that deceives and is intended to deceive another so that he or she shall act upon it to his or her legal injury. Anything calculated to deceive.

free on board (FOB)

A term used in conjunction with a physical point to determine (a) the responsibility and basis for payment of freight charges and (b) unless otherwise agreed, the point at which title for goods passes to the buyer or consignee. *FOB origin* – The seller places the goods on the conveyance by which they are to be transported. Cost of shipping and risk of loss are borne by the buyer. *FOB destination* – The seller delivers the goods on the seller's conveyance at destination. Cost of shipping and risk of loss are borne by the seller.

functional specification

A purchase description that describes the deliverable in terms of performance characteristics and intended use, including those characteristics that at minimum are necessary to satisfy the intended use.

general and administrative (G&A)

(1) The indirect expenses related to the overall business. Expenses for a company's general and executive offices, executive compensation, staff services, and other miscellaneous support purposes. (2) Any indirect management, financial, or other expense that (a) is not assignable to a program's direct overhead charges for engineering, manufacturing, material, and so on, but (b) is routinely incurred by or allotted to a business unit, and (c) is for the general management and administration of the business as a whole.

general accepted accounting principles (GAAP)

A term encompassing conventions, rules, and procedures of accounting that are "generally accepted" and have "substantial authoritative support." The GAAP have been developed by agreement on the basis of experience, reason, custom, usage, and to a certain extent, practical necessity, rather than being derived from a formal set of theories.

General Agreement on Tariffs and Trade (GATT)

A multi-national trade agreement, signed in 1947 by 23 nations.

gross profit margin

Net Sales minus Cost of Goods Sold. Also called Gross Margin, Gross Profit or Gross Loss.

gross profit margin % or ratio

Gross Profit Margin $ divided by Net Sales.

gross sales

Total revenues at invoice value before any discounts or allowances.

horizontal exchange

A marketplace that deals with goods and services that are not specific to one industry.

imply

To indirectly convey meaning or intent; to leave the determination of meaning up to the receiver of the communication based on circumstances, general language used, or conduct of those involved.

incidental damages

Any commercially reasonable charges, expenses, or commissions incurred in stopping delivery; in the transportation, care and custody of goods after the buyer's breach; or in connection with the return or resale of the goods or otherwise resulting from the breach.

indefinite-delivery/indefinite-quantity (IDIQ) contract

A type of contract in which the exact date of delivery or the exact quantity, or a combination of both, is not specified at the time the contract is executed; provisions are placed in the contract to later stipulate these elements of the contract.

indemnification clause

A contract clause by which one party engages to secure another against an anticipated loss resulting from an act or forbearance on the part of one of the parties or of some third person.

indemnify

To make good; to compensate; to reimburse a person in case of an anticipated loss.

indirect cost

Any cost not directly identifiable with a specific cost objective but subject to two or more cost objectives.

indirect labor
All work that is not specifically associated with or cannot be practically traced to specific units of output.

intellectual property
The kind of property that results from the fruits of mental labor.

internet
The World Wide Web.

interactive chat
A feature provided by automated tools that allow for users to establish a voice connection between one or more parties and exchange text or graphics via a virtual bulletin board.

intranet
An organization specific internal secure network.

joint contract
A contract in which the parties bind themselves both individually and as a unit.

liquidated damages
A contract provision providing for the assessment of damages on the seller for its failure to comply with certain performance or delivery requirements of the contract; used when the time of delivery or performance is of such importance that the buyer may reasonably expect to suffer damages if the delivery or performance is delinquent.

mailbox rule
The idea that the acceptance of an offer is effective when deposited in the mail if the envelope is properly addressed.

marketing
Activities that direct the flow of goods and services from the producer to the consumers.

market intelligence
Information on your competitors or competitive teams operating in the marketplace or industry.

market research

The process used to collect and analyze information about an entire market to help determine the most suitable approach to acquiring, distributing, and supporting supplies and services.

memorandum of agreement (MOA)/ memorandum of understanding (MOU)

The documentation of a mutually agreed-to statement of facts, intentions, procedures, and parameters for future actions and matters of coordination. A "memorandum of understanding" may express mutual understanding of an issue without implying commitments by parties to the understanding.

method of procurement

The process used for soliciting offers, evaluating offers, and awarding a contract.

modifications

Any written alterations in the specification, delivery point, rate of delivery, contract period, price, quantity, or other provision of an existing contract, accomplished in accordance with a contract clause; may be unilateral or bilateral.

monopoly

A market structure in which the entire market for a good or service is supplied by a single seller or firm.

monopsony

A market structure in which a single buyer purchases a good or service.

NCMA CMBOK

Definitive descriptions of the elements making up the body of professional knowledge that applies to contract management.

negotiation

A process between buyers and sellers seeking to reach mutual agreement on a matter of common concern through fact-finding, bargaining, and persuasion.

net marketplace

Two-sided exchange where buyers and sellers negotiate prices, usually with a bid-and-ask system, and where prices move both up and down.

net present value (NPV)

The lifetime customer revenue stream discounted by the investment costs and operations costs.

net sales

Gross sales minus discounts, allowances and returns.

North America Free Trade Agreement (NAFTA)

A trilateral trade and investment agreement, between Canada, Mexico, and the United States ratified on January 1, 1994.

novation agreement

A legal instrument executed by (a) the contractor (transferor), (b) the successor in interest (transferee), and (c) the buyer by which, among other things, the transferor guarantees performance of the contract, the transferee assumes all obligations under the contract, and the buyer recognizes the transfer of the contract and related assets.

offer

(1) The manifestation of willingness to enter into a bargain, so made as to justify another person in understanding that his or her assent to that bargain is invited and will conclude it. (2) An unequivocal and intentionally communicated statement of proposed terms made to another party. An offer is presumed revocable unless it specifically states that it is irrevocable. An offer once made will be open for a reasonable period of time and is binding on the offeror unless revoked by the offeror before the other party's acceptance.

oligopoly

A market dominated by a few sellers.

operating expenses

SG&A plus depreciation and amortization.

opportunity

A potential or actual favorable event

opportunity engagement

The degree to which your company or your competitors were involved in establishing the customer's requirements.

opportunity profile

A stage of the Capture Management Life Cycle, during which a seller evaluates and describes the opportunity in terms of what it means to your customer, what it means to your company, and what will be required to succeed.

option

A unilateral right in a contract by which, for a specified time, the buyer may elect to purchase additional quantities of the supplies or services called for in the contract, or may elect to extend the period of performance of the contract.

order of precedence

A solicitation provision that establishes priorities so that contradictions within the solicitation can be resolved.

Organizational Breakdown Structure (OBS)

A organized structure which represents how individual team members are grouped to complete assigned work tasks.

outsourcing

A contractual process of obtaining another party to provide goods and/or services that were previously done internal to an organization.

overhead

An accounting cost category that typically includes general indirect expenses that are necessary to operate a business but are not directly assignable to a specific good or service produced. Examples include building rent, utilities, salaries of corporate officers, janitorial services, office supplies, and furniture.

overtime
The time worked by a seller's employee in excess of the employee's normal workweek.

parol evidence
Oral or verbal evidence; in contract law, the evidence drawn from sources exterior to the written instrument.

parol evidence rule
A rule that seeks to preserve the integrity of written agreements by refusing to permit contracting parties to attempt to alter a written contract with evidence of any contradictory prior or contemporaneous oral agreement *(parol* to the contract).

payments
The amount payable under the contract supporting data required to be submitted with invoices, and other payment terms such as time for payment and retention.

payment bond
A bond that secures the appropriate payment of subcontracts for their completed and acceptable goods and/or services.

Performance-based contract (PBC)
A documented business arrangement, in which the buyer and seller agree to use: a performance work statement, performance-based metrics, and a quality assurance plan to ensure contract requirements are met or exceeded.

performance bond
A bond that secures the performance and fulfillment of all the undertakings, covenants, terms, conditions, and agreements contained in the contract.

performance specification
A purchase description that describes the deliverable in terms of desired operational characteristics. Performance specifications tend to be more restrictive than functional specifications, in that they limit alternatives that the buyer will consider and define separate performance standards for each such alternative.

Performance Work Statement (PWS)
A statement of work expressed in terms of desired performance results, often including specific measurable objectives.

post-bid phase
The period of time after a seller submits a bid/proposal to a buyer through source selection, negotiations, contract formation, contract fulfillment, contract closeout, and follow-on opportunity management.

pre-bid phase
The period of time a seller of goods and/or services uses to identify business opportunities prior to the release of a customer solicitation.

pricing arrangement
An agreed-to basis between contractual parties for the payment of amounts for specified performance; usually expressed in terms of a specific cost-reimbursement or fixed-price arrangement.

prime/prime contractor
The principal seller performing under the contract.

private exchange
A marketplace hosted by a single company inside a company's firewall and used for procurement from among a group of preauthorized sellers.

privity of contract
The legal relationship that exists between the parties to a contract that allows either party to (a) enforce contractual rights against the other party and (b) seek remedy directly from the other party.

procurement
The complete action or process of acquiring or obtaining goods or services using any of several authorized means.

procurement planning
The process of identifying which business needs can be best met by procuring products or services outside the organization.

profit

The net proceeds from selling a product or service when costs are subtracted from revenues. May be positive (profit) or negative (loss).

program management

Planning and execution of multiple projects that are related to one another.

progress payments

An interim payment for delivered work in accordance with contract terms; generally tied to meeting specified performance milestones.

project management

Planning and ensuring the quality, on-time delivery, and cost of a specific set of related activities with a definite beginning and end.

promotion

Publicizing the attributes of the product/service through media and personal contacts and presentations, e.g., technical articles/presentations, new releases, advertising, and sales calls.

proposal

Normally, a written offer by a seller describing its offering terms. Proposals may be issued in response to a specific request or may be made unilaterally when a seller feels there may be an interest in its offer (which is also known as an unsolicited proposal).

proposal evaluation

An assessment of both the proposal and the offeror's ability (as conveyed by the proposal) to successfully accomplish the prospective contract. An agency shall evaluate competitive proposals solely on the factors specified in the solicitation.

protest
> A written objection by an interested party to (a) a solicitation or other request by an agency for offers for a contract for the procurement of property or services, (b) the cancellation of the solicitation or other request, (c) an award or proposed award of the contract, or (d) a termination or cancellation of an award of the contract, if the written objection contains an allegation that the termination or cancellation is based in whole or in part on improprieties concerning the award of the contract.

punitive damages
> Those damages awarded to the plaintiff over and above what will barely compensate for his or her loss. Unlike compensatory damages, punitive damages are based on actively different public policy consideration, that of punishing the defendant or of setting an example for similar wrongdoers.

purchasing
> The outright acquisition of items, mostly off-the-shelf or catalog, manufactured outside the buyer's premises.

quality assurance
> The planned and systematic actions necessary to provide adequate confidence that the performed service or supplied goods will serve satisfactorily for the intended and specified purpose.

quotation
> A statement of price, either written or oral, which may include, among other things, a description of the product or service; the terms of sale, delivery, or period of performance; and payment. Such statements are usually issued by sellers at the request of potential buyers.

reasonable cost
> A cost is reasonable if, in its nature and amount, it does not exceed that which would be incurred by a prudent person in the conduct of competitive business.

request for information (RFI)
> A formal invitation to submit general and/or specific information concerning the potential future purchase of goods and/or services.

request for proposals (RFP)
> A formal invitation that contains a scope of work and seeks a formal response (proposal), describing both methodology and compensation, to form the basis of a contract.

request for quotations (RFQ)
> A formal invitation to submit a price for goods and/or services as specified.

request for technical proposals (RFTP)
> Solicitation document used in two-step sealed bidding. Normally in letter form, it asks only for technical information; price and cost breakdowns are forbidden.

revenue value
> The monetary value of an opportunity.

risk
> Exposure or potential of an injury or loss

sealed-bid procedure
> A method of procurement involving the unrestricted solicitation of bids, an opening, and award of a contract to the lowest responsible bidder.

selling, general & administrative (SG&A) expenses
> Administrative costs of running business.

severable contract
> A contract divisible into separate parts. A default of one section does not invalidate the whole contract.

several
> A circumstance when more than two parties are involved with the contract.

single source
> One source among others in a competitive marketplace that, for justifiable reason, is found to be most worthy to receive a contract award.

small business concerns

A small business is one that is independently owned and operated, and is not dominant in its field; a business concern that meets government size standards for its particular industry type.

socioeconomic programs

Programs designed to benefit particular groups. They represent a multitude of program interests and objectives unrelated to procurement objectives. Some examples of these are preferences for small business and for American products, required sources for specific items, and minimum labor pay levels mandated for contractors.

solicitation

A process through which a buyer requests, bids, quotes, tenders, or proposes orally, in writing, or electronically. Solicitations can take the following forms: request for proposals (RFP), request for quotations (RFQ), request for tenders, invitation to bid (ITB), invitation for bids, and invitation for negotiation.

solicitation planning

The preparation of the documents needed to support a solicitation.

source selection

The process by which the buyer evaluates offers, selects a seller, negotiates terms and conditions, and awards the contract.

Source Selection Advisory Council

A group of people who are appointed by the Source Selection Authority (SSA). The Council is responsible for reviewing and approving the source selection plan (SSP) and the solicitation of competitive awards for major and certain less-than-major procurements. The Council also determines what proposals are in the competitive range and provides recommendations to the SSA for final selection.

source selection plan (SSP)

The document that describes the selection criteria, the process, and the organization to be used in evaluating proposals for competitively awarded contracts.

specification

A description of the technical requirements for a material, product, or service that includes the criteria for determining that the requirements have been met. There are generally three types of specifications used in contracting: performance, functional, and design.

stakeholders

Individuals who control the resources in a company needed to pursue opportunities or deliver solutions to customers.

standard

A document that establishes engineering and technical limitations and applications of items, materials, processes, methods, designs, and engineering practices. It includes any related criteria deemed essential to achieve the highest practical degree of uniformity in materials or products, or interchangeability of parts used in those products.

standards of conduct

The ethical conduct of personnel involved in the acquisition of goods and services. Within the federal government, business shall be conducted in a manner above reproach and, except as authorized by law or regulation, with complete impartiality and without preferential treatment.

statement of work (SOW)

That portion of a contract describing the actual work to be done by means of specifications or other minimum requirements, quantities, performance date, and a statement of the requisite quality.

statute of limitations

The legislative enactment prescribing the periods within which legal actions may be brought upon certain claims or within which certain rights may be enforced.

stop work order

A request for interim stoppage of work due to nonconformance, funding, or technical considerations.

subcontract
> A contract between a buyer and a seller in which a significant part of the supplies or services being obtained is for eventual use in a prime contract.

subcontractor
> A seller who enters into a contract with a prime contractor or a subcontractor of the prime contractor.

supplementary agreement
> A contract modification that is accomplished by the mutual action of parties.

technical factor
> A factor other than price used in evaluating offers for award. Examples include technical excellence, management capability, personnel qualifications, prior experience, past performance, and schedule compliance.

technical leveling
> The process of helping a seller bring its proposal up to the level of other proposals through successive rounds of discussion, such as by pointing out weaknesses resulting from the seller's lack of diligence, competence, or inventiveness in preparing the proposal.

technical/management proposal
> That part of the offer that describes the seller's approach to meeting the buyer's requirement.

technical transfusion
> The disclosure of technical information pertaining to a proposal that re-suits in improvement of a competing proposal. This practice is not allowed in federal government contracting.

term
> A part of a contract that addresses a specific subject.

termination
> An action taken pursuant to a contract clause in which the buyer unilaterally ends all or part of the work.

terms and conditions (Ts and Cs)
All clauses in a contract, including time of delivery, packing and shipping, applicable standard clauses, and special provisions.

unallowable cost
Any cost that, under the provisions of any pertinent law, regulation, or contract, cannot be included in prices, cost-reimbursements, or settlements under a government contract to which it is allocable.

uncompensated overtime
The work that exempt employees perform above and beyond 40 hours per week. Also known as competitive time, deflated hourly rates, direct allocation of salary costs, discounted hourly rates, extended work week, full-time accounting, and green time.

Uniform Commercial Code (UCC)
A U.S. model law developed to standardize commercial contracting law among the states. It has been adopted by 49 states (and in significant portions by Louisiana). The UCC comprises articles that deal with specific commercial subject matters, including sales and letters of credit.

unilateral
See *bilateral contract.*

unsolicited proposal
A research or development proposal that is made by a prospective contractor without prior formal or informal solicitation from a purchasing activity.

variable costs
Costs associated with production that change directly with the amount of production, e.g., the direct material or labor required to complete the build or manufacturing of a product.

variance
The difference between projected and actual performance, especially relating to costs.

vertical exchange

A marketplace that is specific to a single industry.

waiver

The voluntary and unilateral relinquishment a person of a right that he or she has. See also *forbearance*.

warranty

A promise or affirmation given by a seller to a buyer regarding the nature, usefulness, or condition of the goods or services furnished under a contract. Generally, a warranty's purpose is to delineate the rights and obligations for defective goods and services and to foster quality performance.

warranty, express

A written statement arising out of a sale to the consumer of a consumer good, pursuant to which the manufacturer, distributor, or retailer undertakes to preserve or maintain the utility or performance of the consumer good or provide compensation if there is a failure in utility or performance. It is not necessary to the creation of an express warranty that formal words such as "warrant" or "guarantee" be used, or that a specific intention to make a warranty be present.

warranty, implied

A promise arising by operation of law that something that is sold shall be fit for the purpose for which the seller has reason to know that it is required. Types of implied warranties include implied warranty of merchantability, of title, and of wholesomeness.

warranty of fitness

A warranty by the seller that goods sold are suitable for the special purpose of the buyer.

warranty of merchantability

A warranty that goods are fit for the ordinary purposes for which such goods are used and conform to the promises or affirmations of fact made on the container or label.

warranty of title

An express or implied (arising by operation of law) promise that the seller owns the item offered for sale and, therefore, is able to transfer a good title and that the goods, as delivered, are free from any security interest of which the buyer at the time of contracting has no knowledge.

web portals

A public exchange in which a company or group of companies list products or services for sale or provide other transmission of business information.

win strategy

A collection of messages or points designed to guide the customer's perception of you, your solution, and your competitors.

Work Breakdown Structure (WBS)

A logical, organized, decomposition of the work tasks within a given project, typically uses a hierarchical numeric coding scheme.

World Trade Organization (WTO)

A multi-national legal entity which serves as the champion of fair trade globally, established April 15, 1995.

REFERENCES

Atkinson, William, *Beyond the Basics,* PM Network Magazine, May 2003 (Project Management Institute).

Badgerow, Dana B., Gregory A. Garrett, Dominic F. DiClementi, and Barbara M. Weaver, *Managing Contracts for Peak Performance* (National Contract Management Association, 1990).

Bonaldo, Guy, *Interview with Business 2.0 Magazine,* Business Intelligence, February 2003.

Barkley, Bruce T., and Saylor, James H., *Customer Driven Project Management: A New Paradigm in Total Quality Implementation* (McGraw-Hill, 1993).

Bossidy, Larry and Charan, Ram, *Confronting Realty: Doing What Matters to Get Things Right* (Crown Business, 2004).

Bruce, David L., Norby, Marlys, and Ramos, Victor, *Guide to the Contract Management Body of Knowledge (CMBOK)* 1st Edition (National Contract Management Association, 2002).

Cleland, David I., *Project Management: Strategic Design and Implementation* (McGraw-Hill, 1994).

Cleland, David I., and King, William R., *Project Management Handbook,* Second Edition (Van Nostrand Reinhold, 1988).

Collins, Jim, *Good to Great: Why Some Companies Make the Leap...and Others Don't* (Harper Collins, 2001).

Coulson-Thomas, Colin, *Creating the Global Company* (McGraw-Hill, 1992).

Covey, Stephen R., *The Seven Habits of Highly Effective People* (Simon and Schuster, Inc., 1989).

Fisher, Roger, Elizabeth Kopelman, and Andrea K. Schneider, *Beyond Machiavelli: Tools for Coping with Conflict* (Harvard University Press, 1994).

Freed, Richard C., Romano, Joe, and Freed, Shervin, *Writing Winning Business Proposals* (McGraw – Hill, 2003).

Garrett, Gregory A., *Achieving Customer Loyalty*, Contract Management Magazine, August 2002 (National Contract Management Association).

Garrett, Gregory A., *Performance-Based Acquisition: Pathways to Excellence* (NCMA 2005).

Garrett, Gregory A., *World-Class Contracting: How Winning Companies Build Successful Partnerships in the e-Business Age, 4th Ed.* (CCH, 2006).

Garrett, Gregory A., *Managing Complex Outsourced Projects* (CCH 2004).

Garrett, Gregory A., *Contract Negotiations: Skills, Tools, & Best Practices* (CCH 2005).

Garrett, Gregory A. and Bunnik, Ed, *Creating a World-Class PM Organization*, PM Network Magazine, September 2000 (Project Management Institute).

Garrett, Gregory A., and Kipke, Reginald J., *The Capture Management Life-Cycle: Winning More Business* (CCH 2003).

Garrett, Gregory A. and Rendon, Rene G., *Contract Management Organizational Assessment Tools* (NCMA, 2005).

Gates, Bill, *Business @ The Speed of Thought: Using a Digital Nervous System* (Warner Books USA, 1999).

Harris, Phillip R., and Robert T. Moran, *Managing Cultural Differences* (Gulf Publishing Company, 1996).

Hassan H. and Blackwell R., *Global Marketing* (Harcourt Brace Publishing, 1994).

Horton, Sharon, *Creating and Using Supplier Scorecards,* Contract Management Magazine (NCMA, September 2004).

Kantin, Bob, *Sales Proposals Kit for Dummies* (Hungry Minds, 2001).

Kerzner, Harold, *In Search of Excellence in Project Management* (Van Nostrand Reinhold, 1998).

Kirk, Dorthy, *Managing Expectations,* PM Network Magazine, August 2000 (Project Management Institute).

Lewis, James P., *Mastering Project Management: Applying Advanced Concepts of Systems Thinking, Control and Evalution, Resource Allocation* (McGraw-Hill, 1998).

Liker, Jeffrey K. and Choi, Thomas Y., *Building Deep Supplier Relationships,* Harvard Business Review, December 2004.

McFarlane, Eileen Luhta, *Developing International Proposals in a Virtual Environment,* Journal of the Association of Proposal Management, Spring 2000 (Association of Proposal Management Professionals).

Monroe, Kent B., *Pricing: Making Profitable Decisions,* 2d ed. (McGraw-Hill Publishing Company, 1990).

Moran, J. and Riesenberger M., *The Global Challenge* (McGraw-Hill, 1994).

The National Contract Management Association, *The Desktop Guide to Basic Contracting Terms,* 4th ed. (1994).

O'Connell, Brian, *B2B.com: Cashing-in on the Business-to-Business E-commerce Bonanza* (Adams Media Corp., 2000).

Ohmae, Kenichi, *The Borderless World: Power and Strategy in the Interlinked Economy* (Harper Collins Pubs., Inc., 1991).

Ohmae, Kenichi, *The Evolving Global Economy* (Harvard Business School (HBS) Press, 1995).

Patterson, Shirley, *Supply Base Optimization and Integrated Supply Chain Management,* Contract Management Magazine, NCMA, January 2005.

Peterson, Marissa, *Sun Microsystems: Leveraging Project Management Expertise,* PM Network Magazine, January 2003, (Project Management Institute).

Project Management Institute Standards Committee, *A Guide to the Project Management Body of Knowledge* (Project Management Institute, 2001).

Reichheld, Frederick F., *The Loyalty Effect* (Harvard Business School Press, 1996).

Tichy, Noel, *The Leadership Engine* (Harper Business Press, 1997)

Webster' Dictionary, The New Lexicon of the English Language (Lexicon Publications, Inc., 1989).

Wilson, Greg, *Proposal Automation Tools,* Journal of the Association of Proposal Management, Spring/Summer 2002 (Association of Proposal Management Professionals).

INDEX